The Complete DRAWING & PAINTING Course

CW01617615

The Complete Drawing & Painting Course

The artist's practical guide to media and techniques

Edited by
Sean Connolly

SELECT EDITIONS

A QUANTUM BOOK

Paperback edition published by
Selectabook Ltd.
Selectabook Distribution Centre,
Folly Road,
Roundway,
Devizes
Wiltshire SN10 2HR

Copyright © MCMXCVII
Quintet Publishing Ltd.

This edition printed 2004

All rights reserved.
This book is protected by copyright. No part of it may be reproduced, stored in a retrieval system, or transmitted in any form or by any means, without the prior permission in writing of the Publisher, nor be otherwise circulated in any form of binding or cover other than that in which it is published and without a similar condition including this condition being imposed on the subsequent publisher.

ISBN 1-86160-966-3

QUMD&P

This book is produced by
Quantum Publishing Ltd.
6 Blundell Street
London N7 9BH

Printed in Singapore
by Star Standard Industries Pte. Ltd

contents

I N T R O D

Try to remember your first experience with art. It was probably at school, featuring a messy collection of crayons, cutouts, construction paper, and runny watercolors. It is possible that the seeds of artistic expression were sown in these early days, out of this haphazard collection of materials. On the other hand, you might have found the experience unsettling and daunting, and your brush with the arts ended when you closed the tray of watercolors for the last time.

Many adults retain this sense of bewilderment when it comes to drawing and painting. They might have

felt that they had some potential, and they usually are exposed to great works in museums and exhibitions, but somehow there seems to be a barrier to participating. The will is there, but it can easily be crushed by feelings that the world of art is too difficult or highbrow to enter. Too often "Oh, I could never begin to paint that" replaces "I wonder how the artist managed to convey such a sense of depth."

The Complete Drawing and Painting Course is aimed at the novice artist who retains that sense of questioning. It answers many of the questions that novices usually ask, and sometimes are afraid or embarrassed to address. What sort of investment do I need to start painting in oils? Is watercolor the easiest painting medium? Is collage simply a children's exercise, or can it help me develop my own skills? What exactly are pastels, and are they easy to use? What is the first step in painting a landscape?

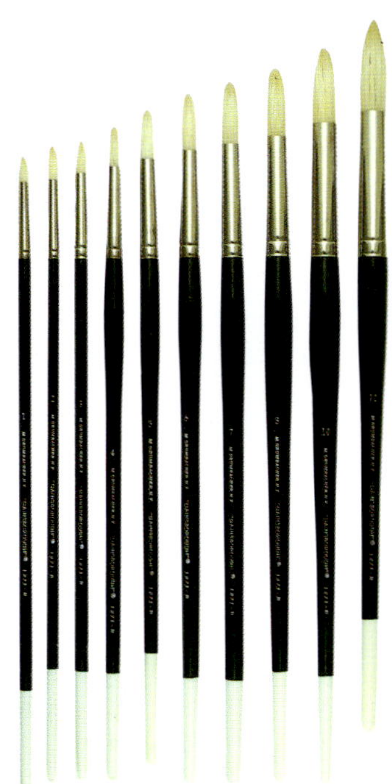

Often the answers to such questions are simple and reassuring, but *The Complete Drawing and Painting Course* also points out areas that pose problems even for the most accomplished artist. The advice is straightforward and frank, covered in three clear sections. Color photographs and illustrations provide an essential framework for understanding the information. Step-by-step exercises, offering the

UCTION

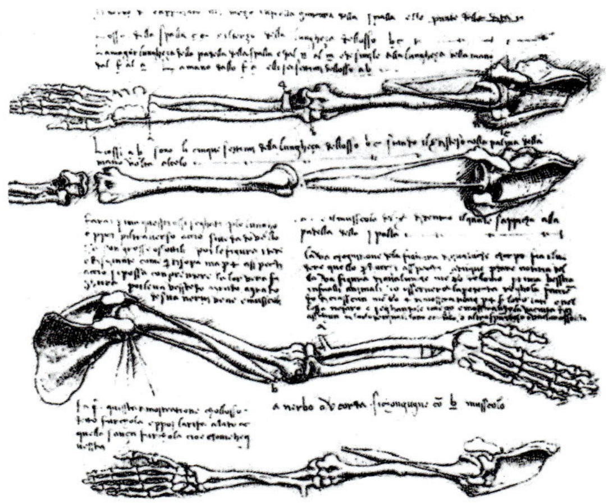

novice a chance to observe or experiment, share the pages with fine reproductions of the Old Masters and contemporary artists.

Part I, "Media, Materials, and Equipment," covers all possible drawing and painting media. It has advice on the development and use of artists' media—including paints and pigments, pencil, charcoal, and combinations—as well as insider's tips on the best brushes, palette knives, supports (papers and canvas), mounts and frames.

Part II, "Techniques," shows that in order to draw or paint effectively, the artist must first be able to see. Then it is a matter of making choices about composition (how the images will be arranged), light and dark, colors, balance, and even rhythm. Clear advice, tied in with easy-to-follow exercises, makes these points while providing pointers on special techniques to achieve the right effects. Part II ends with reassuring advice on problem solving, and how to rescue a work once it is well underway.

In Part III, "Projects," the reader is invited to throw away the training wheels and try a work in one of the main compositional areas. Useful introductions and specific instructions precede the main project in each of five areas: Landscapes, Seascapes, and Skies; Buildings and Towns; Nature and Animals; Still Life; and Portraiture and the Human Figure. Each project follows the lead of an established artist and offers the chance to try the same techniques to achieve similar results.

The Complete Drawing and Painting Course cannot guarantee that your work will sell for millions in auction rooms of New York, Paris, and London. Nor does it pull any punches about everything being easy. However, it will remove the bewildering mystique surrounding art and allow you to recapture the sense of wonder and achievement that you had when things went well in the school art class.

VIRIDIAN
381
Rowney
FINEST ARTISTS'

chapter I

MEDIA, MATERIALS, *and* EQUIPMENT

The first step in learning to draw or paint is to familiarize yourself with just what you will need to use. This might seem obvious, but too many people are either put off by what they see as unnecessary outlay or they go and buy everything for a particular medium only to find most of their purchases gathering dust. These pages provide a sensible guideline for learning about each medium, with practical advice on how to build up an effective collection of materials and equipment. You will also find out how to mount and frame your finished work to best advantage.

DRAWING MEDIA

PENCIL

From childhood we have used pencils to scribble, make notes and record our responses to things seen and imagined. Pencils offer the most direct, and the most versatile, means of allowing our thoughts to flow from the mind through the finger tips to a sheet of paper. The artist is concerned with varying degrees of softness to express different qualities in a drawing. There is usually a choice of twelve grades, from the pale, hard lines of a 6H to the soft, graduated tones of 6B. Most artists tend to work with a medium-soft pencil—grade 2B or 3B—and these can render most of the tones required. Harder pencils are sometimes useful when trying to render structure or architectural subjects. The quality of line and tone will depend to some extent on the choice of paper used. A paper with a heightened grain such as a watercolor paper will enhance the soft grades of pencil; a hard pencil used on the same paper might be too incisive and simply tear into the surface. White cartridge is perfectly adequate for most purposes, but certain papers accept the full range of tone. Mold-made papers, such as Ingres, Fabriano, or Saunders, are especially suitable.

BELOW LEFT AND RIGHT: *The three main types of pencil used for drawing, are: clutch pencil, propelling pencil, and the traditional wooden pencil. For tonal variation graphite and carbon pencils are invaluable. Colored wax pencils are produced in an extensive range of colors, some of which are water-soluble.*

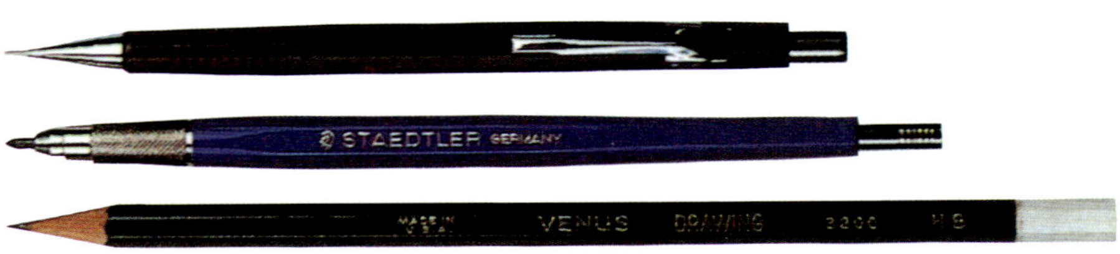

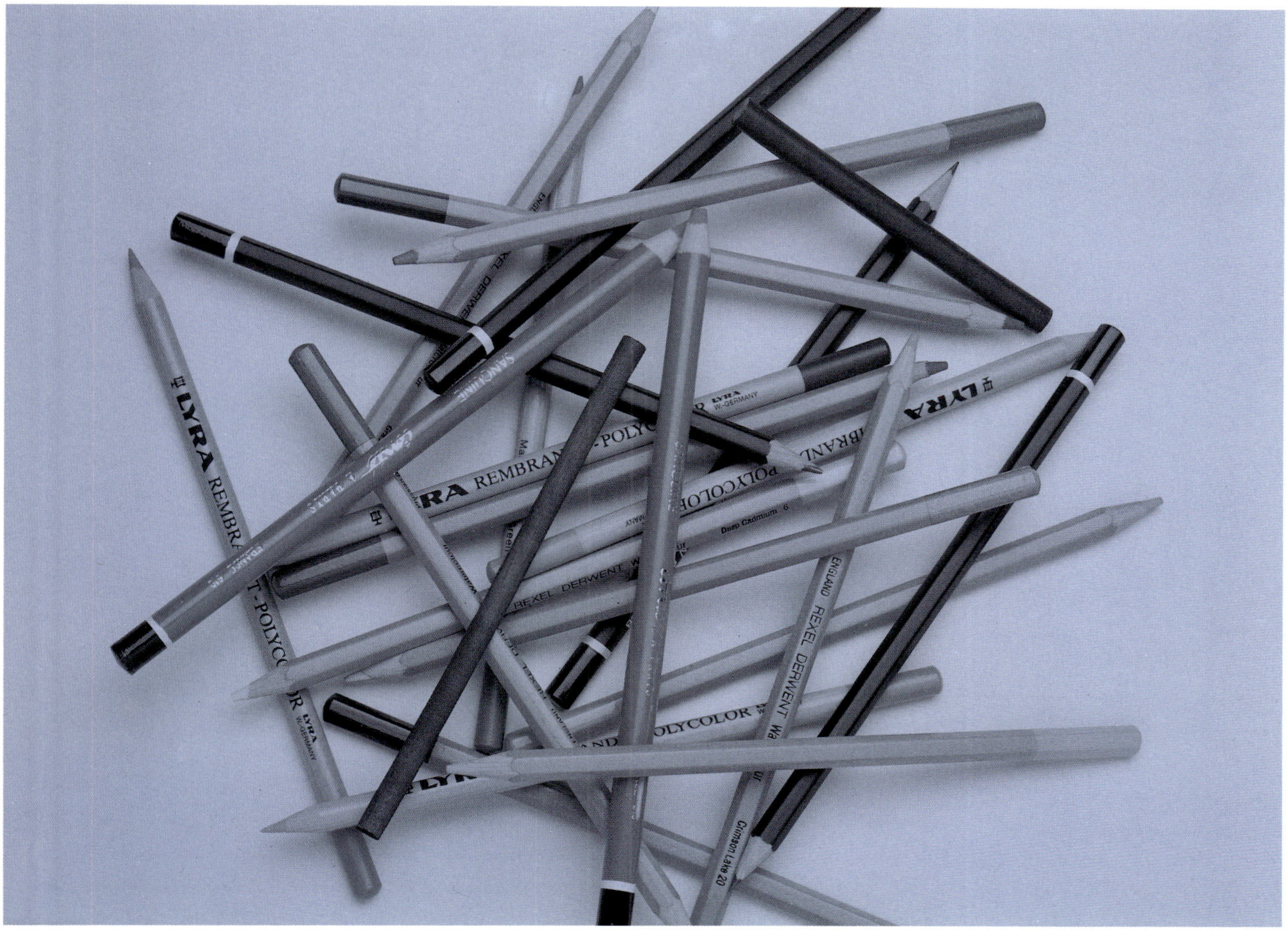

ABOVE: *A range of very hard to soft graphite pencils, colored pencils, and charcoal. By drawing on different types of paper with different grades of pencil, a rich variety of textures can be achieved.*

Pencil covers a wider range of medium than is commonly thought. The lead pencil is now quite an uncommon medium, although still available. The lead pencil's light, silvery, gray line can produce an effect not dissimilar to that of silverpoint which, before the innovation of the modern graphite pencil, was the main linear drawing instrument, particularly among Renaissance artists, although that too is in less common use today. The silverpoint and lead pencils make their mark by leaving a small metallic deposit on the paper, which in the case of silverpoint can barely be seen when the drawing is first done. The metallic deposit tarnishes, and this increases the richness of tone in the line.

The graphite pencil as we know it today is still often incorrectly called a "lead pencil." It is a relatively new drawing instrument and has been in common use only for about 200 years. It comes in a variety of grades. The softest grades are denoted by the letter B and range from B to 8B, which is the softest: F, HB, and H are in the middle of the range. H pencils are the hard range, from 2H to 8H. There are other grading systems but the H and B system is the most common. If in doubt, always test pencils before you buy them.

A useful alternative to the ordinary pencil, particularly for outdoor drawing, is the propeling clutch pencil, for which the "lead" is purchased separately. This is useful in that no sharpening is required and a fine line can be continuously maintained.

The solid graphite stick, normally graded approximately at 3B, is also very useful for larger, tonal, pencil drawings, and is often used in conjunction with a regular pencil. A number of artists recently have been drawing with raw graphite powder, rubbing it into the paper to make large tonal marks, then bringing out highlights with an eraser and more detailed areas with a regular pencil. This method is suitable for very large works.

A pencil can be used in a variety of ways but is most commonly

1

2

3

4

5

6

LEFT:

1 *The graduated tone is achieved by using a 4B (soft) pencil on a smooth paper.*

2 *The same pencil used on a rough watercolor paper renders a totally different quality.*

3 *By indenting lines into the surface of the paper with the blunt rounded end of the pencil, a negative effect is produced when tone is applied.*

4 *Pencil erasers can be used as a drawing tool to create highlights from passages of softly drawn pencil tones.*

5 *Black wax pencil reveals the grain of the paper.*

6 *The dust scraped from a very soft pencil lead can be spread with a finger to create a soft tone. The different grades of pencil shown in the illustration range from hard: 10H, 7H, 3H, and 2H to soft: HB, 3B, 6B, and EE.*

employed in making a line; the result is a crisp, clear drawing. Shadow can be produced by hatching or cross-hatching, which is a set of parallel lines or two opposing sets of parallel lines, respectively. In the detail illustrated, on the right, note that the lines follow the form, adding to the solidity of the drawing and also giving a considerable amount of information about the surface undulations of the form. This approach has been widely used, and two of its greatest exponents were Raphael and Michelangelo. In addition to cross-hatching, darker tonal areas can be shown by a series of regularly spaced dots. The softer variety of pencil can produce very soft areas of tone using the finger or torchon, or by spreading with an eraser. The flexibility of the pencil allows for a great amount of variation and experimentation that can help to decide what is the most suitable approach for a particular subject. The harder, smoother-surfaced papers are generally best for pencil drawing. A good-quality cartridge paper is commonly used and is widely available. Coarser-toothed papers can produce some very interesting results with a softer-grade pencil, but generally the rougher papers are used less commonly with pencil.

A very large selection of colored pencils and crayons is available, most of which are suitable for use in drawing, although some of the wax crayons have a tendency to fade quickly if exposed to strong light.

Wax crayons should really be used only for work of a temporary nature, such as for visualizing an idea in terms of its color scheme. They can be quite useful for children's drawing because the colors do not smudge or blend together easily. The biggest problem (as noted above) is fading, which can be remarkably rapid.

LEFT: *Eight different grades of pencil were shaded across a piece of paper in varying tones to show the differences between grades. The pencils were* (top to bottom): *10H, 7H, 3H, 2H, HB, 3B, 6B, and EE.*

ABOVE: *Blending conté crayon with tortilllon—a piece of paper tightly rolled to make a point—allows more control over small areas than blending with the fingers.*

BELOW: *In this pencil drawing made on a late fall day, the strong lines of perspective of the freshly plowed field lead the eye into the middle distance.*

Rendering line with pen and ink is a technique embedded in Greek, Roman, and Egyptian history. Ancient documents and books were often illustrated with pen drawings. Quills were generally sharpened and dipped in ink, though reeds and bamboo shoots were also brought into use. There are some fine examples of drawings with a quill pen in the notebooks of Leonardo da Vinci, and Rembrandt used a pen very lucidly, often combining the drawn line with washes of sepia ink to give strong tonal contrasts. The modern nib is not much different from the bronze nibs made by the Romans. A great variety of pens were developed, culminating in the modern fountain variety, which houses the ink in a reservoir, usually a rubber tube inside the hollow handle of the pen.

Pen and ink is not a medium for the faint-hearted: decision-making takes place before committing pen to paper and mistakes are difficult to erase. The quality of line is critical to the success of the drawing. That is why the traditional nib is so much better than a mechanical drawing pen, which offers no variety in the thickness of the line. The pen drawings of Van Gogh, for instance, make use of the characteristic strokes of both nib and reed pen, with thick and thin lines used with uneven pressure. Segonzac is another artist whose work demonstrates an exquisite feeling for line.

BELOW: Study of a woman: *Guercino (Giovanni Barbieri). The free lucid line was obtained by using a fairly broad metal nib. Washes of ink were added to heighten the sense of form.*

LEFT: Nibs. *Contrasting linear qualities can be obtained by using fine, italic, thick, and multiple points.*

ABOVE CENTER: View of Arles: *Vincent Van Gogh. This drawing clearly demonstrates how Van Gogh was able to achieve the sense of depth and movement in his pen drawings by using thick and thin pen lines in short strokes.*

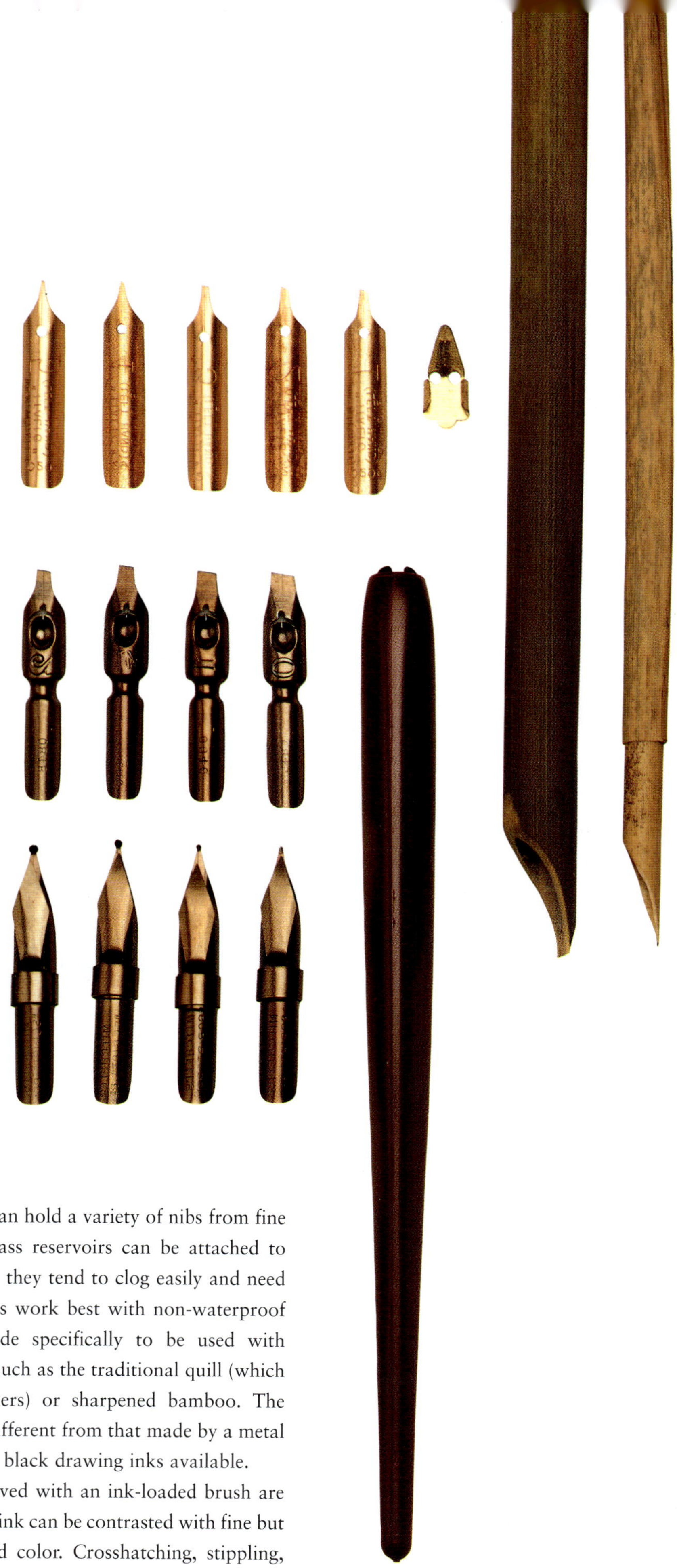

ABOVE RIGHT: *Bamboo pens and quills have very long histories, but are still made today.*

ABOVE MIDDLE: Pen Holders. *Most nibs will fit into a standard holder. For fine lines, mapping pen nibs are fitted into a smaller holder. Brass reservoirs can be attached to most to retain more ink.*

Dip pens are inexpensive and can hold a variety of nibs from fine to broad chisel-edged shapes. Brass reservoirs can be attached to some nibs to retain more ink, but they tend to clog easily and need cleaning frequently. Fountain pens work best with non-waterproof ink, though some pens are made specifically to be used with waterproof drawing implements, such as the traditional quill (which can be made from pigeon feathers) or sharpened bamboo. The quality of line produced is quite different from that made by a metal nib. There are a number of dense, black drawing inks available.

The effects which can be achieved with an ink-loaded brush are numerous. Broad washes of dilute ink can be contrasted with fine but strong lines of more concentrated color. Crosshatching, stippling, splattering, and the sharp freely drawn line can all be used. Drawings can be given a softly graded tonality or high contrast depending on the visual requirements of the artist.

ABOVE: *A pen line drawing in which the building is isolated from its surroundings. This type of drawing usually illustrates a builder's or architect's brochure. There might of course be a power station behind the building, but the aim of this drawing is to concentrate the viewer's mind on the building that is for sale.*

RIGHT: *This pen and ink study has been produced as a two-dimensional abstract design, and although it is a drawing of a plant, the manner of its composition makes it much more an exercise in still life than an accurate representation of natural form.*

CHARCOAL

The technique of drawing with a stick of charred wood has been in existence since man first felt the need to express himself visually. The charcoal in use today is burned in special kilns so that it is evenly charred. The wood used is willow or vine twigs. Charcoal is a particularly pleasant medium to draw with; it can be soft and yet capable of producing sharp, precise lines. The strength of line and tone can be easily modified with a finger tip, allowing contours to be constantly restated. For this reason it is an ideal medium for gaining confidence in drawing.

Originally charcoal was thought of as a means of providing an underdrawing for painting; consequently, most early charcoal drawings are buried under layers of paint. During the nineteenth century it came to be used more frequently as a medium in its own right. The French Impressionists found in charcoal an ideal medium for capturing the fleeting nuances of nature. And in his series of drawings of dancers, Degas produced some of his finest charcoal drawings.

The texture of the paper used can affect the final result. The pronounced grain of a watercolor paper, for example, breaks up the line and thus reduces the strength of the drawing. Charcoal is a medium that should be used decisively; it lends itself to strong, emphatic statements. For that reason it is best to work simply—summarizing the basic shapes and structure rather than getting bogged down with detail.

Stick charcoal is brittle and comes in varying thicknesses. The charcoal made from branches of the vine is the finest in quality. Compressed charcoal is short and stubby and made from compressed charcoal powder. Charcoal pencils are easy to handle and break less often then stick charcoal, but the tones produced tend to be less sensitive. The strong, graphic quality of charcoal can enhance even a poor drawing, but one should guard against any formula for producing striking drawings which are not based on observation. When one has achieved a satisfactory result in a charcoal drawing, it should be sprayed with fixative immediately. An unfixed drawing can be completely ruined by even the slightest brush of a sleeve.

LEFT: Types of Charcoal.
(**1, 2**) *Compressed charcoal pencils are graded from hard to soft. Stick charcoal comes in different widths —thick* (**3**) *medium* (**6**) *and thin* (**7**). *Compressed charcoal* (**4**) *is darker in tone and powdered charcoal* (**5**) *is spread with a paper torchon.*

RIGHT: *It might not be immediately apparent that this drawing was rendered in compressed charcoal. Greater use has been made of the uniformly dense black quality that compressed charcoal can give. Although it can be spread more readily than conté, it produces a harder crisper tone than natural charcoal. Both this and the saplings drawing are on the same type of paper and were drawn in a similar manner. In this drawing, however, there is less subtlety of tone.*

BELOW: Caravaggio: *Octavio Leoni. This charcoal drawing relies on tonal contrast rather than a linear construction. The rich intensity of the dark areas suggests the famous artist's violent life.*

RIGHT ABOVE: Papers for charcoal. *Charcoal reveals the grain of even the most highly textured paper, and this is a quality which should be exploited. Illustrated (*from left to right*) are a smooth Fabriano, a medium Saunders, and a rough Arches.*

1

2

3

1 and 3 *Kneaded bread may be used to create softer patches of light.*

2 *A soft putty eraser can be used to produce sharp highlights from an area of tone.*

PASTEL *(oil and chalk)*

Chalk pastels are bound together with gum and white filler. The crumbling particles are pressed into the surface of a suitable support paper. Unlike watercolor or oil paint, the colors are not mixed before being applied to a support. The color mixing takes place as part of the drawing process itself, by fusing one color into another. This is done with the finger tip or with a paper-felt stump called a torchon. The colors of chalk pastels are neutralized to some extent by the presence of the white filler. Thus we tend to talk of "pastel shades."

Careful examination of a pastel drawing by Degas will reveal his technique of building up color in a web of opposing chalk strokes. Pastel drawings are distinguished from other drawings by the freshness of their color. Degas was much influenced by the pastel drawings of Quentin de la Tour, whose work he collected. But he developed his own techniques and often used a semitransparent paper to produce progressive states of a composition by laying one drawing on top of another, tracing the contours of the first drawing as a basis for the next. By spraying water on to certain parts of an almost completed pastel drawing, he was able to brush certain passages in the drawing into a paste-like texture. Pastel has often been successfully combined with other media; some painters, for

instance, first produce an "underpainting," using oil paint or gouache very thinly, and then gradually build up a pastel drawing on top of it. Degas added pastel to his monotype prints, first painting his subject with oil very thinly on to a copper plate. The image on the plate was transferred to a dampened sheet of paper under great pressure through the rollers of an etching press. He then burnished the pastel into the surface of the print with great delicacy, so that the color became a transparent tint over the original drawing.

One should attempt to work in a way that makes use of the particular qualities of pastel—it is no use trying to render fine detail with a stump of chalk. Work broadly and begin on a large scale with a sheet of paper big enough to allow the arm to move freely across the surface. Mistakes in the drawing can usually be brushed away with a hog's-hair brush. Take care not to destroy the grain of the paper when erasing parts of the drawing. It is the pronounced grain of the paper which anchors the particles of chalk to the surface. The simple, bold statement is usually the most successful; pastels that are overworked lose their "bite" and feeling of spontaneity. Toned or tinted papers make an ideal base for pastel drawings. Watercolor papers can be tinted by using diluted gouache, which can be rubbed into the grain of the paper with a soft pad of cloth.

Oil pastels are quite different from chalk pastels; they are softer and more malleable. The resulting blending of one color with another can give a very rich effect. Oil pastels can be scraped with the sharp edge of a blade, which gives the drawing a kind of sculptural quality. The resistance of the medium makes it most suitable for strong, expressive statements.

Because colors need to be blended on the paper support, rather than on a separate palette, the color range of pastels is vast. Well over 500 tints are manufactured by various artists' colormen. A range of

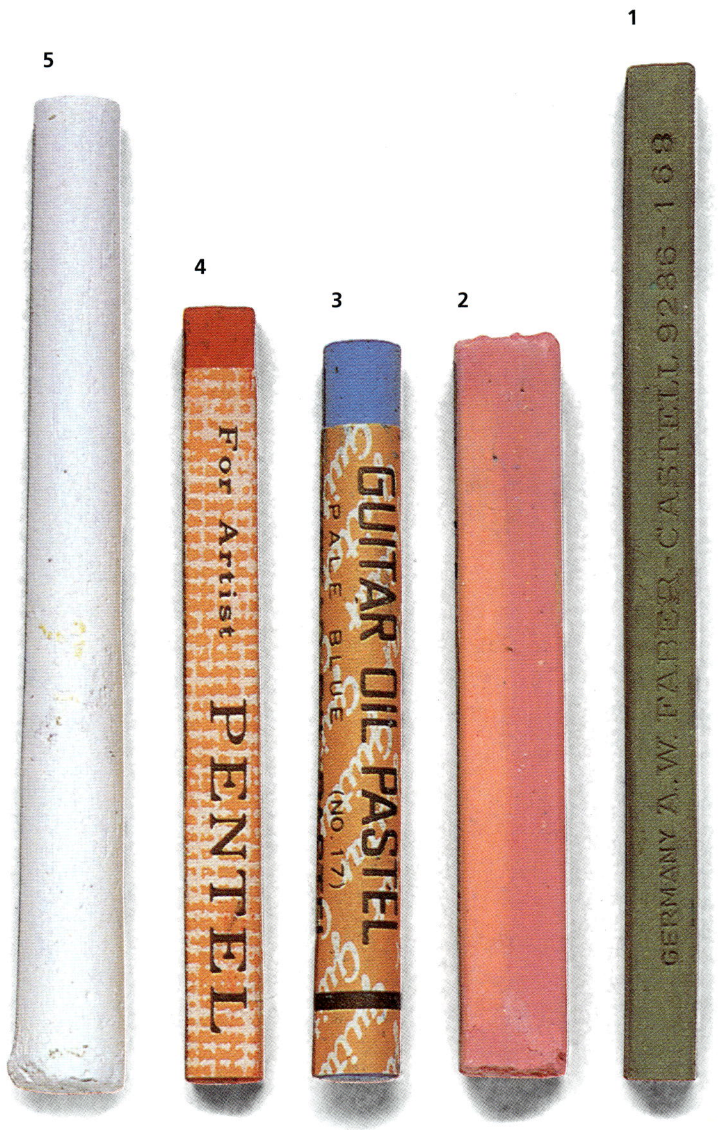

TOP: Dancer II: *pencil and colored crayon on toned paper. The drawing relies on understatement to lend emphasis to the delicacy of the subject.*

ABOVE: Types of Chalks and Pastels. *Pastels are manufactured in varying degrees of hardness.* **1** *Castell Polychromos;* **2** *Inscribe soft pencil;* **3** *Guitar oil pastel;* **4** *Pentel oil pastel;* **5** *chalk pastel.*

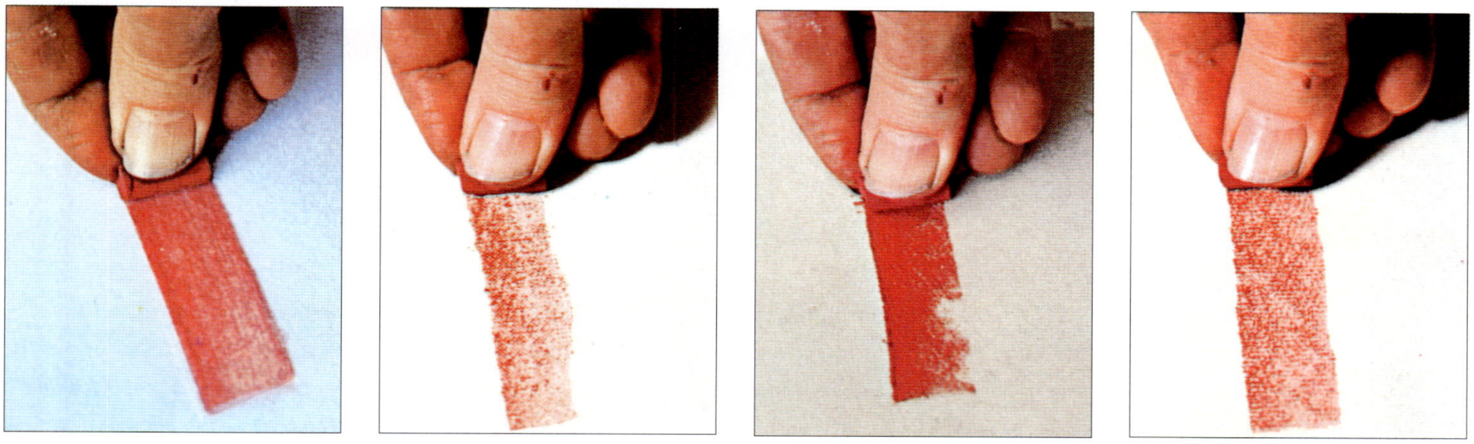

two dozen tints will suffice for most purposes; additional tints can be bought when needed. Graded in soft, medium, and hard, the sticks tend to be used up fairly quickly, especially when working intensely with compacted color. So colors constantly need replacing.

Toned and colored papers, such as Fabriano or Swedish Ingres, make excellent paper supports. One way of understanding color values in pastel is to work on dark-colored paper—brown or even black: all the light areas in your drawing will then have to be imposed on the dark ground with lighter tints of pastel—working from dark to light, which is a reversal of the normal painting process.

It takes some time to adjust to the idea of blending color on the surface of the paper and in your first drawings it is advisable to limit the number of colors to four or five from the same color range such as yellow, ocher, terra-cotta, burnt umber, and dark brown. Your first drawings will then be essentially monochromatic and it will be easier to understand tonal values.

ABOVE: *The effect of working on different surfaces. From left to right: flock paper, sandpaper, canvas, and Ingres paper.*

ABOVE: *Effects of oil pastels.*

The harder the pigment is pressed into the surface of the paper, the more dense the tone will become. But a great deal of surface manipulation of tones can be achieved by spreading and pushing the pigment over a wider area with a finger or a torchon. A gentle touch is sometimes needed to fuse delicate tones together. Preliminary drawing can be carried out in charcoal.

Fixing is done after various stages, or not until the drawing is completed. Oil pastel is really a species of oil painting and it offers much greater resistance than chalk pastel. Turpentine can be used as a thinning agent or to create washes over the drawing. The color can be scraped away with the edge of a blade and reworked.

BELOW: *The range of pastel tints available is vast; one light, one medium and one dark gradation of each color is practicable, and a set of just 12 is probably adequate for sketching outdoors.*

BELOW LEFT: *Drawing with a paper stoop or "torchon." The tip is used to blend chalk pastels into soft delicate tones, particularly in flesh tints. It can also be dipped into powdered pastel.*

PAINTING MEDIA

WATERCOLOR

The fickle nuances, muted tones, and hues of landscape are ideally conveyed in watercolor painting. No other medium offers the same range of atmospheric and luminous qualities. Through watercolor, painters were released from the formal pretentiousness of "Academy" painting. They were able to escape the confines of the studio and gain a more direct contact with nature. Thomas Gainsborough complained to his friend, William Jackson, that he was "sick of portraits" and that he wanted to find some sweet village where he could paint "landskips and enjoy the fag end of life in quietness and ease."

BELOW: Seaside Pavilion: *Moira Clinch. This is a good example of an intricately detailed architectural study that nevertheless retains the freshness and sparkle of more spontaneous sketches.*

LEFT: The Indian village of Pomeioc 1585: *An early record of American life drawn descriptively with a thick brush line and wash.*

BELOW: *A long broad brush is ideal for watercolor painting.*

Watercolor has always been subordinate to oil painting. Even today it is much underrated as a legitimate means of expression. Watercolor painting is characteristically an "English" medium, owing little to any European tradition. The qualities of watercolor are seen at their best in Turner's color beginnings, and topographical studies. Since the end of the nineteenth century, however, watercolor has been widely adopted by amateur painters and this has resulted in its becoming subjected to all kinds of mannerisms and formulas. This is not to decry the fine tradition of watercolor painting among amateurs. Their work is often far more perceptive than that to be found in many a gallery. But the most successful works are usually those that are produced spontaneously, that are not hidebound by technical conventions or overworked to a degree where they become "picturesque." The essence of watercolor lies in the swiftness of the statement; it does not lend itself to the laborious modelling techniques of oil painting.

The English tradition in watercolor painting paralleled the Romantic revival among the great English poets. Tennyson, Wordsworth, Clare, Gray, Cowper, and many others found inspiration in close contact with nature. Turner was first and foremost a watercolorist; when he used oil paints he tended to thin them down into transparent glazes, particularly in his seascapes. His conception demanded a greater lucidity than could be achieved with the usual paste-like consistency of oil-bound pigment. French painters marveled at the English "aquarellists" who exhibited at the Paris Salon of 1824. Corot described how, on seeing the watercolors of Bonington, he was transformed from an errand boy to a painter.

Many painters, including Turner, were indebted to the work of John Robert Cozens, who, in addition to making the usual topographical studies of "The Grand Tour," produced numerous watercolor sketches of desolate and barren landscapes. Constable described his paintings as "all poetry" and Cozens himself as "the greatest genius that ever touched landscape." As a teacher, Cozens did not follow the convention of instructing his pupils to copy either

ABOVE: The White House, Chelsea: *Thomas Girtin. Girtin was one of the first English artists to concentrate on watercolor. In this painting he used just five colors, overlaid to produce a painting of depth and richness of color.*

LEFT: Venice from the Giudecca: *J. M. W. Turner. This painting characterizes Turner's mastery of watercolor.*

his own work or that of the great masters. Believing that such methods served only to weaken his students' powers of invention, he encouraged them to experiment with technique, suggesting that they should develop landscapes from "blots" of color.

The development of landscape watercolor painting in England was an important factor in the formation of England's only recognizable "school" of painting, the Norwich school, founded by John Crome and later joined by John Sell Cotman. These two, together with their children and friends, formed a society whose common aim was to work directly from nature. Working in East Anglia, where flat plains and large expanses of sky produce striking qualities of light, they tended to use natural color values, rather than the color schemes of the Italian schools which had such a dominating influence on painters working elsewhere. Cotman's skill as a watercolorist has never been surpassed, but there are those who feel that technique sometimes replaced real personal expression in his work.

After Blake and Palmer, watercolor became established as the medium most suited to recording various aspects of the English scene. The tradition was maintained by Paul Nash and, later, his students, Edward Bawden and Eric Ravillious. All three were war artists during World War II. They found in watercolor a natural choice in their approach to landscape painting. In the United States a tradition in watercolor painting was established by such artists as Winslow Homer, Thomas Eakins, and more recently, Andrew Wyeth.

The watercolor paintings of Paul Cézanne are worthy of special consideration, and any serious student should study them, even in reproduction. Even Cézanne's most inconclusive watercolors seem to possess the quality of completeness. It was through watercolor that Cézanne discovered the use of colored patches which characterized his later work. Using a limited number of washes, he would overlay blue and green and perhaps yellow ocher in various strengths to give his paintings the quality of vibrant modulation. The nearest points of

ABOVE: Superimposed washes in a single color. *Tonal gradations can be achieved by laying washes of the same strength on top of one another. Each wash must be allowed to dry before the next.*

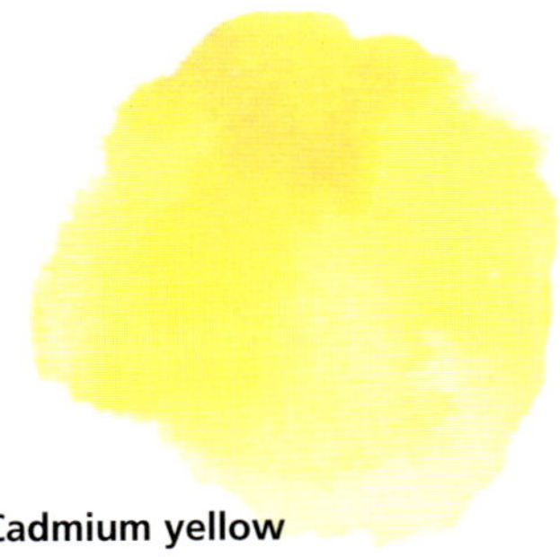

Cadmium yellow

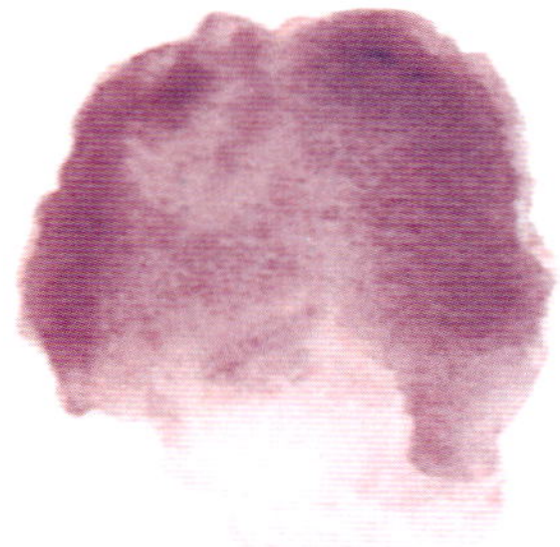

Cobalt violet

Cobalt blue

Cobalt

Lemon yellow

The colors illustrated here are those most generally available, and also the most permanent. From this range one can select a personal palette; a range of colors more suited to one's own particular requirements. It is better to start with a few colours in order to gain experience of mixing colors. White is added to make body color.

Cerulean blue

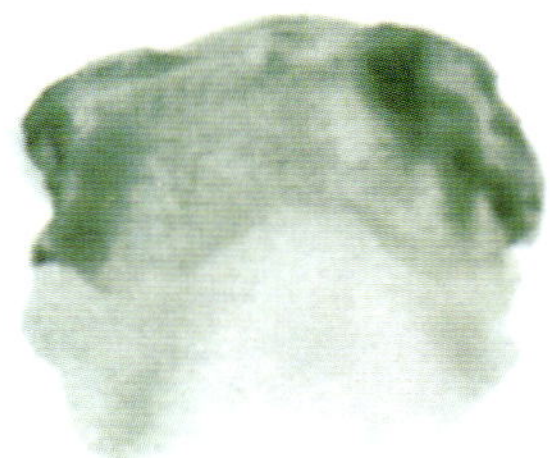

Terre verte

Permanent yellow

Ultramarine

Viridian

Yellow ocher

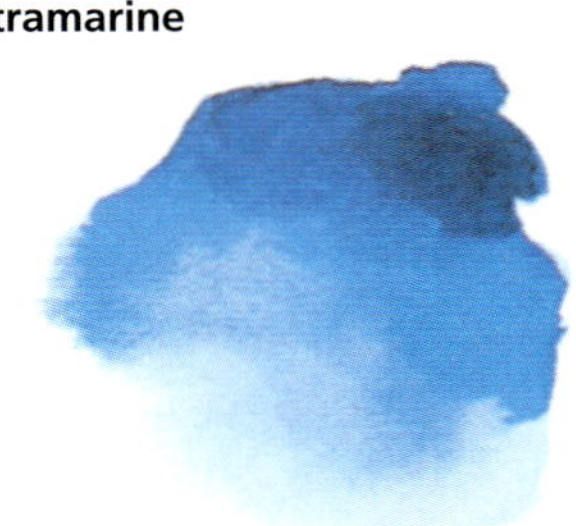

Monastral (phthatocyanine blue)

each object were left white, not as highlights, but to suggest volume. This was in line with the dictum that nature was modeled on the sphere, the cylinder, and the cone.

The important characteristic of watercolor is that the transparent glazes of color appear to be luminous when applied to a white ground. (This luminosity is lost when darker grounds are used). Tonal values are determined by the amount of water used to dilute the raw pigment. The French, who refer to watercolor as the "English method," often prefer to add white paint, which makes the glazes of color opaque. The only difference between watercolor and gouache is the addition in gouache of white to the transparent color. It sometimes happens that one needs a combination of pure watercolor and gouache. In dealing with architecture and water, for instance, or in chalkland landscapes, all the colors tend to be muted

Cadmium red

Burnt sienna

Ivory black

Alizarin crimson

Raw sienna

Lamp black

Indian red

Burnt umber

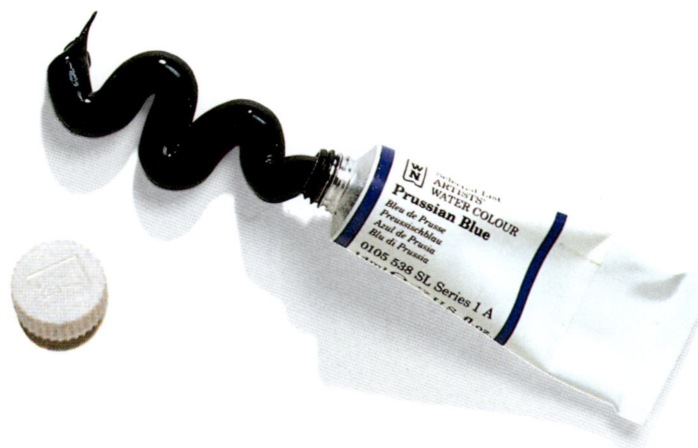

Light red

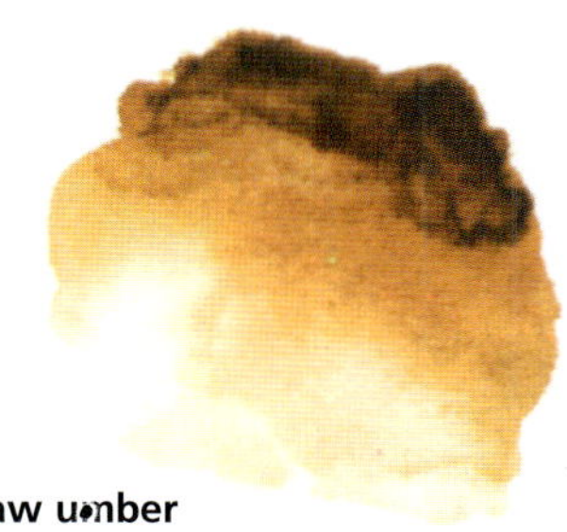

Raw umber

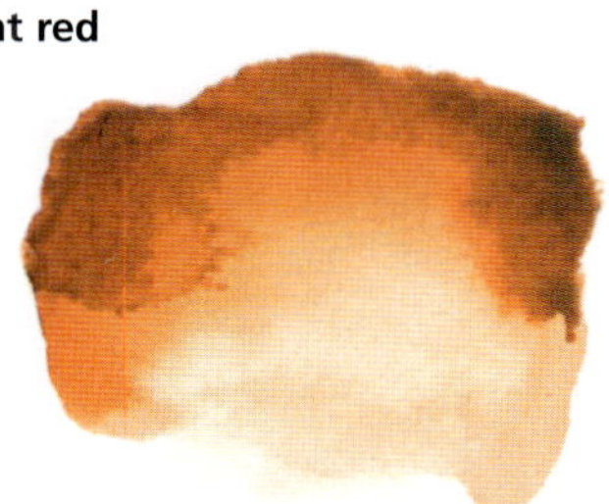

Venetian red

neutrals which are influenced by the presence of chalk.

The powdered pigments are bound in gum arabic, which is soluble in water. Watercolor pigment prepared commercially rarely contains enough gum, and it is useful wherever possible to have your water container filled with a mixture of distilled water and gum arabic. Pigments can be divided into two main groups, mineral and organic, and may be further subdivided as follows:

Mineral

The earth colors: yellow ocher, terre verte, natural ultramarine

Artificial: Cobalt blue, viridian, cadmium

Organic

Animal: Indian yellow, sepia, carmine

Vegetable: The madders, indigo, sap green

Artificial: Prussian blue

The range of colors in your watercolor box should relate to your personal needs. It is, therefore, better to purchase the box and cakes of color separately. A 12-color palette will meet the needs of most painters. Pigments that are bound in gum tend to be less permanent than those mixed with oil, and most manufacturers code the various colors according to their degree of permanence.

The following palette was used by Paul Nash and is a useful guide for selecting your own palette.

Red	Blue	Yellow
Vermilion	Cobalt	Yellow ocher
Light red	Cerulean	Naples yellow
India red	Ultramarine	Lemon yellow
Rose madder		Chrome yellow
Green	**Brown**	**Ivory black**
Cobalt	Burnt sienna	Chinese white
Viridian	Raw sienna	Payne's gray
Terre verte	Raw umber	Sepia

BELOW: *Watercolor can be bought in liquid form though the colors tend to be more fugitive. Round cakes of color are popular though the color range is limited.*

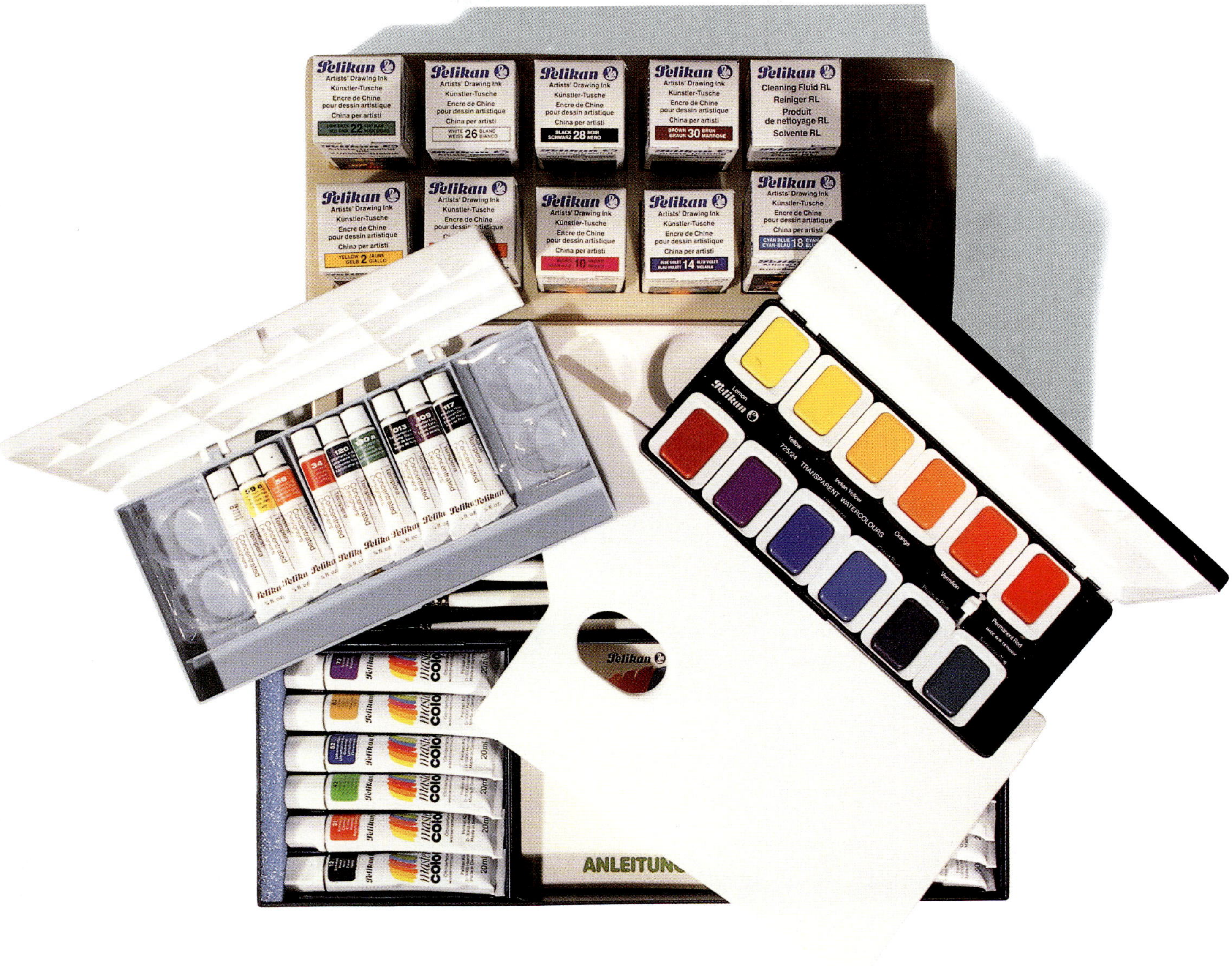

WASHES AND COLOR MIXING

Too much emphasis is placed on the handling of watercolor. Although exercises in applying gradated washes are useful to some extent, the best way to learn to handle watercolor is to work directly from nature. All too often one sees blue skies, for instance, made up of superbly gradated washes which bear little relationship to the rest of the painting. Essentially, there are two main approaches to watercolor. One can begin with a preliminary drawing in pencil or from the start with a loaded brush. Each method has its pitfalls. If the linear statement is too dominant, there is a tendency merely to fill in color in the areas determined by the drawn lines. On the other hand, color masses which simply merge into each other are difficult to control. It is essential to establish a homogeneous relationship between the drawn lines and the washes of color. Pencil lines can usually be partially cancelled out by washes of color, as can a preliminary drawing with brush and watercolor. Alternatively, pen and watercolor work quite well together. Again the subject might determine the best way of working—architectural subjects might work best with a combination of pencil or pen and color washes, whereas plant studies or pure landscape might be best dealt with using a brush for both the drawing and the planes of color. Make sure that you have enough water to replenish the waterpot from time to time—nothing is worse than trying to get a clean color with muddy water. Try also to carry an extra plate or saucer for color mixing, so that sufficient quantities of color can be mixed for large areas of flat color in the painting.

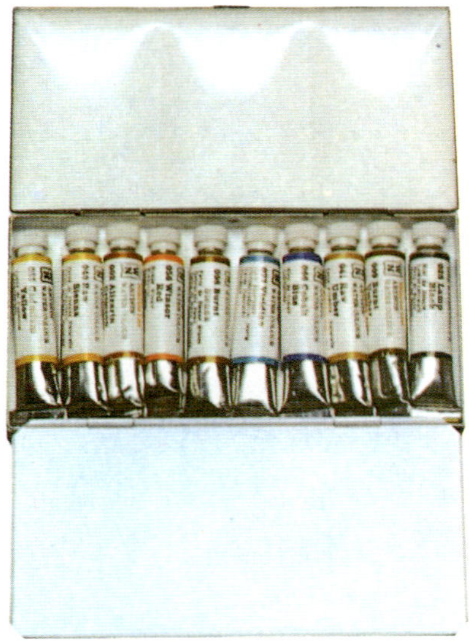

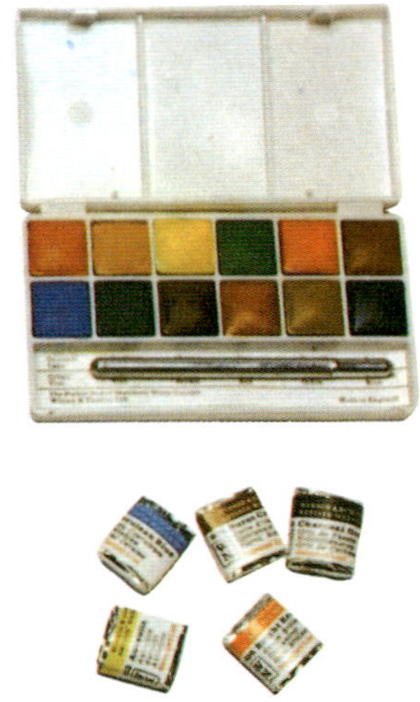

LIGHTING

For indoor work it is vital to organize a good system of lighting. Working by a window with light coming over your left shoulder (or right shoulder if you are left-handed) can be quite satisfactory if the window faces north and gives an even and relatively unchanging light. It is less so if the window faces the sun, since the light may constantly change from brilliant to murky and may even throw distracting patches of light and shade across your work. An artificial light of the fluorescent "daylight" type will enable you to work in a poorly lit room or corner and to continue working when the light has faded—winter days can seem very short for those dependent on daylight. Such light can be used either instead of natural light or to supplement it, and there is one type with a screw base that can be fitted to the edge of a table or an adjacent shelf.

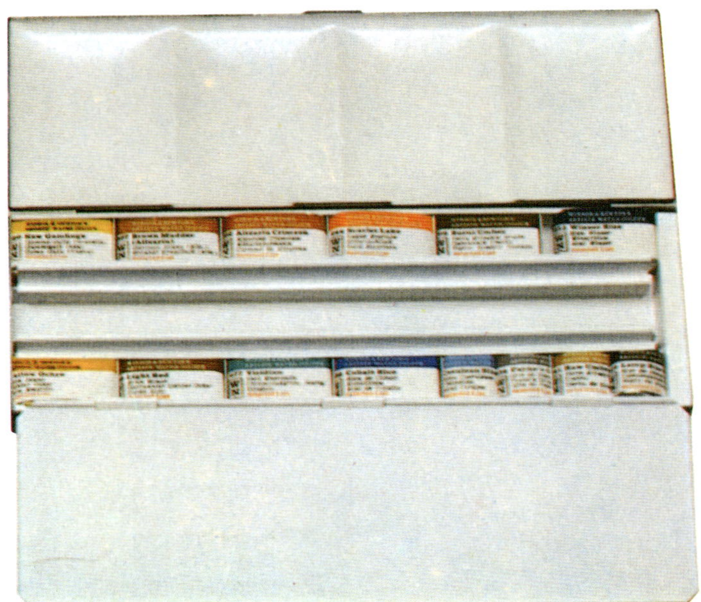

ABOVE: *Ideally, the semi-moist cakes of color are of the best quality. Tubes of watercolor can be used on their own or to supplement the colors in a paintbox. Pocket watercolors are ideal for sketching and avoid the burden of carrying too much equipment.*

BOARDS, PALETTES, AND OTHER EQUIPMENT

You will need a drawing board, or possibly two boards of different sizes, to support the paper and stretch it where necessary. A piece of plywood or blockboard is perfectly adequate provided the surface is smooth and the wood soft enough to take drawing pins. For outdoor work a piece of hardboard can be used, with the paper clipped to it, though the paper must be heavy enough not to require stretching.

If you buy paints in paintbox form you will already have a palette; if not, you will need one with compartments for mixing paint. Watercolor palettes are made in plastic, metal or ceramic, in a variety of sizes, and some have a thumbhole so that they can be held in the non-painting hand when working outdoors. Water containers are

LEFT: *Any plate or dish can be used for mixing watercolor, but there are several specially made palettes on the market. The thumbhole variety is especially useful for outdoor work.*

another necessity for outdoor work; there is nothing worse than arriving at your chosen spot to find that you have forgotten the water. Containers can be bought, plastic soft-drink bottles can be used to carry the water, and any light (unbreakable) container such as a yogurt pot will suffice to put it in.

Various other items, though not strictly essential, can be useful and inexpensive aids for watercolor work and can easily be replaced when necessary. Small natural sponges can be used instead of brushes to apply washes, to sponge out areas and to create soft, smudgy cloud effects; paper towels, blotting paper, and cotton wool can be used in much the same way. Toothbrushes are useful for spattering paint to create textured effects, to suggest sand or pebbles on a beach, for example. A scalpel, or a razor blade, is often used to scrape away small areas of paint in a highlight area. And both masking tape and masking fluid can serve to stop out areas while a wash is laid over the top, leaving a hard-edged area of white paper when removed.

APPLICATION

Pure watercolor, being transparent, must be applied from light to dark. The paper itself is used to create the pure white or light tones which, with opaque paints, would be made by using white alone or mixed with colored pigment.

Any area required to be white is simply "reserved," or left unpainted, so that when it is surrounded with darker washes it will shine out with great brilliance. Pale tones are created in the same way, with a light-colored wash put on first and then surrounded with darker tones. Light reflected off the paper, back through these thin skins of paint known as washes, gives a watercolor painting a spontaneity and sparkle which cannot be achieved with any other medium. Hence watercolor's popularity with artists both past and present.

The two most important facts about watercolor are, first, that it is always to some extent unpredictable, even in the hands of experts, and, second, that because dark is always worked over light, some

starter palette

These colors will provide a perfectly adequate range for most needs. Some artists work with fewer. From left to right: cobalt blue, Prussian blue, viridian, yellow ocher, cadmium yellow, lemon yellow, cadmium red, alizarin crimson, burnt umber, Payne's gray, and ivory black.

using gum water

Gum water, which is gum arabic diluted in water, adds richness to watercolors and keeps the colors bright. It can also be used, as here, as a sort of resist method to create highlights.

1 *The tree and hedge are painted in with pure watercolour.*

2 *A further wash of green is applied, this time mixed with gum water.*

3 *The area of the central tree is spattered with water, flicked on with a household brush.*

4 *The central tree is blotted with a rag, so that wherever the water has touched, small areas of paint are lifted off, the gum being soluble in water.*

5 *The lighter patches of color give an extra sparkle to the tree, while the addition of the gum water imparts richness to the dark green on either side.*

1

2

3

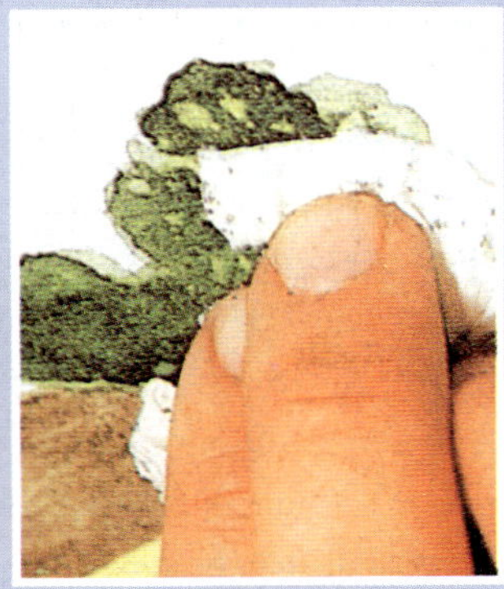

4

5

planning is needed before beginning the painting. It is not always necessary to do a detailed and complicated drawing on the paper, only enough to work out the basic shapes and design; this really should be done, however, or you will begin without really knowing which areas are to be left white or pale and how they will fit into the painting as a whole.

Thus the first step in any painting is to establish where the first wash is to be applied; and the first step in watercolor technique is to learn how to put on the wash.

LAYING A FLAT WASH

The wash is the basis of all watercolor painting, whether it is a broad, sweeping one, covering a large expanse, such as a sky or the background to a portrait, or a much smaller one laid on a particular area. Washes need not be totally flat. They can be gradated in both tone and color, or broken up and varied. But the technique of laying a flat wash must be mastered, even if you subsequently find that you seldom use it.

The support should be tilted at a slight angle so that the brushstrokes flow into one another, but do not run down the paper. For a broad wash a large chisel-end brush is normally used; for a smaller one, or a wash which is to be laid against a complicated edge, a smaller round brush may be more manageable. Laying a wash must

ABOVE: *Small natural sponges are a invaluable aid to watercolor painting, both for applying paint and for correcting or modifying areas. Rags, kitchen paper and cotton buds should also form part of the basic equipment.*

be done quickly or hard edges will form between brushstrokes. Therefore mix up more paint than you think you will need. Start by damping the paper with clear water (this is not actually essential, but helps the paint to go on evenly). Working in one direction, lay a horizontal line of color at the top of the area, then another below it, working in the opposite direction, and continue working in alternate directions until the area is covered. Never go back over the wet paint because you feel it is uneven or not dark enough, as this will result in the paint's "flooding" and leave blobs and patches. A final word of caution: if the doorbell or the telephone rings while you are in the middle of a wash, ignore it; otherwise you will return to a hard edge which is impossible, or at least very difficult to remove.

Leave the wash to dry before working on adjacent areas of the painting. Not until the wash is completely dry will you be able to establish either how even it is or what its true color value is (watercolor dries much paler than it appears when wet). The ability to assess the precise tone of a wash comes only with experience, but

flat wash

A flat wash in a vivid color is being laid on dampened paper with a broad, flat-ended brush. It is not strictly necessary to dampen the paper (many artists prefer the slightly "dragged" look given by working on dry paper) but dampening facilitates an even covering. Tilt the board slightly so that the brushstrokes flow into one another, and work backward and forward down the paper until the whole area is covered.

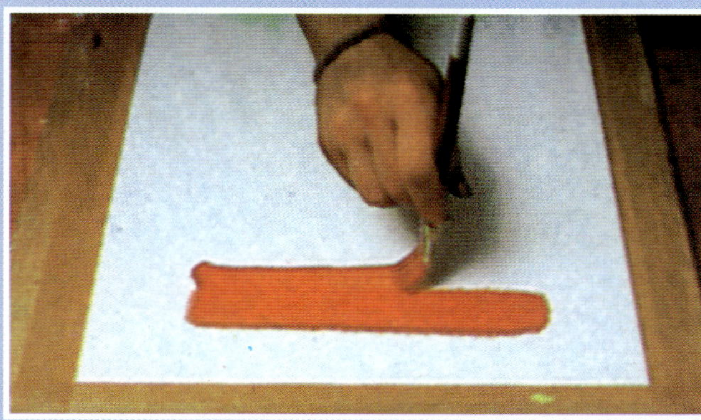

sponge wash

Often a wash needs to be slightly textured or varied in strength, for which purpose a sponge is useful.

1 *The wash is mixed with a brush and tested on a piece of spare paper.*

2 *Enough paint is mixed to cover the area and the sponge is dipped into it. For a lighter covering, some of the paint can be squeezed out.*

3 *A variegated effect is achieved by applying the paint quite thickly with the first stroke, much more thinly with the second.*

4 *The final wash can be worked into with the sponge while it is still wet in order to lighten some areas and produce a soft, shimmering effect.*

1

2

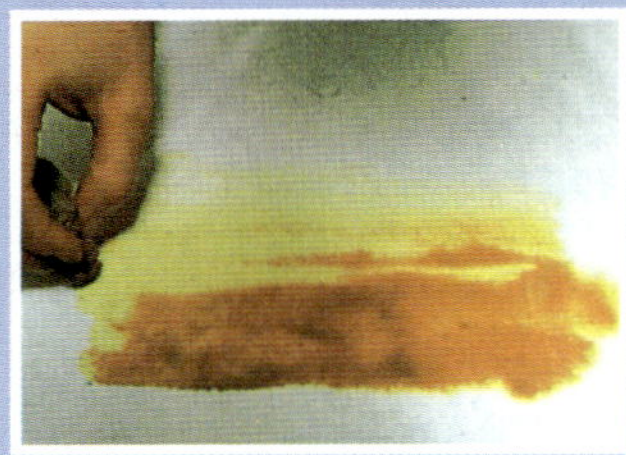
3

4

variegated wash

1 *The paper is dampened with a sponge and a thin wash of color is applied, also with a sponge.*

2 *A second color is then flooded on, using the tip of the sponge so that the two run together.*

3 *A brush is now used to touch in darker areas on the still-wet paint. Very subtle effects can be created by this wet-into-wet technique, but they are always to some extent unpredictable.*

1

2

3

it can be helpful to lay down one or two patches of flat color on a spare piece of paper and allow them to dry as a preliminary test. Washes can be laid on top of the first one to strengthen the color or darken the tone, though too many will turn the painting muddy. Purists claim that more than three layers spoils the quality.

Another method of laying a wash is to use a sponge. This is particularly useful when a slightly variegated or textured wash is required, as the sponge can either be filled with paint for a dense covering or used relatively dry for a paler effect. A sponge can also be used in conjunction with a brush. If, for instance, you rinse it in clean water and squeeze it out you can remove some of the paint laid by a brush while it is still wet, thus lightening selected areas—a good technique for skies or distant hills or to create a soft shimmering effect. Watercolor painting is well suited to representing changing weather conditions, especially the cloudy and watery skies of the northern hemisphere.

GOUACHE

Gouache is sometimes called "body color." Like watercolor, it is bound in gum arabic and is soluble in water. It is characterized by a rich, matt, opaque surface which lacks the transparency of watercolor and the gloss of oil paint. It is a fine medium for architectural subjects, or for figures in interiors, since it lends itself to fine detail. Historically it was used primarily for manuscripts, although in the seventeenth century it became more widely used as a medium for painting by Italian and Dutch artists, including Zuccarelli and Van Dyck. In the eighteenth century, Paul Sandby used both watercolor and gouache extensively. Toulouse Lautrec produced some of his finest café paintings using gouache on scraps of brown paper and card. Edouard Vuillard painted his evocative, atmospheric interiors

TOP: *The color is diluted almost to the consistency of watercolor to register the main forms in the landscape view.*

ABOVE RIGHT: *Colors in the middle-distance are intensified to concentrate attention on that part of the composition.*

using a dry-brush technique. Among contemporary artists, the gouache paintings by Keith Vaughan, Ceri Richards, and Graham Sutherland are outstanding.

Gouache is an ideal medium for recording the changing conditions of light in landscape painting. It dries quite rapidly and with a limited palette one can continually modify tones in such a way that the right balance is achieved. The opacity of the color makes it possible to rework certain passages of the painting in a way that is not possible in watercolor. Gouache paints are opaque and tend to dry lighter than when first applied. The pigment is ground together with a white filler which gives them their opacity. They have been in use for a much longer period than watercolor, although recently they have been replaced to some extent by acrylic paints, which are also water soluble. Nevertheless, gouache is a very adaptable medium with a wide range of colors available. The color can be used thickly or it may be watered down to a fine wash. It can be used on both white paper and colored paper, on cardboard and even on manila wrapping paper.

The opacity of gouache, and the fact that light colors can be laid on dark, makes it very different in character from watercolor. It can be used in varying consistencies, but there is no point in using it thinly as a substitute for watercolor. It should be exploited for its own inherent qualities. The colors can be very rich, especially when they are close in tone. It is common practice to work from neutral

TOP CENTER: *The darker tones of the trees provide a visual link from the foreground to the distance.*

ABOVE LEFT AND RIGHT: *The various parts of the painting begin to work together. The detail in the foreground is understated in order to focus on the valley and hills.*

colors toward the darkest tones. Dry brushwork—where the brush is starved of color—is another technique that works well in gouache. The surface of the paint can be scraped down with the edge of a sharp blade and gum arabic can be added to give the paint surface a slight glaze.

RIGHT: *Gouache or body color comes in tubes and the color range is extensive.*

OILS

ABOVE: Autumn at Argenteuil: *Claude Monet (1840–1926). The French Impressionists were very much influenced by Constable's landscape paintings, and Monet in particular took the preoccupation with the effects of light almost to the point of an obsession. He frequently worked outdoors, and would paint several versions of the same scene in different lights, building up the paint in thick impastos to achieve the ever-changing effects suggestive of motion which he sought.*

In recent decades there has been an amazing proliferation of new materials for artists and designers, so much so that a visit to one of the larger artists' suppliers can leave an uninitiated person feeling confused and bewildered. There are pencils, pens, crayons, and pastels in every color of the rainbow; there are acrylic paints, both in tubes and in pots; there are watercolors in tubes, pans, and boxes; there are gouaches and poster paints; there are even special paints for fabrics and ceramics. Indeed, special materials are now available for almost any surface that could conceivably be painted or decorated. And, often tucked away unobtrusively in one corner, there are oil paints.

Why, then, are oil paints still so popular with professional artists and "Sunday painters" alike? There are two main reasons for this, the first being that oil paint is the most versatile of all the painting media, and can be used in any number of ways to suit all styles, subjects and sizes of work. The second is that it is the easiest medium for a beginner to use. Which is not to say, of course, that a novice will automatically be able to create a masterpiece at first try—that is most unlikely. But because oil paint can be manipulated, scraped off and overpainted, built up and then scraped down once again, it enables you to learn by trial and error, uninhibited by the thought of having "to start all over again," or waste expensive materials. This is not true of any other medium: acrylic, for example, cannot be moved at all once it has been laid down, and watercolor—a lovely medium but a tricky one—quickly loses all its qualities of freshness and translucence if overworked. Of course, an overworked oil painting will not be a perfect picture, but it may at least be a creditable one, if only because of the knowledge gained in painting it.

Oil paint, though regarded as a "traditional" painting medium, is actually quite young in terms of art history. In Europe, before the

RIGHT: Olive Trees: *Vincent Van Gogh (1853–90). The Impressionists' use of paint was free and daring by the academic standards of the day, but Van Gogh's was the most innovative by far, and even those accustomed to the newer styles found his paintings perplexing and even shocking. No one had hitherto dared to represent the sky or foliage as a series of thickly-painted swirls, as in this painting, or the ground as broken lines of bright, unblended color.*

LEFT: Self Portrait: *Rembrandt van Rijn (1606–69). Rembrandt shocked many of his contemporaries by his bold use of paint, which produced thick, textured surfaces. The popular Dutch paintings of the time were characterized by a very smooth finish, with no visible brushstrokes, while in Rembrandt's later work brushstrokes and the paint itself are used to suggest texture, the paint being used almost as a modeling medium in places.*

ABOVE: Man in a Turban: *Jan van Eyck (active 1422–41). In his oil paintings, van Eyck used much the same methods as previously used for tempera work, building up thin layers of paint, one over another, the technique known as glazing. However, oil paint used in this way gives a depth and luminosity of effect which cannot be achieved with tempera.*

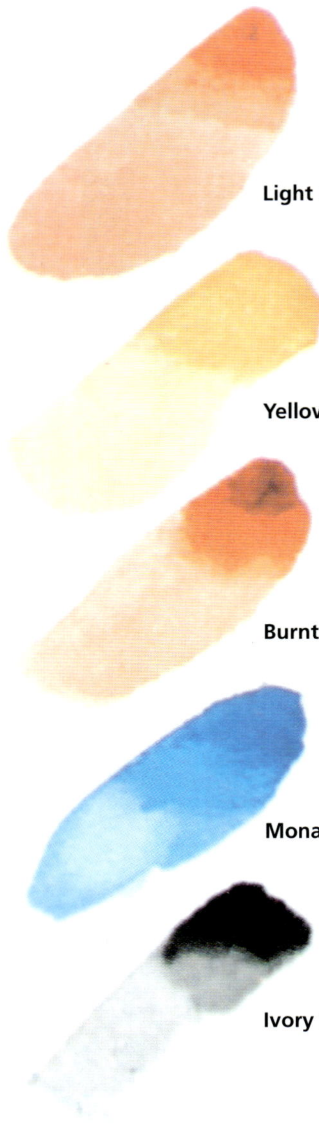

invention of oil paint in the fifteenth century, artists painted with tempera, which is color pigment bound with egg yolk. This was a difficult medium to use as it dried very fast, and thus called for a deliberate and meticulous approach.

The Flemish painter Jan van Eyck (*c.*1390–1441) was the first to experiment with raw pigments bound with an oil mixture, when he found that one of his tempera paintings had split while drying in the sun. Not only did the oil paints dry without cracking, but, as van Eyck discovered, they could be applied in thin, transparent layers which gave the colors a depth and luminosity hitherto unknown.

The early painters in oil, like van Eyck, used the paint thinly, with delicate brushstrokes that are almost invisible to the eye. But the full potential of oil paint was not really exploited until it was taken up by the Italian painters of the fifteenth and sixteenth centuries, notably Giorgione (1475–1510) and Titian (*c.*1487–1576).

In Titian's hands, and later in those of the great Dutch painter Rembrandt (1606–1669), oil paint was at last used with a feeling for its own inherent qualities. Both artists combined delicately painted areas of glazing (thin paint applied in layers over one another) with thick brushstrokes in which the actual marks of the brush became a feature rather than something to be disguised. Rembrandt's later paintings must have seemed quite shocking to a public accustomed to the smooth, satin finish of other contemporary Dutch paintings—a common complaint was that they looked unfinished.

The English landscape painter John Constable (1776–1837), and the French Impressionists later in the nineteenth century, took the freedom of painting to even greater lengths by using oil as a quick sketching medium, often working outdoors. In Constable's day the camera had yet to be invented, and artists had of necessity to make a great many sketches as references for their finished works. Constable's wonderful sky and landscape studies, made rapidly, often on scraps of paper and cardboard, were never intended as finished works of art; but to our eyes they are much more pleasing, and

ABOVE: Appledore: *Thomas Girtin. This Devon fishing village is almost unchanged since Girtin painted it. He produced this painting using only five colors carefully overlaid to create subtle tones.*

ABOVE: Snowstorm: *William Turner (1775–1851). This painting demonstrates the wonderful atmospheric effects that Turner obtained by the use of transparent glazes of oil color.*

infinitely more exciting, than his large polished studio paintings, because they have the quality of immediacy that landscape painting seems to demand.

The Impressionists, who drew inspiration from Constable, applied their paint in thick dabs and strokes of broken color to depict what was their main preoccupation—the ever-changing effects of light on the landscape. Vincent Van Gogh (1853–1890), who was not an Impressionist but is sometimes grouped with them because he was working at much the same time, used both the color and the texture of the paint to express his emotions and to define forms, treating the paint almost as a modeling medium. We are so familiar with Van Gogh's paintings through countless reproductions that it is hard to appreciate how strange, indeed even offensive, those great, thick, swirling brushstrokes must have looked to his contemporaries (Van Gogh sold only one painting during his entire lifetime).

BELOW: *A suggested "starter palette." From right to left: white (above), yellow ocher, cadmium yellow, cadmium red, alizarin crimson, cobalt violet, ultramarine, Prussian blue, and viridian.*

The palette chosen depends on the subject to be painted: for instance, violet might not be needed at all, cobalt blue might be used instead of the other two blues, an additional green, such as chrome oxide, added, and a different yellow chosen.

The photograph shows the colors mixed with varying amounts of white.

OIL PAINT TODAY

The very diversity of painting techniques in the past has had the effect of freeing us from any preconceptions about the medium. It is what you want it to be; there is no "right" or "wrong" way of doing an oil painting. Today's paintings use oil paint in so many different ways that it is often hard to believe that the same medium has been used. Interestingly, the art of tempera painting is now undergoing a revival, and some artists working in oil use a similar technique, applying thin layers of transparent glazes to produce a luminous, light-filled quality. Other artists apply paint thickly with a knife, building it up on the surface of the canvas so that it resembles a relief sculpture.

New painting mediums—oils, varnishes and extenders—are constantly being developed in recognition of these different needs; for example, you can choose one type of medium if you want to build up delicate glazes, another if you want to achieve a thick, textured surface using the impasto technique.

Oil paints can be mixed with other types of paint and even other media; for instance, they can be used in conjunction with oil pastels for quick and dramatic effects; they can be drawn into with pencils; and some artists even mix paint with sand to create areas of texture.

CHOOSING PAINTS

Materials for oil painting can be costly; so it is advisable to work out your "starter kit" carefully. Begin by buying the minimum and adding extra colors, brushes, and so on when you have progressed to the stage of understanding your particular requirements. For example, someone who intends to specialize in flower painting will need a different range of colors from someone whose chosen theme is seascapes, while a person working on a miniature scale will use brushes quite unlike those needed for large-scale paintings.

Oil paints are divided into two main categories: artists' and students' colors. The latter are less expensive because they contain less pure pigment and more fillers and extenders, but in general they are a false economy for that very reason; they cannot provide the same intensity of color as the more expensive range. However, students' colors are fine for practising with, and it is possible to combine the two types using the students' colors for browns and other colors where intensity is not a prime requirement, and artists' for the pure colors such as red, yellow and blue. A large-size tube of white works out most economical, since white is used more than most other colors.

Paints in the artists' range are not all the same price—a trap for the unwary. They are classified in series, usually from 1 to 7 (different manufacturers have different methods of classification), series 7 being extremely expensive. The price differences reflect the expense and/or scarcity of the pigment used. Nowadays, because

there are so many excellent chemical pigments, it is seldom necessary to use the very expensive colors, such as vermilion, except in very special cases.

It is often said that all colors can be mixed from the three primaries, red, yellow, and blue. To some extent this is true, but they will certainly not provide a subtle or exciting range, and in any case there are a great many different versions of red, yellow, and blue. The illustration shows a suggested "starter palette," which should provide an adequate mix of colors for most purposes. In general you will need, as well as white, a warm and a cool version of each of the primaries, plus a brown and a green and perhaps a violet or purple. Strictly speaking, greens are not essential as they can be mixed to arrive at the right hue, and there really is not much point in spending more time in mixing than you need. Viridian is a good choice, since it mixes well with any color. Other useful additions to your palette are rose madder in the red group; a lemon yellow such as Winsor or cadmium lemon in the yellow group; cerulean blue and Antwerp or cobalt blue in the blue group; and sap green and chrome green in the greens. Good browns and grays are burnt sienna, burnt umber and Payne's gray. Flake white dries quickly and is resistant to cracking, but it contains poisonous lead; for this reason some artists prefer to use titanium white, which is nontoxic. The use of black is often frowned upon, and many artists never use it as it can have a deadening effect, but it can be mixed with yellow to produce a rich olive green, and many landscape artists use it for this purpose.

PAINTING MEDIUMS

Oil paint can be used just as it comes from the tube, or it can be a combination of oil and a thinner (what artists call a medium). If you try to apply undiluted paint accurately in a small area, you will see why such mediums are necessary; without them the paint is not easily malleable.

The most popular medium is the traditional blend of linseed oil and turpentine or white spirit, usually in a ratio of 60% oil and 40% thinner. Linseed oil dries to a glossy finish which is resistant to cracking—but be sure to buy either purified or cold-pressed linseed oil, which dry without yellowing. Boiled linseed oil, the sort found in hardware shops, contains impurities which cause yellowing.

Linseed oil is slow to dry, which may not suit your way of working and can produce a rather churned-up paint surface. There are several faster-drying mediums available, such as drying linseed oil, drying poppy oil, stand oil (which also makes the paint flow well and disguises brushstrokes) and an alkyd-based medium sold under the name of Liquin.

Turpentine is the most commonly used artist's thinner, though in fact oil of turpentine is just as good and is less likely to cause the headaches and allergic reactions which artists sometimes complain of when using turpentine. Oil of turpentine also has less odor, and stores without deteriorating.

LEFT: *This painting was begun with a monochrome underpainting in dilute cobalt blue, an unusual but deliberate choice of color, as the blue is repeated throughout the picture. The flowers and drapery were then built up in thicker paint, the method known as "fat over lean," the background and foliage being left quite thin.*

Special ready-mixed painting mediums are sold for specific purposes. Linseed oil, for instance, is not suitable for glazing as it will dribble down the surface of the canvas, but Liquin is excellent for this purpose. Another alkyd medium, Oleopasto, has been developed specially for impasto work. It is designed to extend the paint and add body to it so that it can be applied in thick layers, with the brush or knife marks clearly visible.

GENERAL PAINTING TECHNIQUES

Although there are really no hard-and-fast rules in oil painting, it is helpful to have an idea of the various ways in which artists go about things so that you can experiment with different techniques, color schemes and compositions as you evolve your own particular style. Rules are often useful in a negative way: once you know a rule, you can break it for reasons of your own, or "bend" it, as many artists have done with the rules of perspective. Constable and the French Impressionists broke the rules of their times, thus freeing painting from the very rigid set of procedures to which artists had previously been forced to adhere, but their knowledge of all the theories of painting was very thorough indeed.

If you are painting a very simple subject, such as an empty landscape with a wide expanse of sky, there is often no need for an underdrawing or underpainting, except perhaps a line or two to delineate the horizon. However, for a more complex subject such as a figure study, or perhaps a landscape including people or buildings, a preliminary drawing on the canvas is usually advisable. This

one should avoid bright and light colors, as you will want to build up to these as the painting progresses. Nowadays artists often use acrylic paint for underpainting, as this dries much faster than even thinned oil paint, enabling the next stage to proceed immediately.

A good general rule for oil painting—and a very old one—is to work "fat over lean." This simply means that in the initial stages the paint should be used fairly thin (diluted with turpentine only), becoming thicker and oilier as the painting progresses. Working in this way reduces the risk of the paint cracking as it dries out. If, however, "lean" paint is brushed over a layer of "fat" paint (containing a greater proportion of oil) what happens is that the lean layer dries first, and when the fat layer beneath it eventually starts to dry it contracts, causing the dry layer on top to crack.

Not all paintings, however, are done in stages in this way; many are completed at one sitting, with a minimum of drawing or underpainting or even none at all. This is known as alla prima painting, and is much used for landscape or quick portrait studies where the painter wants to record his impressions rapidly in a free and spontaneous manner. The paint is used thickly, with each color laid down more or less as it will finally appear. When oil paints are used in this way, the colors blend into each other, particularly when one is laid on top of another. This is a feature of alla prima painting, known as working "wet-into-wet," and was much exploited by the Impressionists, particularly Claude Monet (1840–1926) in his outdoor paintings. For anyone who has not used oils before, alla prima is a good way of starting, as it will give you an immediate "feel" for the medium and force you to work fast without being overconscious of each brushstroke.

ACRYLICS

Acrylic paints have been in general use for only about 20 years or so. They are made by combining colored pigment with a synthetic resin. Acrylics are water soluble and dry very rapidly. One particular advantage for the beginner is that because no traditions or established techniques prevail, one is free to make use of the medium in a completely personal way. Acrylics can be used in thin washes of color or as a thicker impasto. For those artists who previously tended to combine watercolor with gouache, acrylics offer an alternative method. They can be painted on almost any surface—from canvas to cardboard—and even on unprimed surfaces. They are ideal for use on a large scale, and are especially suitable for mural painting, since they do not crack or gather dust so readily as other paints. A completed painting can safely be cleaned from time to time with soapy water. Acrylics are being used increasingly by both students and professional painters.

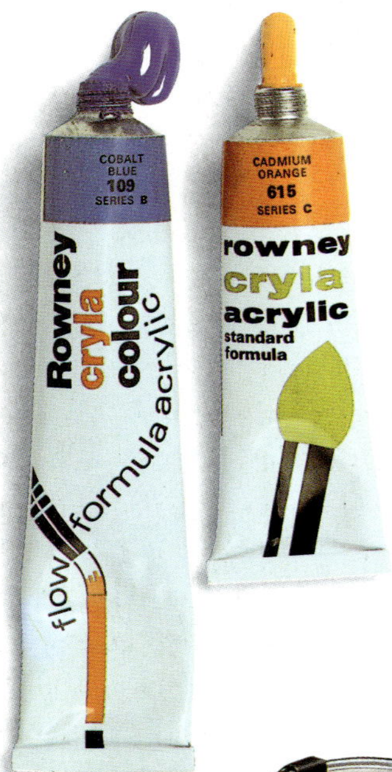

ADVANTAGES OF ACRYLIC

One of the advantages of acrylic is its speed of working. It dries rapidly, in minutes if need be, and permanently. Alternatively, drying can be prolonged to suit individual working requirements. Acrylic dries throughout so thoroughly, it can be varnished immediately with either a matt (eggshell) or glossy finish.

Another advantage is that acrylic is both tough and flexible.

WHY ACRYLICS?

They are simple and clean to handle; flexible; water resistant; tough. Acrylics can simulate other paints: smell good; need little special equipment; dry fast; can be cleaned; can be repaired; adhere permanently. Acrylic paint does not peel, crack, or split, and it is water-resistant. The surface of dried acrylic can be gently cleaned should the need arise, and can be repaired easily if damaged.

Perhaps the most advantageous characteristics of acrylic paint are its adhesive qualities. It can be applied, without difficulty, to almost anything, and remain, permanently, without flaking or rubbing off. Unlike oil paint, which can damage the surface of certain materials if applied without the appropriate priming, acrylic can be used without any special preparation if the situation demands.

Among other things, it will adhere satisfactorily to all kinds of wall surfaces, cloth, paper, cardboard, hardboard, wood, plastic—almost any object or surface suitable for a painting or decoration.

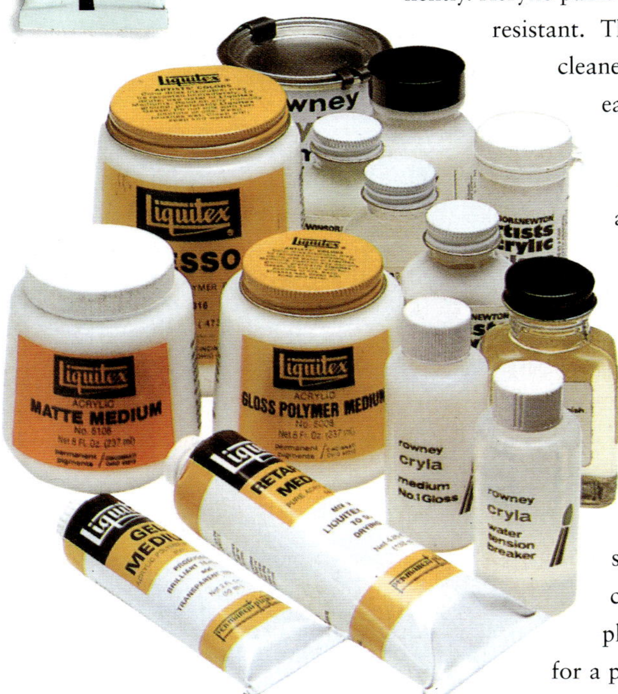

ABOVE: Sofa: *Terence Millington.*

LEFT: *Mediums are used with acrylic paints to give a heavier impasto, to add gloss, or conversely to make more matt, and to make them more liquid. Gesso primers can be used for both acrylic and egg-tempera paints.*

TOP LEFT: *Rowney Cryla colors are just one example of the many different types of acrylic paint available.*

FAR RIGHT: Girl Lying in a Hammock: *Leonard Rosomon.*

THE NATURE OF ACRYLIC PAINT

Acrylic is unlike any other paint, but it has affinities with all of them, since all paints contain the same ingredient: pigment. A pigment used in watercolor is identical to that used in oil and acrylic. The quality is equally high, its brightness and durability the same, and the care used in manufacture just as thorough.

The major difference between one paint and another is not the color but something much more fundamental: the binder. The binder largely decides the character and behaviour of the various paints. Binders also play a large part in permanence and drying qualities, brilliance and speed of working. They also determine what kinds of diluents (also known as solvents) and varnishes may be used in conjunction with them. For instance, water is the diluent for watercolors and gouache, and turpentine for oil, because of the liquid binders used.

A brief look into the history and development of paint will provide valuable insight into what may be achieved when it is used with imagination.

The history of painting reveals that before the establishment of paint and equipment manufacturers and suppliers most artists made their own materials. They ground their own paint, prepared their own supports and primings, even made their own brushes.

In studios in the fifteenth century the apprentices who worked under the master ground the colors and made the supports. It was all part of the artist's training.

Irksome as it may appear to us today, for them it was a normal part of the process of painting to know how paints were made as well as how to use them. It gave them, in effect, an enormous respect for their materials and was instrumental in achieving a high level of craft which, in turn, richly enhanced the creativity of their work.

Today, luckily, we can buy brushes and paint of a consistently high standard whenever we need them. And though we can buy every kind of support to suit all mediums, prepared for oil, tempera or acrylic—canvas, hardboard, cardboard, even paper for oil paint—we can, if we prefer, make our own with ready-to-be-assembled stretchers and prepare our own canvas or board with ready-made primings—not necessarily to save money, which it undoubtedly does, but for the satisfaction it will give.

Pigments are the coloring materials of paint, and are usually made in the form of powders. From the earliest, pigments had to be bright and clear, and able to withstand prolonged exposure to light. Certain colors were apt to fade and did not produce the subtle tints and shades we would admire today, but were more likely to produce a dead or muddy effect.

Throughout history, bright color was preferred for both practical and aesthetic reasons, having close associations with joy, celebration, pleasure, and delight. To express these emotions, bright, rich hues were in constant demand, and the search for pigments that possessed these qualities has been constant over the centuries.

By the Middle Ages the range of colors was quite extensive, and put to complicated use on walls, illuminations, panels, in books and on woodwork. An all-purpose paint like acrylic would have suited them admirably.

After the Renaissance, pigments reached a peak of brightness and variety. Thereafter a more expressive and realistic style emerged and the medium more suited to this was oil paint. Realistic paintings moved away from bright colors to rich, somber hues, which brought a new range of pigments into being. An interest in bright color returned again in the nineteenth century due, in part, to Constable and Turner, the designs of William Morris, and the Impressionists.

Delight in bright color today means a wide range of pigments, and the list of those available is long. The names of pigments often echo places: burnt Sienna, Venetian red, Naples yellow, Prussian blue, Chinese vermilion; or recall the materials they are derived from: cobalt blue, rose madder, emerald green, ivory black, sap green,

geranium lake, and so on. Though interesting sounding, the names give little indication of the quality or behavior of colors, and some are sold under two or three different names.

To simplify the situation, the names of absolutely necessary colors are listed further on, and you may want to look at a color chart to see the full range. The number of colors needed to produce a variety of tones and tints need not be large. Pigments today are bright, durable (unless specified) and capable of a great deal of mixing.

Briefly the requirements for a reliable pigment are that it should be a smooth, finely divided powder; insoluble in the medium in which it is used; able to withstand the action of light without changing color under normal exposure; and it should be chemically inert and unaffected by materials with which it is mixed, or by the atmosphere. Moreover, it should possess the proper degree of opacity or transparency to suit the purpose for which it is intended, and should conform to accepted standards of color and color quality.

The raw materials used to provide the pigments are customarily classified as inorganic or organic. Inorganic materials are those of purely mineral origin such as the natural earths: ochers, raw umber, which can be calcined like burnt umber and burnt sienna, and the artificially prepared colors like cadmium yellow and zinc oxide, the basis of the famous "Chinese white" which was introduced in 1837 by Winsor & Newton.

Organic pigments include animal and vegetable substances, as well as complex synthetic substances. Vegetable sources furnished color like gamboge, indigo (now not available) and madder. Animal sources produced cochineal which was made into carmine, and Indian yellow was an incredible color made in India from the urine of cows fed on mango leaves. It has now been replaced by synthetically made colors. Other artificially prepared organic colors include alizarin, or anilines (now largely discontinued for artists' colors, but occasionally used as constituents of household paints and printers' inks).

Many of these organic colors are no longer produced, and have been replaced by newer and more durable colors that have been

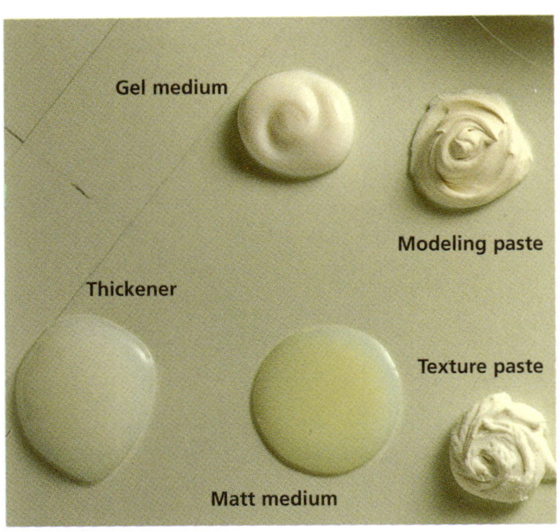

how acrylic paint is made

1 *The first constituent is the powdered pigment.*
2 *The pigment is mixed with acrylic adhesive.*
3 *The paint is then milled between steel rollers.*
4 *After it has been inspected, the paint is put into tubes.*

1

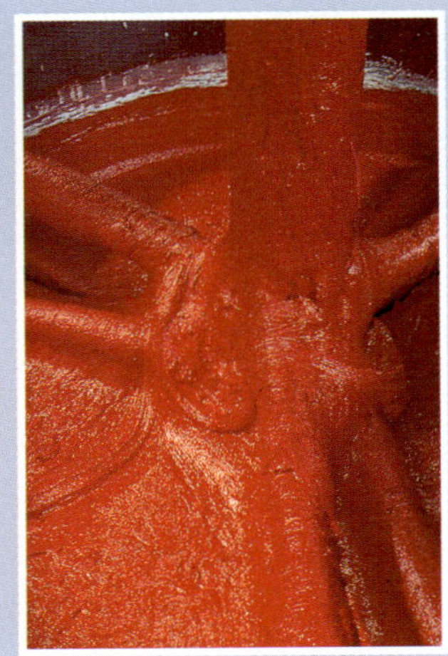
2

3

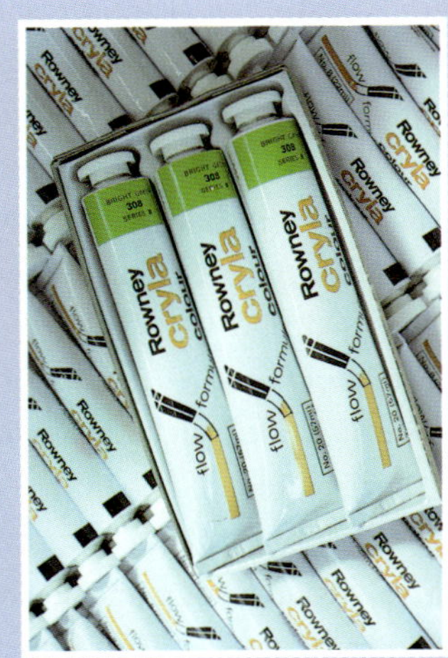

4

developed successfully over the years. Notable among these is the phthalocyanine range, the first of which was a very intense blue, known under the trade name of Monastral blue and a very suitable replacement for the less reliable Prussian blues, whose color effects and pigment properties it closely resembles.

The range has now increased to include yellows, reds, and greens, and a splendid violet, all of them available in oil, watercolor and acrylic. These colors are classed as organic and are produced by a chemical process from an organic dyestuff. They are very intense with a high degree of durability and, like acrylic paint itself, are a modern and flexible addition to the artist's means of expression.

TEMPERA

Tempera, or egg-tempera as it is generally known, is paint made by blending pure color pigment with egg yolk. It is thinned with distilled water, which evaporates once the color has hardened. Tempera is one of the most permanent media available. It is essentially an emulsion made up of oil and water constituents. When the paint is dry it cannot be dissolved, even with hot water.

Tempera is characterized chiefly by the dryness of the color. It does not yellow or darken with age. The preparation involved in mixing it can be formidable, but the results more than justify a little patience. It is possible to purchase egg-tempera ready-mixed in tubes, but most tempera artists prefer to mix their own colors. The colored pigment is first ground with water into a soft paste (the colored paste can be stored in airtight containers). Mix the tempera immediately before use in an equal quantity of pigment to egg yolk. The white of the egg should be removed altogether. The egg is first cracked over a bowl, preferably with a knife so that it breaks evenly. Allow the white of the egg to run into the bowl, holding the yolk back. Then pass the yolk from one half of the shell to the other several times—this gets rid of the remaining white. The yolk can then be punctured and poured into a cup. Add three spoonfuls of cold water and stir. The mixture is then poured into a stoppered container and thoroughly shaken to emulsify yolk and water. Then mix equal parts with the colored pigment paste to make the tempera. As with gouache the paint is thinned for use with water.

There are other recipes for tempera, using either linseed oil and

BELOW: *Pigments for tempera painting:* **1** *Zinc white* **2** *Titanium white* **3** *French ultramarine* **4** *Cerulean blue* **5** *Viridian* **6** *Cadmium yellow* **7** *Scarlet lake* **8** *Cadmium red* **9** *Venetian red* **10** *Indian red* **11** *and* **13** *Burnt and raw sienna* **12** *Burnt umber* **14** *Yellow ocher* **15** *Raw umber* **16** *Ivory black*

5 6 7 8 9 10 11 12 13 14 15 16

making tempera

1

2

3

4

5

6

7

8

9

1 *Dry powdered pigment is transferred to a small jar.*

2 *Distilled water is added sparingly to make a thick paste.*

3 *Replace the top securely and shake the bottle vigorously.*

4 *The egg is broken and the yolk separated by allowing the white to drain through the fingers into a bowl.*

5 *Make the yolk dry by passing from one hand to the other. Hold the yolk carefully and make an incision to allow the liquid to run into a glass container.*

6 *Distilled water is added and stirred to a consistency of cream.*

7 *The pigment and egg yolk binder are now blended together with a palette knife.*

8 *The paint is tested on a piece of glass.*

9 *When dry the paint is scraped off and stored for use. If it is too dry, add more egg.*

ABOVE: Christina's world: *Andrew Wyeth. Wyeth is best known for his tempera paintings. The luminosity of the painting and the fine working of the detail is offset by the pale wash of the sky which reveals the gesso ground.*

glue or gum arabic and wax. Many early manuscripts were decorated with illustrations drawn with egg-tempera and it is worth noting that not only have they survived well, but in many cases they look as fresh as the day they were painted. Giotto and Botticelli used tempera for fresco painting. That is why there are so many fine examples of their work still intact. Today artists tend to use a gesso ground. Hardboard can be a most suitable support—some artists prefer to paste cotton or linen on to hardboard before priming with gesso. Gesso primer can be bought ready-mixed or made from gilder's white mixed with size. At least four coats of primer are required, allowing approximately half an hour drying time between each coat. The surface can then be smoothed with a damp sponge, and when dry rubbed with a fine sandpaper.

Painting in tempera requires a little more organization than working with oils. Tempera dries quickly and brushes need to be rinsed frequently in warm water. Glazing with tempera can be very rewarding. Layers of transparent color can be built up quite quickly. Dry-brush working can also be very effective. The brush takes up paint, most of which is put down on scrap paper, leaving the brush "starved" of color. Part of the paint surface can be scraped away with the edge of a blade to reveal the gesso ground and then repainted with a different, transparent glaze of color so that the scraped texture shows through. The surface of a tempera painting can be fine, but also sculptural, as layers of paint are scraped away and reworked.

Many other media can be used in combination with paints; indeed, the mixing of media is now commonplace, whereas in the past it was regarded as breaking the rules. Watercolor used with pen and ink has a long history; in the days before watercolor became recognized as a medium in its own right, it was used mainly to give touches of color to drawings or to tint black and white engravings. Nowadays there are many other media—some old and some new—that can be used with watercolor to good effect.

One traditional way to change the nature of watercolor paint by thickening it is to mix it with a little gum arabic, which gives it both texture and lasting luster. Soap can be used in much the same way, and it makes the paint easier to scrape back. Soap can also be used to make imprints of objects such as leaves or flowers. Coat the object with soap, apply paint to it and then press it on to the paper.

Watercolors can be drawn into with pens, pencils, crayons, or pastels, and areas can be stressed or lightened with gouache or Chinese white. Watercolor pencils and crayons, a relatively new invention, are particularly suitable for this purpose. When dry they behave like crayons or hard pastels, but if dipped in water or used on wet paper they will dissolve, forming a wash. Using these, or

collage

1 *Acrylic medium can be used for collaging. Cut the canvas shape and paint one side with medium.*

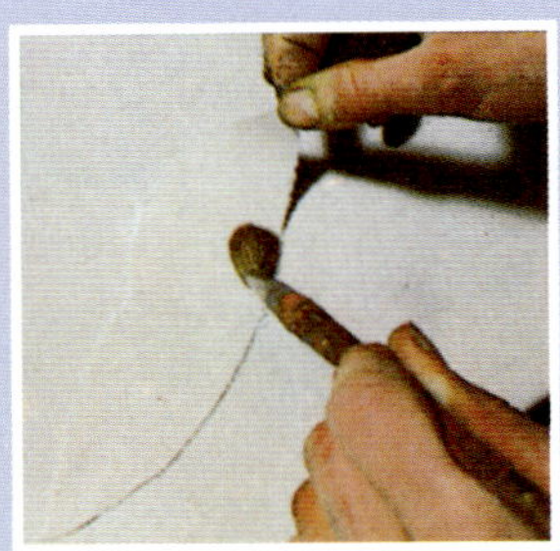

2 *Press the shape onto stretched canvas. Rub it down with a clean, dry brush.*

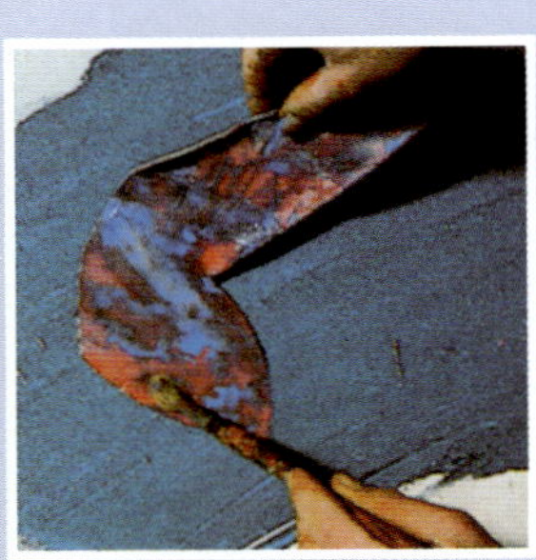

3 *Collage can also be done using the adhesive qualities of acrylic paint.*

collage

The word collage comes from the French coller *to tick—an apt description for a picture or design that is made up from pieces of paper, cloth, or other material and stuck to a firm support.*

This method of creating images was extensively used by the Cubists, the two main innovators being Picasso and Braque, both painters. In his later years Matisse used pieces of colored paper as a substitute for painting.

Collage can literally transform discarded bits of cloth and wood and other materials into interesting schemes of color, tone, form and texture.

Another sort of collage can be made from waste pieces of wood sawn off frame moldings. When stuck together in varying combinations, interesting ideas for three-dimensional designs emerged, not apparent in the original material. When the discarded bits were reassembled, completely new forms were created.

You can see even from a few examples the potential of collage, and in particular its pronounced three-dimensional qualities. None has paint added to them in these instances, though it can be tried with equal success.

ordinary pastels, on top of watercolor can turn a painting that has "gone wrong" and become dull and lifeless into something quite new and different. It is always worth experimenting with such media on a painting that you are less than happy with; you may evolve a personal technique that you can use again. Wax oil pastels can create interesting textured areas when laid underneath a wash, as can treating the paper, or parts of it, with oil of turpentine before painting, which has a similar effect. Wax resist and collage, illustrated here, are other ways to utilize or modify the qualities of paint media. The possibilities are almost endless, and experimentation is sure to reward you with interesting discoveries.

ABOVE: *East Guldeford Church, Romney Marsh. A drawing in pen and ink with spatter. The reeds appear as negative shapes painted with white gouache.*

wax resist with acrylics

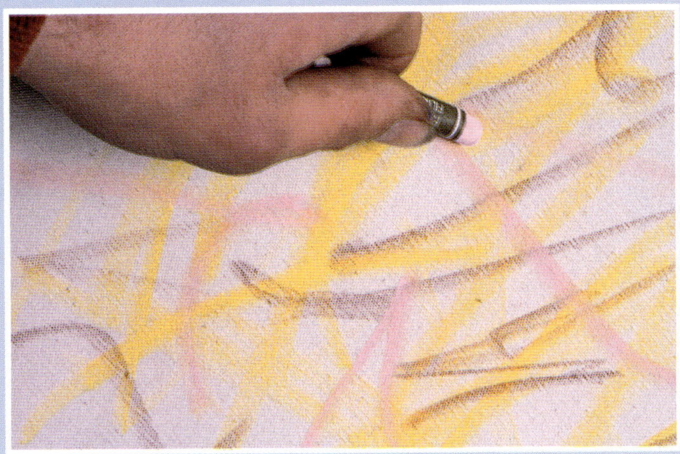

1 *Wax resist. Wax crayon is applied to the support. Candles or any fatty, waxy material will do.*

2 *The next step is to paint acrylic over the crayon.*

3 *The wax resists the paint, allowing a textured pattern to show through.*

MATERIALS

SUPPORTS

WATERCOLOR

Anything upon which a painting or drawing is executed is called a support. The luminous character of watercolor is dependent on a suitable paper support. Paper of good quality is important; inexpensive papers, such as machine-made cartridge paper, do not hold the washes very well. Essentially there are three different types of paper surfaces which are used for watercolor—hot-pressed (HP), cold-pressed (CP), also known as "not," and rough.

Cold-pressed papers tend to be used more frequently than the others. Hot-pressed papers are used more for combined techniques, such as pen and wash, or for combining gouache with watercolor. Rough-textured papers are attractive to handle, but the pronounced tooth is unsuitable for delicate or detailed brushwork. There are numerous handmade papers, many of which have a toned surface such as "De Wint." The maker's name appears as a watermark and should be read the right way round to denote the right side to work on. Watercolor papers are selected by weight as well as for their surface qualities. The weight is measured by the ream (480 sheets). An average weight for a sheet size A2 would be 90lb. Stretching dampened paper with gummed tape is necessary only with the lighter weights of paper. Papers such as Arches (French) and Fabriano (Italian) are best purchased in large rolls which are less expensive. They can be cut into smaller sheets. Cold-pressed paper, which is

BELOW: *The textured surface of the watercolor paper can influence the finished painting.*

ABOVE: *There is a wide variety of white and toned watercolor papers available to the artist. The tone of the paper, however, should not be too dark, since the transparent glazes of watercolor would be lost.*

BELOW: *Handmade papers are delightful to work on—the right side of the paper is determined by reading the manufacturer's watermark in the right direction. Where no watermark is used, the right side is that which has been coated with size.*

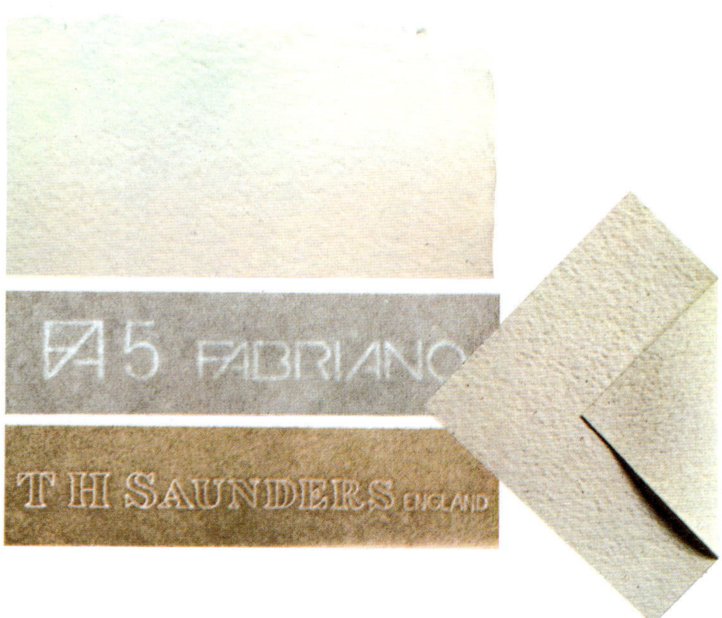

slightly textured, is the most popular and is suitable for both broad washes and fine detail. Rough paper, as its name implies, is much more heavily textured, and the paint will settle in the "troughs" while sliding off the "peaks," giving a speckled effect which can be effective for some subjects but is difficult to exploit successfully. Among the best-known makes of good watercolor papers are Saunders, Fabriano, Arches, Bockingford, Strathmore in the US, Ingres in the UK, and R.W. S. (Royal Watercolour Society), some of which also include hand-made papers.

Hand-made papers are made from pure linen rag and specially treated with size to provide the best possible surface for watercolor work. Such papers are sized on one side only and thus have a right and a wrong side, which can be checked by holding the paper up to the light so that the watermark becomes visible. Many of the better machine-made papers also have a watermark and hence a right and wrong side.

Some papers have surfaces which are tough enough to withstand a great deal of preliminary drawing and erasing without damage, but others do not. Bockingford paper, for instance, although excellent in many ways, is quickly damaged by erasing, and the paint will take on a patchy appearance wherever the surface has been spoiled. One of its advantages, however, is that paint can easily be removed by washing out where necessary; the paint, moreover, can be manipulated and moved around in a very free way. Arches paper and Saunders paper are both strong enough to stand up to erasing, but

stretching the paper

1

2

3

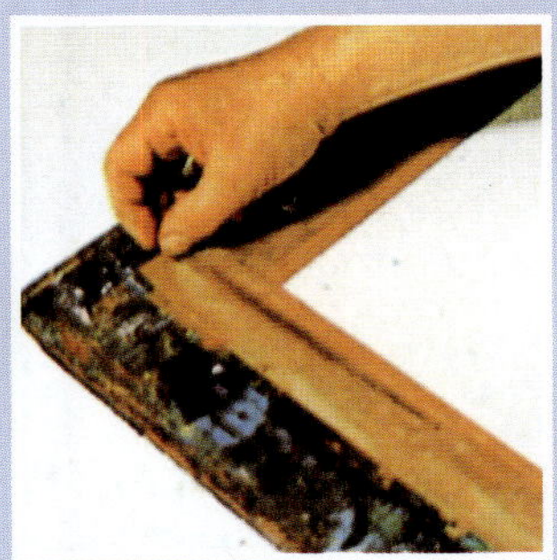
4

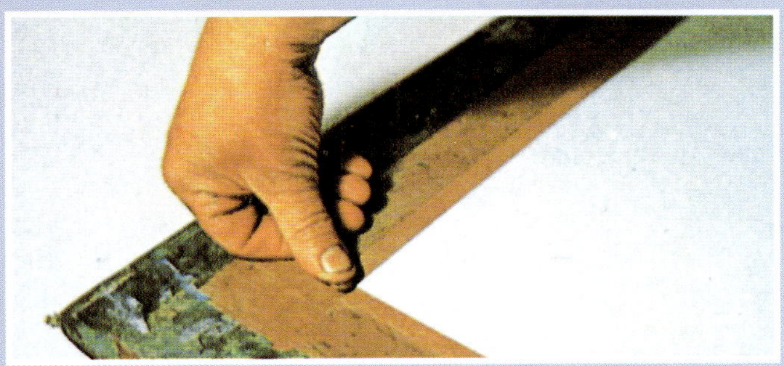
5

1 Cut the paper to size and place it right-side-up in a bath or tray of water. Leave it to soak for a few minutes.
2 Lift out the paper and drain off the excess water.
3 Lay the paper on a drawing board at least 1 in larger than the paper all around. Make sure that the paper is still the right way up.
4 Smooth the paper quite flat and stick gumstrip around the edges, starting with opposite sides.
5 Finish by putting a thumb tack in each corner. Do not dry the paper in front of a fire, which will buckle it.

mistakes are difficult to remove from the former, which holds the paint very firmly. Saunders paper is a good choice for beginners: it is strong, stretches well and has a pleasant surface with enough grain to give a little, but not too much, texture.

Watercolor papers vary widely in weight, or thickness, and the lighter ones need to be stretched or they will buckle as soon as wet paint is applied to them. The weight is usually expressed in pounds and refers to the weight of a ream (480 sheets), not to each individual sheet. The thinner papers, ranging from 70 to 140 pounds, must be stretched; any paper weighing 200 pounds or more can be used without this treatment. Watercolor boards can be bought. These have watercolor paper mounted on heavy board, so that the stretching has already been done. They are particularly useful for outdoor work, since no drawing board is needed.

Stretching paper is not difficult, but since the paper must be soaked, it takes some time to dry thoroughly and needs to be done at least two hours before you intend to start work. Cut the paper to the size required (if you do not want to use the whole sheet) and wet it well on both sides by laying it in a bath or tray of water. When it is well soaked, hold it up by the corners to drain off the excess water, then lay it right-side-up on a drawing board and stick down each edge with the gummed brown paper known as gumstrip (do not use masking tape or clear adhesive tape). Finally, place a drawing pin in each corner. The paper will dry taut and flat and should not buckle when paint is applied. Occasionally, however, stretching does go wrong and the paper buckles at one corner or tears away from the gumstrip; if that happens there is no other course but to repeat the process. Drying can be hastened with a hairdrier, but it is not a good practice to leave the board in front of a fire. Ideally the paper should dry naturally.

OIL/ACRYLICS/TEMPERA

Stretched canvas is the most common support for oil painting. A variety of cloth can be adapted for use, but linen is considered to be most suitable. Coarse and fine weaves of linen are equally attractive—the coarse weaves being used generally for very large canvases. Cotton can be bought ready primed for use. Wood panels are suitable so long as the wood is of sufficient thickness to avoid warping or buckling. The wood should also be well-seasoned and not kiln-dried. Hardboard, or masonite, is inexpensive and easy to handle and prepare; it is undoubtedly the most popular support used by students and beginners. The *smooth* side, *not* the textured side, should be used. Sandpaper the surface with a medium-grit sandpaper before priming. Cardboard and binder's millboard are ideal supports for oil painting and acrylics, though the paint must be applied fairly thinly. Plywood is light and, if primed with a number of coats, highly suitable for painting in oil. Prepared canvas—linen or cotton—can be bought ready for stretching on to a wooden frame. Stretchers are sold with small wooden wedges which, when knocked into the slotted corners of the frame, give the canvas a final tension.

ABOVE: *Firm supports for oil and tempera painting: Although canvas is still the most widely used support for oil painting, wood can also be used including: mahogany (7), hardboard (2), blockboard (3), and plywood (5). Thinner boards require additional support to prevent warping and buckling. Chipboard (4) requires no support. Heavy duty cardboard is absorbent and should be sized. Canvas boards can be bought ready-primed for use. Metal supports are rarely used, but copper (8) is the best surface to work on. Various types of paper can be pasted to a firm support and sized (1).*

DRAWING

A number of supports can be used for drawing. With natural charcoal a variety of papers can be used—but for the beginner a medium-toothed hot-pressed paper will probably secure the best results. The heavier-toothed papers require a little more confidence as the marks are smudged and moved less readily. Compressed charcoal and conté can be used on a grained (toothed) paper, but some of the quality of hard, black line which these media can make is lost. If the drawing is intended to be predominantly linear, a harder-surfaced paper is more suitable. Some very interesting drawings in conté can be produced on a common, hard cartridge paper; that medium produces marks that are slightly greasy and do not require a toothed paper to adhere to the surface.

With all these mediums, colored papers specially produced for charcoal and pastel drawing can be very helpful. The colored papers can reduce the starkness of black against white, if such a contrast is not required.

Pastels behave very similarly to charcoal and conté, and come in a variety of grades from very soft to a stick as hard as a 2B pencil. Many beginners find that their first approach to color is through this medium. When using pastels care should be taken in the selection of the paper. With the harder variety of pastels, which behave more like crayons, a hard, smooth paper can be quite suitable and a very clear and detailed image can be produced. With soft pastels, a paper with a tooth (grain) is almost essential for a satisfactory result because the tooth of the paper is necessary to hold the soft pastel marks. (If soft pastels are used on smooth paper, as fast as the pastel is put on the paper it will come off, because there is nothing to hold it.) There are a great variety of tinted and colored papers available, many of them produced specifically for use with pastels. Many paper manufacturers produce pads showing the full range of their pastel papers. It is a good idea for the beginner to obtain one of these pads to experiment with various colors, tints, and grades of paper, to find what is most suitable for the type of pastel drawing he or she wishes to do.

BELOW: *This drawing was done with a single pencil of medium hardness. The reflections and different surfaces are competently rendered, but a greater range of tones would have enlivened the overall gray: using pencils of different hardness would have made this easier.*

MAKING MARKS WITH DIFFERENT MATERIALS

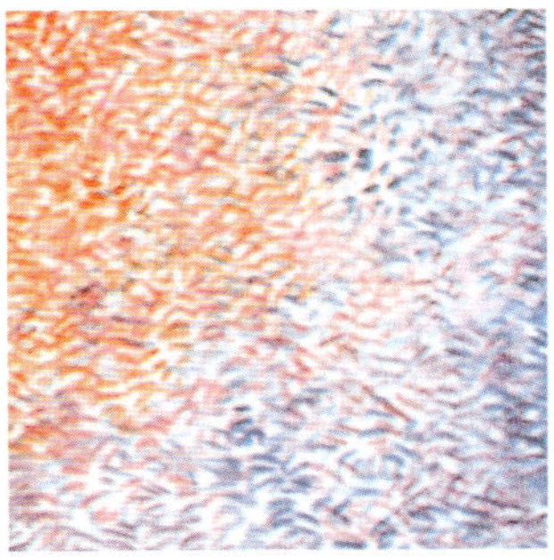

1 *A web of color made by using different colored pencils in short overlapping strokes.*

2 *The grit-like texture made with a wax pencil such as a Chinagraph.*

3 *Soft atmospheric tones created by blending crayon dust.*

4 *The lines of a 4H pencil are softened by burnishing with a finger.*

5 *A soft 4B pencil drawn over colored crayon.*

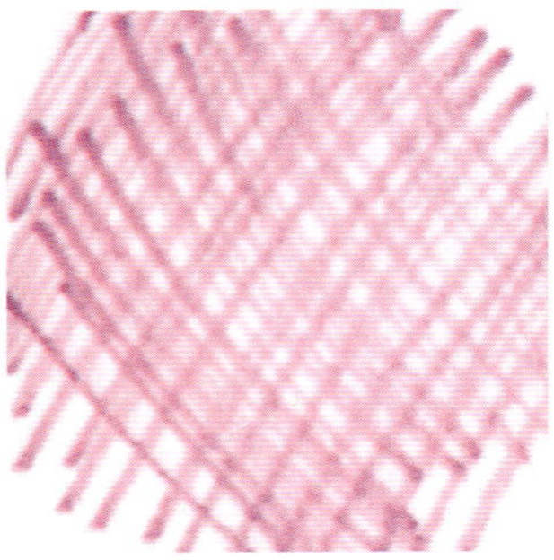

6 *The line of a Caran d'Ache pencil blurred by first damping the watercolor paper.*

7 *Black marks transferred from carbon paper.*

8 *Blended tones of Caran d'Ache pencils.*

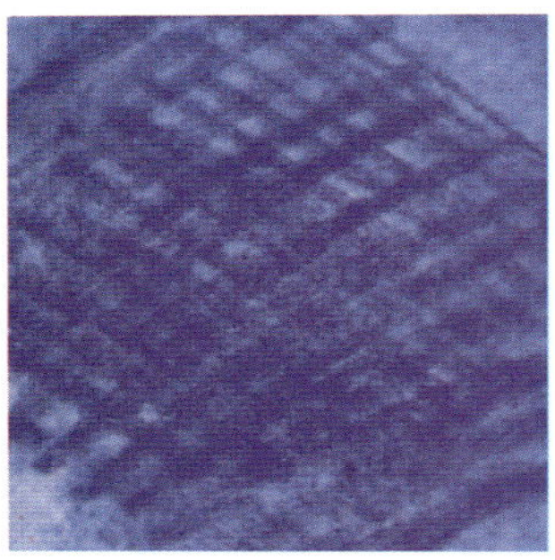

9 *A wash dilutes the cross-hatched lines of a Caran d'Ache pencil.*

10 *Soft tones produced by rubbing graphite dust into the paper.*

11 *Gradations of color made with colored crayons reveal the texture of the paper.*

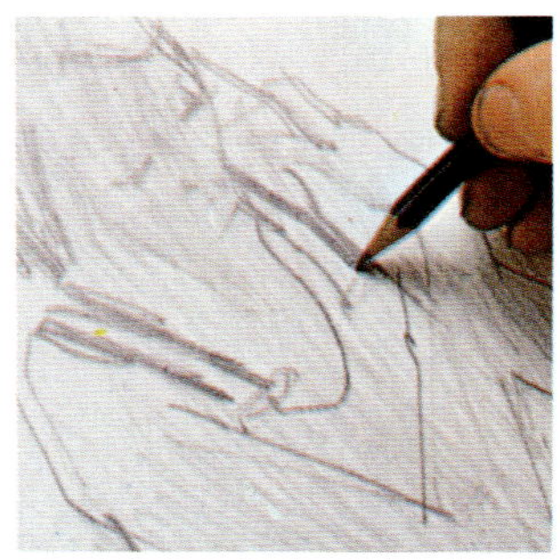

12 *2B and 5B pencils used in the same drawing.*

13 *Using a 2B pencil to block in tone.*

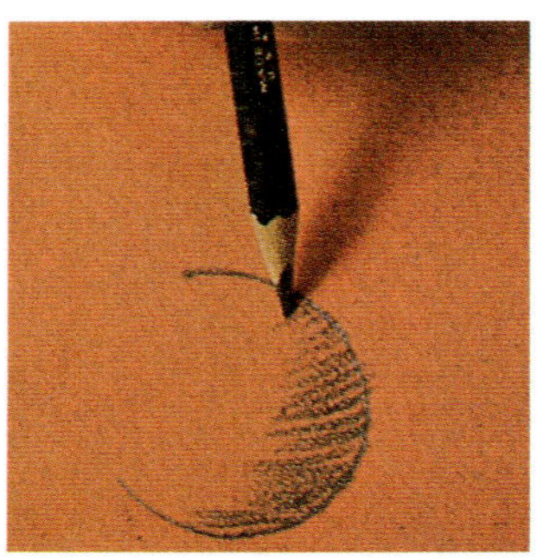

14 *Colored paper makes a good ground for tonal drawing.*

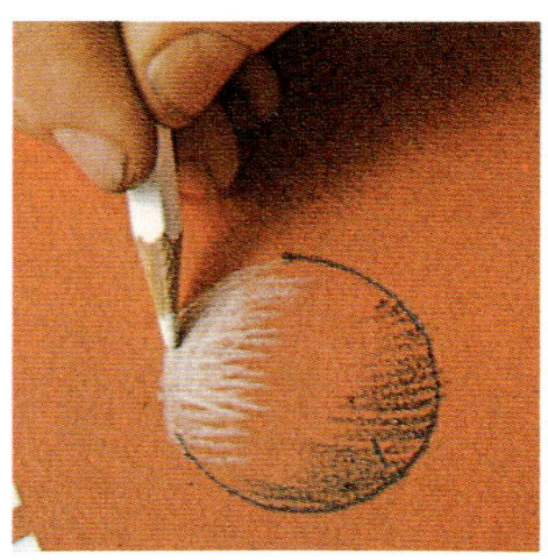

15 *Highlights are added using a white pencil.*

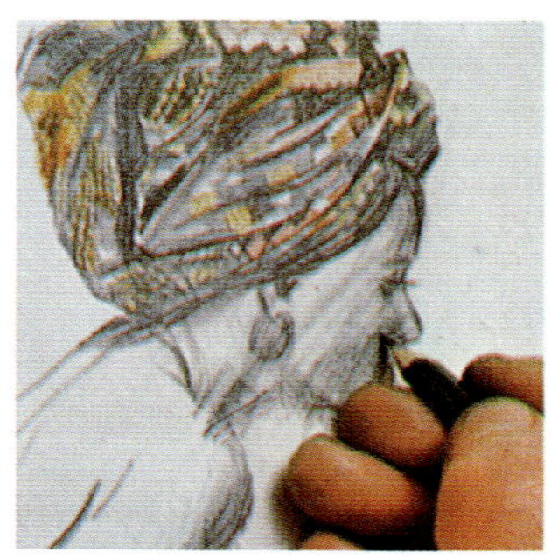

16 *Combining black and colored pencils.*

SABLE BRUSHES

Sable brushes are delightful to work with in all media; they can be used for watercolor, oil, and acrylic with equal success. Having specially fashioned points, they can make the most delicate lines and strokes. In addition, they are constructed to hold the paint well, and so spread it with ease and fluency.

The advantage of a sable brush over most of the others is that it responds so sensitively to the touch, allowing the most gentle of marks to the broadest of washes to occur with the slightest pressure of the hand. Your intentions are carried out immediately with a sable, which in effect becomes an extension of the hand.

They are also expensive, and so must be carefully treated on all counts. If sables are used with acrylic paint, they must be scrupulously washed of all color after use. Acrylic dries hard very quickly, so always keep water handy, to ensure that there is little chance of that happening. Get into the habit of dipping your brush into the water when not in use.

The range and the variety of sable brushes may appear bewildering initially, but a good start can be made by narrowing the choice down to two; a number 3 for fine work, and a number 7 for broad, both round in shape. Other sizes can be added later.

To these can be added ox-hair or squirrel brushes which, though a great deal less expensive than sable, are very useful to do those jobs that would otherwise be impossible. Large areas, for example, which would need a very expensive sable to do the job, could be done just

BELOW: *Brushes come in many sizes. Most ranges are numbered from 1 (the smallest) to 12. Extra large brushes (numbered up to 36) are also available.*

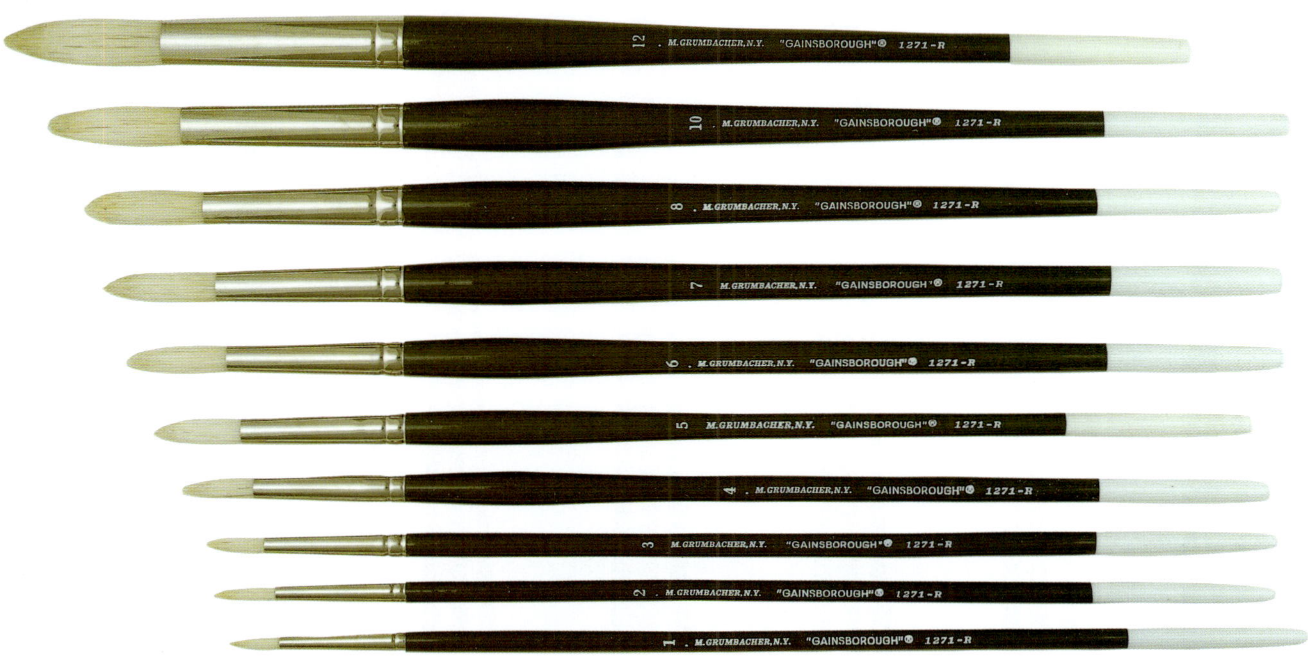

as satisfactorily with an ox-hair or squirrel brush.

A good all-round selection of brushes must contain a few soft and hard brushes to meet all possible contingencies.

The best hard brushes are hog's-hair.

HOG'S-HAIR BRUSHES

Hog's-hair brushes were mainly used for oil paint, until the introduction of acrylic, for which they are admirably suited. They differ from sables in a number of ways: whereas the majority of sables are round in shape, hog's-hairs come in four quite distinct shapes: round, bright (or square), flat, and filbert, which are capable of a great variety of marks.

Hog's-hair brushes are made from real bristle, and are dressed and shaped according to the natural curve of the hair. They are so skilfully put together that they always retain their shape no matter how much paint is on them and how vigorously they are used. Though sturdier than sables, they must still be treated with care by keeping them clean, and not doing too much mixing with them.

Choosing a selection of these brushes may be done in the same way as with sables: a small and a large from each type—say a 3 or 4 small, and a 7 or 8 large, depending on individual preferences.

Other brushes that may be found to be useful are household and nylon brushes. Household brushes, the kind that are used for painting woodwork around the house, come in various sizes, and are extremely useful for the kinds of painting that are too arduous or rough for sables and hog's-hair—for example, priming supports, and painting sculpture, models, and other kinds of designs, in preparation for painting with sables.

SYNTHETIC BRUSHES

Nylon brushes have improved a great deal since they were first introduced. They are available in a large variety of sizes and shapes, perform well, clean easily and, as sable brushes have become very expensive, are good alternatives to sable and the finer hog's-hair. Synthetic fibers are robust and wear well under vigorous use. They are cheaper than other brushes and well worth trying.

CLEANING AND CARE OF BRUSHES

Looking after brushes is part of painting. If treated properly, they will give good service and do their job well.

Washing brushes after use is more thorough an operation than cleaning them during work. It does not mean a swirl round in clean water. Color has a habit of remaining deeply embedded in the ferrule and must be removed, or it will ruin the brush in time. Therefore make it a practice to wash them with warm water and mild soap (not a detergent). Lather in the palm of the hand, watch all the hidden paint emerge, rinse well in plenty of warm water, shake out the excess, and shape the points before allowing them to dry upright in a jar or bottle.

If brushes are unfortunately encrusted with dried paint, you can try one of these two methods. Soak them in warm water for a few hours. Warm water will soften the paint, and then it may be removed by easing it off very carefully, preferably with the fingers. Avoid using any kind of sharp implement, like a knife, to do this part of the job. You may damage the hairs irrevocably if you do. Once the point or edge of a brush is damaged, the brush is then virtually useless. Or try a solvent.

Acrylic has a tendency to be more coarse in texture than watercolor or gouache—a good reason to avoid vigorous mixing and application, especially with sables, and, instead, to use a palette knife more often. One way of avoiding vigorous handling is to hold the brush lightly so that it almost falls from the hand, rather than gripping it so tightly that the hand becomes tense and so the brush takes the strain, which will in turn show in the brushmarks.

This may seem obvious, but for those unused to the behavior of brushes, tension may easily be the result of unfamiliarity with them. Brush marking and manipulation exercises and experiments will be of considerable help in overcoming this problem.

PAINTBOXES

Theoretically, any old cardboard box will do to keep paints, brushes and media in, but if you are intending to carry paints around with you it is worth investing in a proper box with separate compartments for paints and brushes. Most of these are wooden, with a carrying handle, and are sold with their own palette which fits into the lid.

Alternatively you can improvize your own paintbox from a toolbox or fishing tackle box, which are less expensive and much lighter to carry.

OIL PAINTING ACCESSORIES

Other essential items include dippers for your painting medium, which can be attached to the palette; glass jars or tin cans to hold oil of turpentine for cleaning brushes; and of course a large supply of rags or paper towels (oil paint is very messy and needs to be cleaned up frequently)

BELOW LEFT: *Soft sable brushes are produced in a series of sizes. The brushes illustrated are all size 5 made by different manufacturers. A number of synthetic sable brushes are available and though they are generally of good quality they do not retain as much watercolor in the bristle as real sable.*

BELOW: *The brushes are a mixture of synthetic, mixed hairs, ox-hair, sable, and squirrel-hair.*

ABOVE: *Flexible palette knives were originally used solely for color mixing. They can be used instead of a brush, as a tool for laying on a thick impasto of oil or acrylic paint. Additionally, they can be used to scrape away paint when a particular passage in a painting needs to be removed.*

Another useful painting aid is a mahl stick, which steadies your hand when you are painting small details or fine lines. The traditional mahl stick has a bamboo handle with a chamois cushion at one end. The stick is held across the canvas with the cushioned end resting lightly on a dry area of the painting, and you rest your painting arm on the stick to steady yourself as you paint. Mahl sticks are sold at artists' suppliers, but a piece of doweling or garden cane with a bundle of rags tied to one end is quite adequate, and can be rested on the side of the canvas or board if the paint surface is wet.

For anyone who intends to do a lot of outdoor work, a pair of canvas separators is very useful. These are designed to keep two wet canvases apart without damaging the paint, and have a handle for carrying. It is necessary to have two canvases of the same size with you, even if you intend to use only one.

VARNISHES

Ideally, paintings should be varnished to protect them from dust and to restore the colors, which tend to become toned down as the paint dries. Many people associate varnish with that dark-brown, sticky look that was such a feature of Victorian paintings, but several clear synthetic varnishes are now available, both matt and gloss. Most varnishes, however, cannot be applied for at least six months, even a year if the paint is very thick, as it takes this long for it to dry out thoroughly. The exceptions are the temporary varnishes, such as retouching varnish, which can be applied when the paint is "skin dry," that is, in about two weeks to a month. It can also be used to brush over an area that may have become dull and matt during the painting, as sometimes happens, and can be removed if necessary by rubbing gently with distilled turpentine.

PALETTES

Palettes come in a variety of shapes, sizes and materials, designed to suit your individual requirements. Thumbhole palettes are designed for easel painting. They have a thumbhole and indentation for the fingers, and the palette is supported on the forearm. Before buying a palette, try out different sizes and shapes to see which feels the most comfortable.

New wooden palettes should be treated by rubbing with linseed oil to prevent them absorbing the oil in the paint. You can even improvize your own palette, from any nonabsorbent surface, making it any size and color you like.

A sheet of glass with white or neutral-colored paper underneath it would be suitable, or there are disposable palettes made of oil-proof paper—these are a boon for outdoor work, and remove the necessity for cleaning. The nearest object I have found to fulfil all the conditions for the ideal palette is a large china plate.

A porcelain or glazed pottery surface is easy to keep clean. If paint dries on it, it can be cleaned with hot water. A few minutes' soaking is all that is needed. For more stubborn cases, soak for a longer time in hot water; paint should then scrape off quite easily.

A white plate is an advantage. White allows mixtures to be accurately gauged; a colored surface plays optical tricks and is best avoided.

The lip or edge on a plate is only important if the mixtures are rather liquid. For stiffer mixtures, using thicker paints, a pad of paper palettes has advantages. Mixing is done on the top layer, which

BELOW: *There are many forms of palette. The traditional palette with thumbhole may be held in one hand while painting. Small pots may be used to mix colors separately. Alternatively, you may wish to keep the colors together in a larger palette with several wells. The palette used is the artist's personal choice.*

the ideal palette:

- *holds paint well on the surface*
- *is easy to keep clean*
- *has a smooth nonporous surface*
- *is white in color*
- *has a lip or edge*

choose a palette that is:

- *large enough*
- *practical for your purposes*
- *suits your style of working*

can be torn off and discarded. Paper palettes are not very practical for more liquid paint, or washes, as the paper tends to wrinkle and the paint to spill over the edges.

Another possible palette is a sheet of plain white plastic. The advantage here is that it can be bought in any size. Most palettes tend to be small, useful for taking outdoors for sketching trips, but not nearly large enough for working in the studio.

A sheet of firm, white plastic, glued to an old kitchen table, will make not only a good surface for mixing paint on, but can double up as a working desk.

If there is any disadvantage in a plastic palette it might be in the way acrylic paint clings to it. Some kinds of plastic also have a tendency to stain, unless kept scrupulously clean. Plastic palettes can be obtained at most art supply stores.

CHOOSING A PALETTE

The choice of palette will depend, broadly speaking, on how you paint—large or small, with thick paint or thin paint or washes.

For thick paint you will want plenty of room for mixing and holding the amount to be used. For thin paint and washes a lip or edge to the palette is mandatory, or the paint will spill. For washes, china saucers are very satisfactory and, being small, are easy to keep clean. They will stack neatly and so will not take up too much room on the painting table.

Choosing a palette will entail a certain amount of experimentation in the early stages, but from my personal experience one fact stands out sharp and clear: you cannot have too many palettes.

PALETTE SURFACES

Many surfaces will do as palettes. A sheet of glass, though a bit slippery, with a sheet of white paper underneath, is possible. Enameled metal or marble tops will do at a pinch. A surface to avoid is any kind of metal that is uncoated or untreated—with enamel or plastic, etc. Metal is liable to corrode, and if it does, will contaminate the paint. Also avoid old or dirty surfaces, or spongy surfaces like leather or rubber.

As a last resort, a piece of ordinary hardboard, or thick cardboard, primed with white emulsion—as for supports—will serve. If it should stain, after cleaning give it another coat of emulsion, and it will be ready for use next time. Such a surface is a little more porous as a palette than plastic or china, but with successive coats of paint it will become less so.

One kind of palette that can be carried in the hand, and is useful for outdoor painting, is made of hardboard and coated with a thin sheet of plastic on both sides. It is very light and can be held easily by placing the thumb through the hole specially made for this purpose.

When painting with acrylic, it is more likely that mixing will be done on the painting table, in container-like palettes, rather than on flat surfaces. There is a danger of acrylic paint drying on the palette before it is even used. For this reason the less absorbent the palette, the better. A plastic one, or even a piece of glass, is preferable to a wooden palette. The paints can also darken noticeably as they dry, especially if thinned with water. The answer is to try as many palettes as possible, as and when the need arises.

EASELS

An easel is a necessity. You may manage to produce one small painting by propping up your canvas on a table or shelf, but you will very soon find out how unsatisfactory this is. Without an easel you cannot adjust the height of your work—essential if you are doing a painting of a reasonable size, as you must be able to reach different areas of it easily and comfortably—and you cannot tilt the work, which you often need to do either to avoid light reflecting on its surface or to catch the best light for working.

There are several different types of easel on the market, from huge, sturdy studio easels to small sketching easels that are light and easily portable. Your choice will be dictated by the space in which you are working, whether you intend to work mostly indoors or outdoors, and by the size of your work and the type of painting you are doing. If you intend to work outdoors frequently you will need a sketching easel (though small sketches can be done by propping the canvas or board against the open lid of a paintbox). If, on the other hand, you know you are unlikely to paint anywhere but indoors, the heavier radial easel could be a good choice, but this cannot easily be dismantled and put away, so you might choose a portable easel for space reasons.

RIGHT: *A selection of wooden sketching easels.*

There are three main types of sketching easel: the box easel, the wooden sketching easel, and the aluminum sketching easel. The first type combines an easel and a paintbox, and can be folded up into a case for carrying. These were at one time very expensive, and the best ones still are, but less expensive versions are now appearing on the market, and for an outdoor painter they are a good choice, as everything can be carried in one piece of luggage.

Wooden sketching easels are inexpensive, but are not recommended, as the blocks which slide up and down in slots to enable you to adjust the height of the work tend to become warped, so that they either do not slide at all or are impossible to fix in position. There is nothing more infuriating than having to fight your easel, which often involves knocking it over, just when you want to work particularly fast because the light is changing.

The metal sketching easel, on the other hand, is excellent, and suffers from none of these disadvantages because metal cannot warp. It is easy to adjust, holds the work firmly, and has the additional advantage of being adjustable to a horizontal position for watercolors (you may find that you want to experiment with other media from time to time). It is also quite adequate for indoor work, provided you are not working on a vast scale, and can be tucked away unobtrusively in a corner when not in use.

The problem with all sketching easels except the heavier version of the box type is that because they are light, and thus easy to carry, they are also vulnerable to gusts of wind, the canvas or board acting as a most effective sail! Some artists manage to anchor their easel by pushing tent pegs into the ground and tying the easel legs to them, or by hanging a heavy stone from the center of the easel.

ABOVE: *A large free-standing easel suitable for large works of art, such as oil paintings.*

WORKSPACE

Few nonprofessional painters are fortunate enough to have access to a studio; nor indeed are all professional ones. Most people have to make do with a small, underequipped room or just a corner of a room used by other people for other purposes. This can create problems, but these are surmountable with a little organization.

One problem is that oil paint is a messy medium and has an almost magical way of appearing on objects that seemed to be nowhere near it when you were painting. You get it on your hands without noticing, then you go and make a cup of coffee and it will be on the kettle, the mug, the spoon, and so on, ad infinitum. If you are working in a corner of a room, clean up as often as you can, including wiping your hands, never wander about with a loaded paintbrush, and cover the equipment table with plenty of newspaper. A more serious problem is lighting. The best light for painting is, of course, daylight, but daylight is unpredictable and changes all the time, not only in variable weather conditions but also according to the time of day. If you have a north-facing window you are lucky, as north light (or south light if you live in the southern hemisphere) changes much less, but many rooms face east or west, in which case enables you to work out the composition and the position of the main elements within it, and to plan the balance of dark colors and light ones. For a portrait or figure painting you will need to establish how you want to place the figure in relation to the background, and you will need to get the proportions of the figure right. If you start an ambitious painting with inadequate drawing you will be forever altering parts of it, which will not only spoil your enjoyment, but will also produce a labored and overworked painting. Careful planning at the start enables you to be more spontaneous later.

Underdrawings can be done either in pencil or charcoal, the latter being preferable, as it is a broad medium, easier to use freely. To avoid loose charcoal mixing with the paint and muddying it, brush it down lightly with a rag before starting to paint —you will still retain the main lines of the drawing.

Underpainting—another form of drawing but done with a brush—can be made either in monochrome or an understated version of the finished color scheme, in both cases using a paint well thinned with turpentine. If you find a blank canvas somewhat intimidating, you will find that an underpainting overcomes the problem by providing a "stepping stone" from which you can build up the succeeding layers of color with confidence.

A monochrome underpainting should concentrate on the main masses of light and shade, as in the example illustrated, and a colored

LEFT: *This small painting was done by the* alla prima *method, with the paint used quite thickly and put down rapidly with little subsequent alteration.*

RIGHT: *Oil paints come in a huge variety of colors.*

ABOVE: *A versatile range of easels that will support canvas, block, frame or sketching boards. A large box easel (center) will hold paints, brushes and other equipment.*

you will sometimes have the sun shining directly on to the work and reflecting off the paint surface, while at other times you will have almost no light at all.

Always try to position your easel so that the light source is behind you and coming over your left shoulder if you are right-handed.

Good light is vitally important: if you look in a good light at a painting done in a poor one you will see why. What were intended to be subtle gradations of color and tone now appear as crude mixtures of bright colors and dingy ones, while what you thought of as nicely blended, unobtrusive brushwork is actually quite clumsy and obvious.

One way of coping with this problem is to use artificial lighting which, while not as perfect as northerly daylight, is at least constant. The best lights for painting are the fluorescent "daylight" ones, which can be bought either as ceiling lights or as lamps which can be fitted on to a shelf, table or windowsill. Look carefully at what is available before buying, as mistakes are expensive, and work out where the light source should be placed so that it does not reflect off the paint. One method is to fix a lamp over the window so that it boosts the available light, but a certain amount of trial and error may be involved before you arrive at a satisfactory solution.

THE FINISHED PRODUCT

MOUNTS

The mounting and presentation of paintings and drawings is a craft in its own right. Every work of art needs a separator of some kind. It is essential to isolate a drawing or painting from its immediate surroundings, so that it can be seen clearly at full value. Watercolors, gouaches and drawings require window mounts with generous borders. White or cream or various-colored mounts can be matched against the painting. More often than not a neutral tint makes a better separator than a strong color, though in some instances a richly colored mount can enhance the work. Window mounts also serve the more practical purpose of keeping the painting or drawing from coming into contact with the glass. The window shape cut from the cardboard should be set above center so that the bottom margin is proportionally larger than the remaining sides. There are a number of mount-cutters which are easy to use currently on the market—they have an adjustable blade which can be angled to cut a bevelled mount. If possible, always use an acid-free tape for fixing your drawing or painting to the mount. This prevents the work from becoming discolored at a later date. Acid-free mounting board is also recommended, but it can be very expensive.

LEFT: *Mount widths. The width of the mount has an immediate effect on the framed picture as a whole. If the mount is too small, it can give the picture a cramped and restricted look. An equal all-round width works well with some images. If the mount is large in comparison with the picture, it is usually better if the picture "sits" high up in the frame—make sure the mount margin at the bottom of the picture is deeper than that of the other three sides.*

ABOVE: *Choosing a color. The landscape is painted in muted, earthy colors. With a picture like this, it is usually advisable to choose a color that harmonizes with the subject. The light beige mount makes the picture look darker; the dull olive green immediately picks out the green tones in the composition; black emphasizes the linear content. Sometimes a mount of an unrelated color works: the rich magenta contrasts attractively with the greens and browns in the picture.*

It is important to differentiate clearly between the mount—the "window" which is placed upon the artwork—and the backing cardboard onto which the artwork is stuck before the process begins. Confusion arises because this backing is often referred to as the mount. The means by which the artwork is stuck to this backing is also referred to as "mounting." This section discusses the general principles of mounts and mounting.

THE BREATHING SPACE

Many artpieces are mounted as well as framed. In other words, the picture does not make direct contact with the frame but is surrounded by a wide margin which separates the picture from the frame. This is the mount. It is "breathing space" between the picture content and the frame itself.

There are no rigid rules governing whether you should or should not have a mount within your frame but, as a basic guideline, consider the artpiece itself: does it, for instance, contain large areas of empty space in its composition, as in the case of a line drawing on a plain white background? This sort of picture would look effective with only a small amount of border, or possibly with none at all. On the other hand, a more crowded picture would benefit from a substantial border of space between the image and the frame.

The mount should be chosen before the frame, because it comes next to the artpiece. A great deal of mystery has been attached to the "proportions" of the mount—the amount of space which should be left at the bottom, sides, and top of the image. In fact, the choice is personal and there is nothing magical about the measurements.

Beginners often make the mistake of cutting mounts for their

TOP RIGHT: *Common moldings*
1 *Box*
2 *Reverse slope*
3 *Flat*
4 *Half-round*
5 *Raised bead and flat*
6 *Box*
7 *Spoon*
8 *Composite made from planed timber and architrave molding*

LEFT: *Tools for framing, from left to right clockwise.* **1** *Set square/ruler* **2** *Plastic ruler* **3** *Hand drill and bits* **4** *Tenon saw* **5** *Craft knife* **6** *Screwdriver* **7** *Pin hammer* **8** *Pincers* **9** *Miter box or clamp* **10** *Nail punch* **11** *Panel pins/tacks*

personal and there is nothing magical about the measurements.

Beginners often make the mistake of cutting mounts for their work that are far too dark and heavy. A black mount may at first seem exciting placed against a pen drawing, but unfortunately in most cases the mount draws so much attention to itself that it presents a stronger image than the drawing. Darker-colored mounts, such as burgundy and olive green, should therefore be used with great caution in the framing and mounting of drawings. These strong colors really work only in conjunction with a robust piece of work.

Drawings never look very satisfactory when framed to the actual size of the drawing without a mount; generally, therefore, all drawings and works of a graphic nature require a cardboard mount to separate the image from the frame.

For the beginner, the advice of a good professional framer can be invaluable: their experience can often enable them intuitively to choose the right mount and weight of frame for the work. For the more ambitious there is readily available a wide selection of wood and metal moldings and mounting cardboard, and with the minimum of equipment and a little skill it should not be too difficult for the student to mount and frame his or her own work.

The cutting of a good bevel-edged cardboard mount could be more difficult than the making of the actual frame, however, and the following suggested sequence may be usefully noted. It is best if you cut your own mount internally about one-eighth of an inch smaller all round than your actual drawing, allowing on a small drawing about two inches between the mount and the frame. Fashions tend to change in relation to whether the mount should be an equal width all the way round or whether the bottom of the mount should be slightly wider. The original reason for the extra width was to allow space for a title or written description of the work to be shown on the mount. Visually, this title becomes part of the drawing, thus leaving an equal space to the other sides. Even when a title is not written, some artists prefer to have an extra weight of mount at the bottom, which can give the framed drawing a sense of stability.

Once the mount is finished, select the molding you require and cut the miters. However, do not attempt to cut without an accurate 45-degree miter block. When all four miters are cut, assemble the frame and pins. The size and number of pins depend very much on the size of molding and the weight of the drawing and glass. Do not attempt to drive in the pins without first drilling guide holes. Failure to do so almost inevitably results in the splitting and damaging of the molding.

Once the frame is assembled, cut the cardboard mount on the outer edges to fit the frame rebate snugly. Cut a backing to suit. At this point measure the internal dimensions of the rebate and get a piece of picture glass cut at your nearest glass-cutter's.

This sequence has been suggested for a beginner when assembling a frame because there is nothing more infuriating than making a frame and then discovering that the glass or the mount is a fraction too small or too large to fit. By making all the final measurements to fit the frame, rather than the frame to fit a predetermined glass measurement, the beginner should avoid such frustration.

FRAMING

Framing any painting needs careful consideration; an overly decorative gilt mounting, for instance, may be too overbearing on a simple landscape painting. Most professional framers will allow you to test sample mitered corners of different types of molding against your own painting to guage whether any of them is suitable. Prints and drawings work well in a stainless-steel or self-assembly aluminum frame. Charcoal and pencil drawings work best in a simple half-round or box wooden molding. Watercolors, if properly mounted, can be enhanced by narrow half-round gilt or silver wooden frames. Larger moldings are best for oil and acrylic paintings.

An artist is not always the best judge of how his work is best framed; he is often so close to the work that he finds it hard to make the right choice. For this reason I would suggest that much can be gained by seeking a second opinion, either from a frame-maker or from a fellow artist whose opinion you value. Remember that the main purpose of a frame is to act as a separator: it is better to be formal than flamboyant.

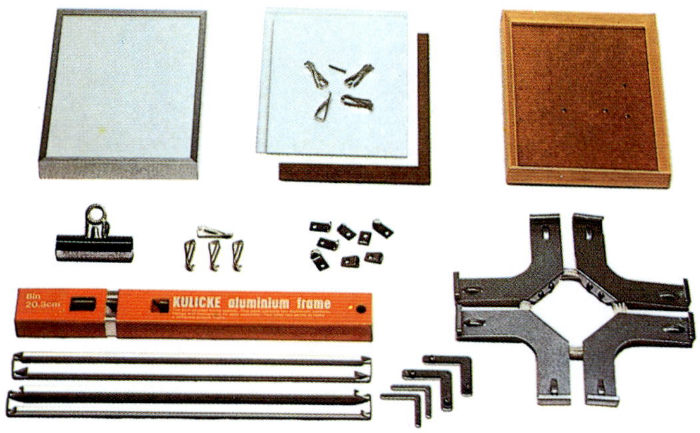

ABOVE: *Ready-made frames and clips:* **1** *Emo interchangeable metal frame,* **2** *Emo framers' pack, containing a piece of glass, a piece of fiberboard and a number of small clips,* **3** *Ready-made frame,* **4 5** *and* **6** *Bulldog, spring, and mirror clips,* **7** *and* **8** *Kulicke and Daler metal frame kits,* **9** *Hang-it frame kit*

BOUGHT FRAMES AND MOLDINGS

A fine, grained frame with a raised inner edge stands complete at the top right of this selection. The group of grained woods and veneers illustrates the range of frames and moldings available. At the bottom left-hand corner are two types of frame for an oval picture, including a gold slip oval that would enhance a particularly treasured period miniature. A more formal style of room cries out for the more formal, polished frames that are typical of those grouped together here. Among the narrower frames is an elegant tortoiseshell and gold, two sides of which are illustrated at the top left. Next to it is a corner piece in antique walnut veneer. Some solid and grand frames lie across the center of the group, including one with fan-shaped wooden inlays. Take care when choosing frames of this sort—consideration should be given not only to the type of picture to be framed, but also to the suitability of the frame to the environment .

COLORFUL PAINT FINISHES

Some highly decorative paint finishes are featured in this group of moldings. All ready-cut frames, they combine a traditional period flavor with modern experimental finishes. The yellow marbled frame across the center is faked. Yet the result is a tasteful version of a traditional marbling technique. It contrasts strongly with the simple green and turquoise ovals that lie next to it in the group. To their bottom right is a series of specimens including a "faux" or "made" (imitation) malachite, and two elegant and narrow samples finished in stippled red and sponged blue. At the extreme top left of the whole group is a marbled dark blue frame, followed by frames sporting a variety of decorative finishes, including two rectangles with painted motifs and decoration over white and green stippled backgrounds.

chapter II

TECHNIQUES

Every drawing or painting depends on a number of choices. Some of the most important decisions are made before anything is put down on paper or canvas. Viewpoint, color balance, perspective, and tone are factors that dictate the composition, providing the foundation of a successful work. "Putting it all together" is a process that begins with the eye and moves on through the sketchbook. With this foundation in place you can begin to practice the drawing and painting techniques to achieve the effects you have chosen. And even if you take a wrong turn, there is usually a chance to put things right, or at least to take your work in a new direction.

exercise

PERCEPTION: THE MIND'S EYE

You might think it odd that the first thing it is suggested you do in a book about drawing is to write something, but it is essential to be aware of how we use our eyes in the everyday business of conducting our lives, and to discover what adjustments we have to make to our perceptual processes to make successful representational drawings.

ABOVE: *This pencil drawing was obviously done from memory by an untutored eye. Without the table in front of you it is very difficult to remember the relationships among the objects to be drawn. Many objects have been left out, and some have been added that were not actually there.*

As an exercise, perhaps at the end of an evening meal, leave the dining table and walk into the adjoining room. Write a full description of the table in the room you have just left. It will probably contain the following sort of information. "There are four dinner-plates on the table, knives and forks, water-pitcher, coffee cups, drinking glasses. The table is a round, mahogany table." This first description will probably be quite limited, constructed almost as a list enumerating the various items you can remember.

Now return to the room you were in. Sit looking at the table in front of you, and write another description. You will probably once again begin by making a list of objects, but you may well discover there are quite a few things that you had left out. Your second description of the objects will now probably be much more elaborate and individually detailed, one or two favorite objects being singled out for particular attention. The table itself, for example, might be described as an early Victorian, round, mahogany table with ornate central pillar and carved tripod legs on small castors. You might also begin to describe your reasons for any particular attachment to this table. You might then likewise choose to describe in much greater detail the salt and pepper mills, how you came into possession of them, and any story attached to them.

The reason for suggesting that you carry out both of these descriptions is simply to make you use your eyes. You were first asked to stretch your memory, and you may have been quite surprised at how many things you had forgotten to include in your first description. In the second attempt you consciously used your eyes to gather considerably more information than your memory could hold. You should by now have proved to your own satisfaction that you are quite an observant person and quite capable of assimilating in considerable detail what is visually presented to you, but that you find it much harder to reproduce it all from memory.

A problem arises, however, when you try to translate this method of observation into a drawing. Leaving the objects exactly where they are on the table, make a drawing of the room in front of you. You will probably end up with a drawing not dissimilar to the one illustrated. Most beginners find it exceedingly difficult to draw a table from wherever they are viewing it. It is impossible to see it as a complete circle, and there is a strong compulsion visually to tilt the surface so that all the objects you wish to draw can be clearly seen. This is due not to any lack of ability to see, but to using the information seen in a way that is not compatible with the act of drawing, but

ABOVE: *A pencil drawing of the same subject matter. Here, however, the drawing was made with the table and chairs in full view. Again, little attempt has been made to render the drawing with any perspective, although all the objects are recorded more tellingly, with the patterns on the plates, the chair seats, and indication that the bottle and saucers are of a darker color. There is clearly far more information in this drawing.*

that corresponds completely with the act of verbal description. For example, to describe verbally all the objects on the table it is necessary to isolate them visually one by one, find an appropriate word or sentence, and move on to the next object. In your first drawing most beginners still want to use the visual information in a verbal way. One reason for wanting to tip the table is a wish to separate each object so that an individual descriptive drawing can be made of it. In exactly the same way, your written description enumerated the objects on the table.

Now try again to draw the table. Place a chair about eight or ten feet away, sit down and try to draw the objects on the table from this one fixed viewpoint. It soon becomes apparent that not all the objects on the table can be fully seen. One object may partly obscure another, and a proportion of the whole table may be partly obscured by a chair that is in your line of vision. You will probably still find

LEFT: *You can see from these two photographs that they have been taken from different angles. It is obvious that the photographs are of the same table, but the visual information they contain is very different. This is even more apparent when the two photographs are transformed into two line drawings (below).*

an urge visually to tilt the table at a far greater angle than it actually is. You will also probably find that you tend to draw one object first in its entirety, then move on to the next, and so on, and that you try to fit the table and chairs round the objects.

This exercise will have been much more difficult than you imagined at first it would be. There is absolutely nothing wrong with your eyes, nor with the visual information that you are receiving. The problem is that you have not been using the information in a genuinely pictorial way.

The main problem most beginners have in perceiving the interrelationships of all the objects is thus due in some degree to the fact that they tend to perceive the world in a solely three-dimensional way. To appraise most objects fully it is normal to pick them up or walk round them, using your eyes all the time to take in details of color, form, weight, and texture. It is not until beginners actually start to make a representational drawing of what he or she sees from a fixed viewpoint that the full realization occurs that it is impossible to see an object in its entirety. For example, if you were to move the chair on which you sat to do your first drawing just one foot to the right or to the left, all the visual relationships of the objects on the table—such as the spaces between them and the shapes of the objects themselves—change. From your first position you might for instance have been able to see a cup; you knew the handle was there, but you could not see it. From your second position, the cup has not moved, but you can now see the handle. Pictorially the object has changed its shape. What beginners are always fighting against when they first start to draw is their *perceived experience* of an object as distinct from their actual view of the object.

We all receive through our eyes far more information than can possibly be represented in a single representational drawing. We therefore have to be selective, using only the visual information that can be recorded from a fixed viewpoint.

exercise

THREE DIMENSIONS INTO TWO

One great advantage of drawing is that there is no need for a lavish studio or even a room set aside for it, and the equipment used can be of the most simple type. Some of the most beautiful drawings have been done with a piece of burned stick and colored earths on cave walls. The right pencils, the right ink and a perfect easel cannot in themselves make anyone draw any better. There is only one requirement: to see.

Collect together four or five cardboard cartons of various sizes, and a couple of bottles, and place them in a natural way on a table that itself should preferably be rectangular. Put your paper on a piece of board and sit on a chair with another chair facing you, propping the board up on that chair, so that it becomes an easel. There is a good reason in this exercise for this odd way of sitting. Look carefully at what is in front of you and try to draw the cartons on the table as accurately as possible from the fixed viewpoint you have chosen.

At your first attempt you will almost certainly come up against a problem. Your mind, through your previous experience of cartons, knows that they have got sides, tops and bottoms and will not believe what your eyes are now telling you—that the tops of the cartons do not appear as perfect rectangles. Even though you are looking across the top of the cartons and your eye is giving you that information, your mind will try to tilt them up so that their squareness or rectangularity can be fully seen.

Try a second drawing. This time, do not look at the cartons individually as boxes but run a line with your pencil from where you have drawn the edge of the table around the shape of all the boxes, making a single outline shape. Your first drawing may well have got into difficulties because your mind was telling you that the boxes were all individual and separate objects, and you were trying to draw one, then another, hoping they would all relate to each other in the particular arrangement in front of you. The eye is also seeing them as individual boxes. In your second drawing you are attempting to see them as a whole shape, not individually. You have now taken the first step to translating what is three-dimensional form into two-dimensional form.

Now move the boxes around into a different pattern, making sure that there is a gap between one or two of the boxes. Again draw purely linearly, starting from where you draw the edge of the table. When you come to the gap between two boxes, try to become aware not of the next box but of the negative space between the boxes. In your two-dimensional translation, the negative space is just as important a shape on the paper as the positive shape of the box itself. You are translating this third image into a series of flat patterns on a flat surface.

Think of your sheet of paper as a flat sheet of glass through which you are viewing the boxes. This can be very useful in helping to understand the two-dimensional nature of drawing. If you can obtain a piece of glass or a sheet of clear, stiff plastic, mask off an area as

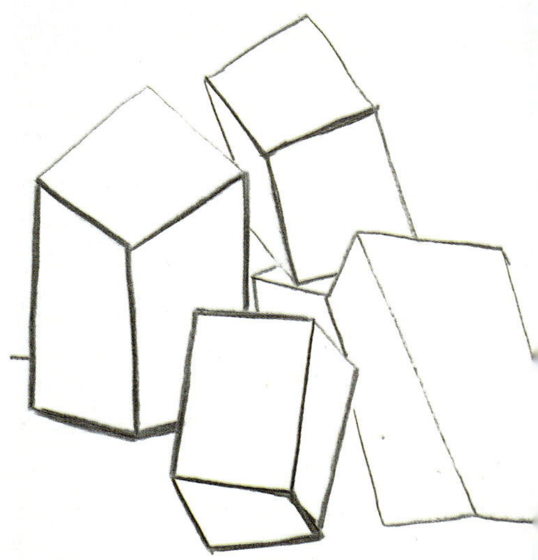

ABOVE: *In this drawing the student has drawn the boxes as they would normally be conceived: showing five individual objects and their relationship to one another. The table has almost been disregarded, conceived as of secondary importance. The drawing is descriptive but not visually representational.*

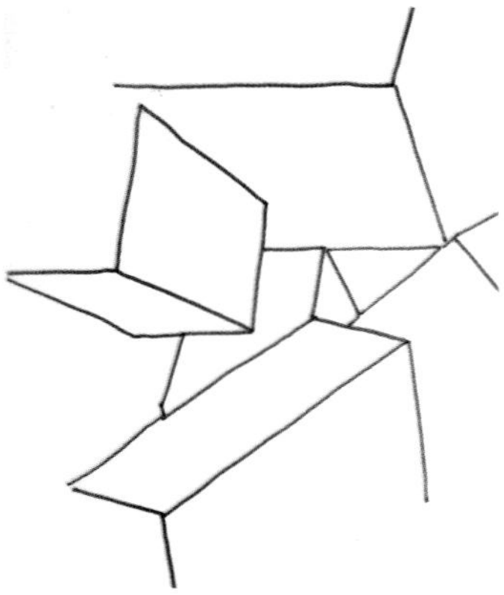

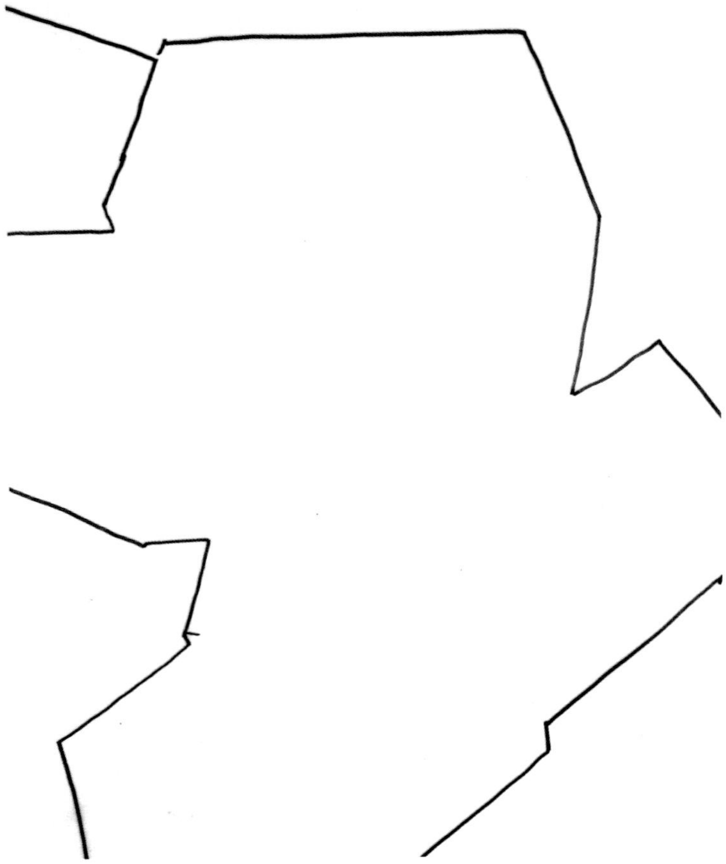

TOP: *The second stage in the drawing, after the simple silhouette (right). It is a careful observation of the center, where all the boxes make a negative shape relative to one another. This is drawn in the correct proportion and relationship to the outer line drawing.*

RIGHT: *In this simple line drawing the five cartons have not been seen as individual shapes but have been approached, along with the table, as a flat silhouette, creating a two-dimensional pattern on the paper. It is impossible to make a drawing like this without conceiving of the cartons as one total shape.*

illustrated, the same size as the piece of paper on which you are going to draw. Prop up the piece of glass in front of you so that the boxes are viewed through this glass screen. With a felt-tip pen start marking out the form of the boxes on the glass screen. You will then see how the eye transposes the boxes into a two-dimensional surface—the glass screen. You will also realize how important a fixed viewpoint is in representational drawing. The slightest movement of the head alters all the relationships between the boxes that you have already drawn on the glass.

In this exercise you might find it easier to close one eye when drawing. Put a mark representing the most obvious corner of the nearest box. Before you make another mark, always make sure that the first mark you made is correctly aligned with the corner of the box that it represents on your glass screen. This ensures that when you make further marks on the screen they are in the correct relationship one to another.

You may well be wondering why you were asked to prop a board up on a chair and draw in that particular manner. The sheet of glass or plastic is acting as a transparent picture plane. A picture can be thought of as a rectangular surface through which we see the world. The window we call the "picture plane" and it is the most important concept to understand in representational drawing and painting. How does this glass picture plane through which we are viewing the boxes relate to our drawing paper?

KEEPING THINGS IN PERSPECTIVE

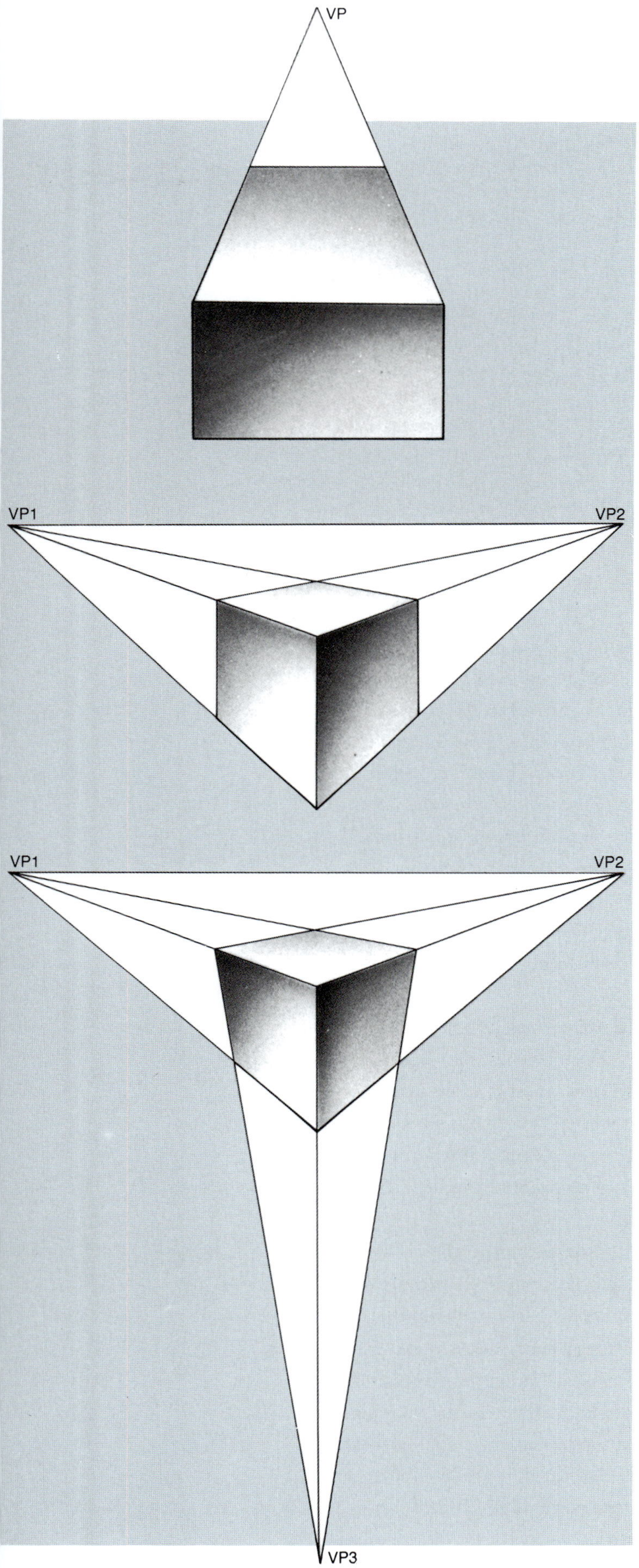

When we look across a valley from a high vantage-point, we see all the elements in nature that make up a landscape, arranged at varying distances from each other. Trees in the foreground, middle distance, and far distance are perhaps linked by paths, hedges, and rivers. To draw these things "in perspective" means only that we need to find a way of representing the distance of one object from another—in other words, "fixing" their position in our drawing.

There are certain ground rules which act as a useful guide in doing this, but as with all art theory, there is no real substitute for training the hand and eye to register things directly without recourse to drawing systems.

The picture plane is a kind of imaginary vertical screen, which is transparent and which is positioned on the ground at a distance from the artist, depending on where he intends his drawing to begin. The "picture" he conceives lies behind this imaginary screen, although some objects in the immediate foreground would touch it. The precise position of the viewer on his side of the picture plane is critical. This will determine how high the eye is from ground level and whether he is in the center or to one side of the picture. The base of the picture plane is called the ground line. It is from the ground line that one's measurements begin.

TOP: *One point perspective. As the parallel lines recede, they appear to converge at the vanishing point. If only two sides of the cube are visible, it can be drawn in perspective from a single vanishing point.*

MIDDLE: *Two point perspective. When three sides of the cube are visible, two sets of parallel lines converge at separate vanishing points.*

BOTTOM: *Three point perspective. When the cube appears either above or below the artist's view of the horizon, it is necessary to draw both vertical and horizontal lines converging on three separate vanishing points.*

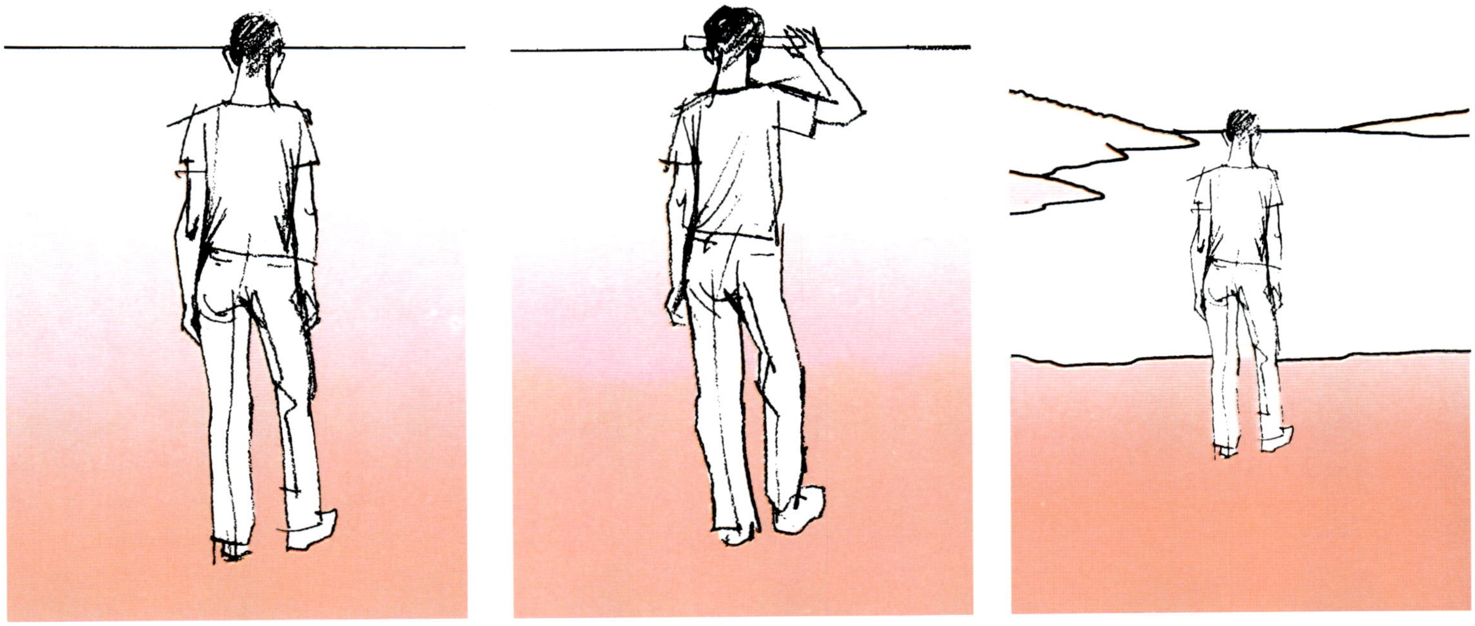

ABOVE: *The horizon line is placed at sea level. You can try this out standing on a beach by holding a ruler up at eye-level. In a more undulating landscape, the horizon line will probably be partially concealed, but it can still be established in the drawing.*

The artist stands on one side of the picture plane, and on the other side all the things that can be seen are disposed at various points toward the horizon. The horizon line is parallel to the ground line and is the same height as the eye of the viewer. On the horizon line is a point we call the "vanishing" point. This may be in the center, or to one side, depending on the position of the viewer. When the vanishing point has been established on the horizon line, then all vertical lines remain vertical and all lines which are parallel to the ground line remain parallel. Imagine, for instance, that you are standing immediately facing the side of a tall building. Then neither the vertical nor horizontal lines will converge. For them to do so it is necessary to move backward, or to one side.

The lines other than those which are vertical or parallel to the ground line are drawn toward the vanishing point. In a landscape, for example, objects of roughly the same size—trees or telephone poles—appear to become smaller as they recede into the distance, and as they get smaller they seem to be nearer the horizon line. Although they diminish in size, there is no distortion in their shapes when seen from the front.

In the diagram on the next page you will notice that the tree in the foreground coincides with the picture plane and the size remains constant. One can therefore find the actual height or width of any object by assessing it in relation to the ground line. On the other hand, the size of an object as it appears in perspective can be determined by taking a line from the ground line to the vanishing point. All the horizontal lines which appear at right angles to the picture plane will converge on the horizon at the vanishing point. If you were drawing a box placed in the center of your line of vision, there would be one vanishing point. If, however, you were to draw

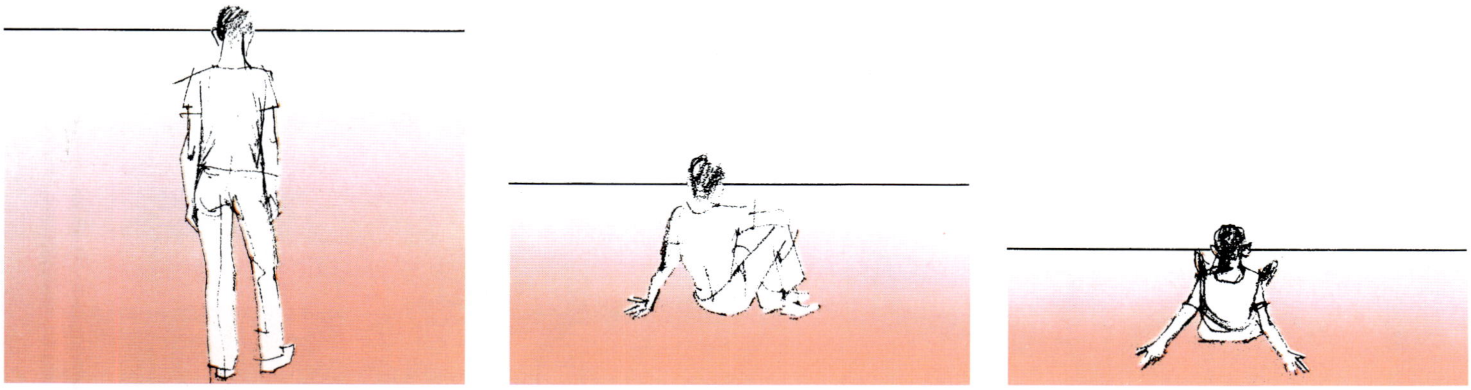

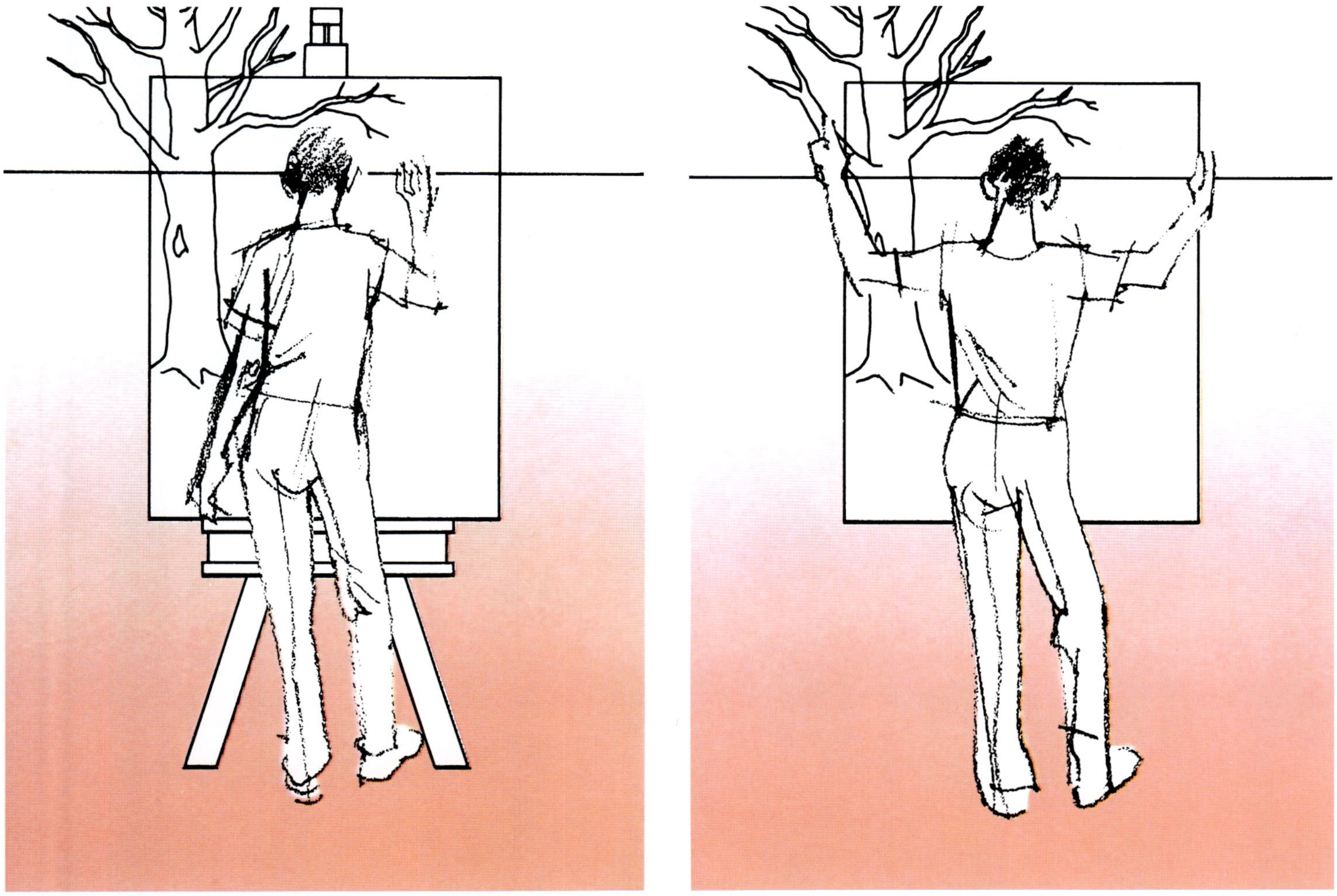

TOP: *These three illustrations show how the horizon line changes according to the way you position your body. In a standing position for instance, most of the ground plane is visible. But the subject itself should suggest the best eye-level for your drawing.*

two separate boxes several feet distant from each other, there would be two sets of parallel lines, each set with its own vanishing point. Strong diagonal lines which incline steeply upward have their vanishing point above the horizon; conversely, those inclining sharply downward have their vanishing point below the horizon line.

ABOVE: *The picture plane is an imaginary transparent screen separating the artist from the subject. The image that you see through this plane is what is transferred to your paper or canvas. When starting to draw, the horizon line should be established first.*

ABOVE: *A pencil and wash study of the glass roof of a Victorian railway station, London. This drawing relies upon a painstaking control of perspective as well as silhouette to create a cavernous expanse of glass and steel.*

ABOVE: *A vacation sketch book study in pencil; the strong perspective gives a sense of towering scale. Again, a squared viewing frame helps to find and isolate the pictorial value of subject matter like this, so easily overlooked.*

RIGHT: *Leonardo da Vinci's pen and ink preparatory study for the background to* The Adoration of the Magi. *Note the vanishing point to the right of center.*

AERIAL PERSPECTIVE

This is a way of using color and tone to give a sense of space in a painting, and to indicate recession. It is particularly important in landscape painting. If you look at an expanse of landscape, such as one with fields and trees in the foreground and distant hills or mountains beyond, you will see that the colors become paler and cooler in the distance, with details barely visible. The objects in the foreground will be brighter and have much clearer areas of contrast, or tonal differences, which will become smaller in the middle distance and may disappear altogether in the far distance, so that the hills or mountains appear as pure areas of pale blue. It takes some experience to use aerial perspective successfully; if you accidentally mix a rather warm blue on your palette and try to use it for the distant hills you will find that they seem almost to jump forward to the front of the picture. The same applies if you combine a pale color with a much darker one; there will then be a greater tonal difference than is actually present and the background will begin to vie with the foreground.

Aerial perspective can, of course, be either exploited or ignored.

Sometimes, for instance, you might be more interested in creating a flat pattern or you might want simply to use areas of vivid color.

LINEAR PERSPECTIVE

This, like color theory, can be a very complex subject, almost a science. During the Renaissance, when the laws of perspective were first being formulated in a systematic way, artists vied with one another to produce more and more elaborate perspective drawings; for example, Paolo Uccello (*c.*1396–1475) made a study of a chalice broken down into a series of separate receding surfaces which is quite breathtaking in its intricacy. However, unless your particular interest is architecture—you might perhaps want to make a series of detailed studies of the interiors of churches, for instance—it is most unlikely that you will need to understand more than the most basic rules, which are helpful when faced with the problem of how to make buildings look solid or how to indicate that they are being viewed from above.

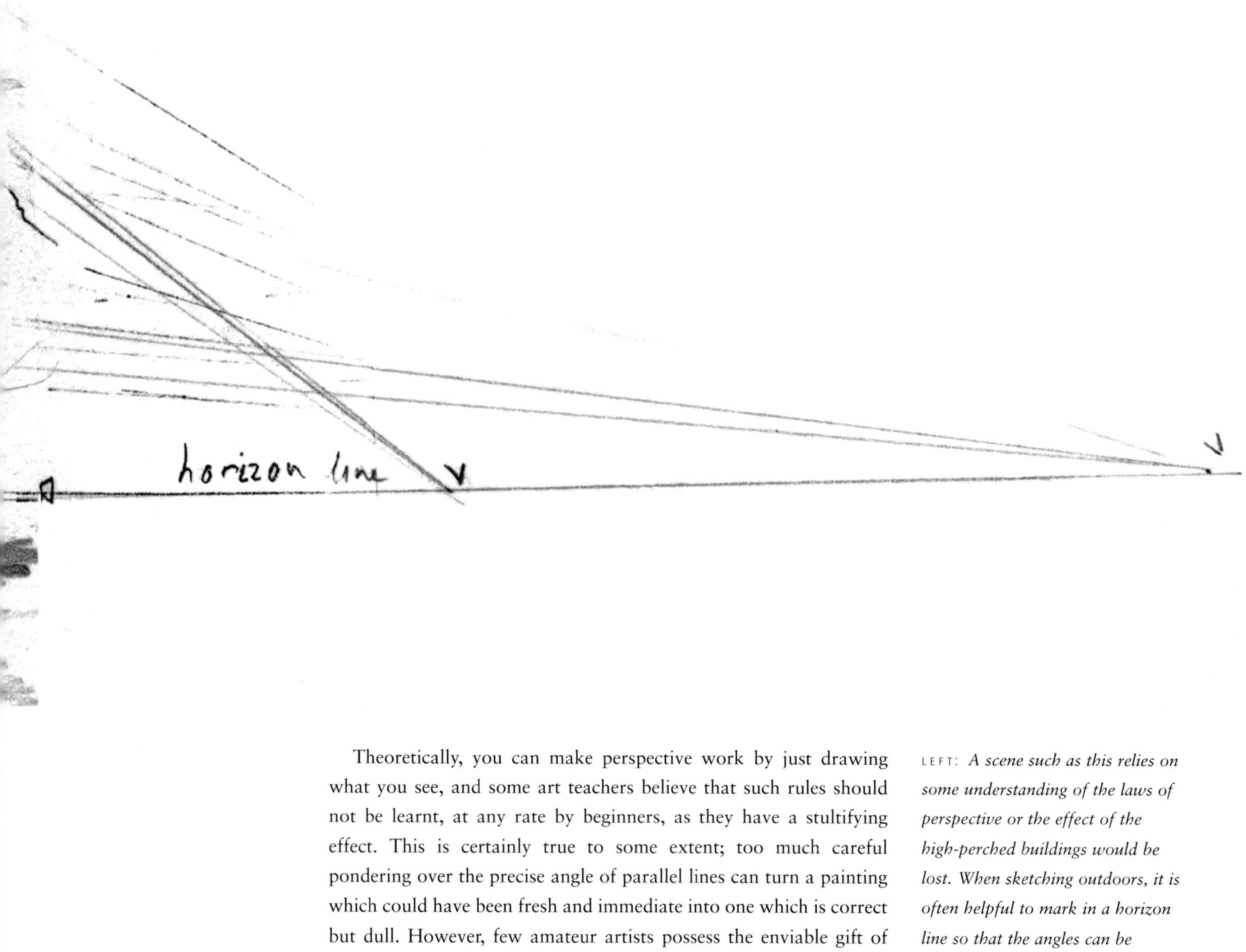

Theoretically, you can make perspective work by just drawing what you see, and some art teachers believe that such rules should not be learnt, at any rate by beginners, as they have a stultifying effect. This is certainly true to some extent; too much careful pondering over the precise angle of parallel lines can turn a painting which could have been fresh and immediate into one which is correct but dull. However, few amateur artists possess the enviable gift of being able to turn direct observation into drawing or painting with any degree of ease, and a knowledge of the basic rules can have a liberating effect rather than the reverse, as long as you don't allow yourself to become too bound up in them.

The primary rule, which many people learn at school, is that all receding parallel lines meet at a vanishing point, which is on the horizon. It is easy enough to learn such rules, but far less easy to apply them. A single building has several different planes, or sets of parallel lines, and a group of buildings, such as a farmhouse with barns and outhouses, has even more, as the buildings are often set at

LEFT: *A scene such as this relies on some understanding of the laws of perspective or the effect of the high-perched buildings would be lost. When sketching outdoors, it is often helpful to mark in a horizon line so that the angles can be related to it; the eye alone cannot always judge such angles truthfully.*

RIGHT: *To artists such as Uccello and Michelangelo, the mysteries of proportion and perspective were studied in a logical and scientific manner. The Renaissance totally re-evaluated the concepts of representational art, and most artists of the period experimented with drawing through a grid screen to understand how the proportions of the same object alter radically from different view points. We are now so familiar with seeing pictures — both photographic and drawn — that it is often difficult for the beginner to believe that this particular approach to drawing has only recently been universally accepted as a representation of the world.*

random angles to one another. Where, you may ask yourself, is this horizon at which they will all meet, and how is it determined? This is dependent on your chosen viewpoint. If you are high up, on a cliff or hilltop, the horizon will be level with you, so that you have very little sky and a large expanse of land or sea. You will be looking down at the group of buildings, and the parallel lines receding from you will slope up to the horizon. If you are at a low angle, perhaps sitting on the ground, the horizon, still at eye-level, will also be low, giving a large expanse of sky. The buildings will be above the horizon and the receding parallels will slope down to it.

In the case of parallels running directly away from you, the vanishing point would be within the picture area, but for different planes at angles to them it will be a hypothetical one which can be some way outside the picture area to the right or left. If you are painting outdoors, the viewing frame is helpful in establishing where the various lines are leading to, or a small pocket ruler can be held up in front of your eye and lined up with a rooftop.

Of course, many artists choose either to ignore or to exaggerate the rules of perspective so as to create their own personal effects. For example, an artist who is more interested in the patterns suggested by a particular scene might paint the buildings quite flat, with no perspective at all, as a child would, while another might choose to "see" a subject from above, with the horizon so high that there is no sky area at all.

grasping perspective

Perspective governs everything we see; even in a simple landscape of fields and hills the way in which a wall twists and narrows or the furrows of a plowed field change direction explain the lie of the land and help to create a feeling of form and recession.

1 *The furrows in a plowed field run across our vision, the spaces between them becoming progressively smaller as the field recedes.*

2 *Now our viewpoint is altered, so that the furrows run away, converging at a vanishing point on the horizon.*

3 *In this mid-view, between that of the two previous examples, the lines still converge on the horizon, but the vanishing point is some way outside the picture.*

4 *This wide-angle view shows that we do not really perceive the lines of the furrows as straight.*

5 *The vanishing point must always be on the horizon—that is, at our own eye-level—if the ground is flat, but it will be within the picture area only if viewed square-on.*

6 *If there is a dip in the ground the furrows will follow it, thus taking their vanishing points from the angle of the indentation, which theoretically alters the horizon line. This is an important point to remember in landscape painting, as the land is seldom completely flat.*

7 *When viewed from a distance, the two sides of a church tower appear to be vertical.*

8 *However, when seen more closely, the side walls appear to converge. The lower the viewpoint, the more sharply they do so.*

9 *When seen from above, the sides appear to converge at the bottom.*

10 *When the tower is seen from an angle, each side will have its own vanishing point. When drawing or painting buildings it is all too easy to forget this.*

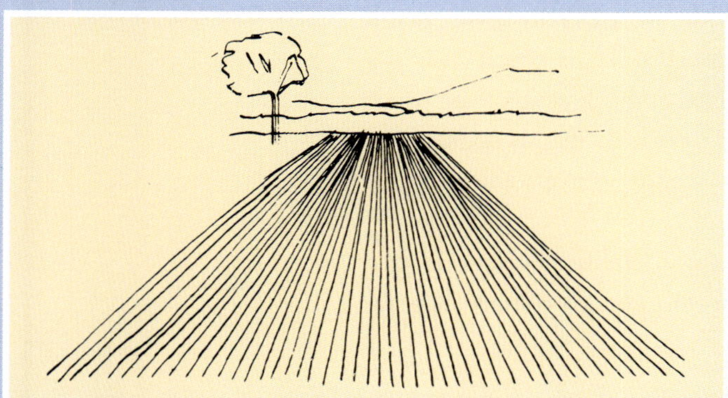

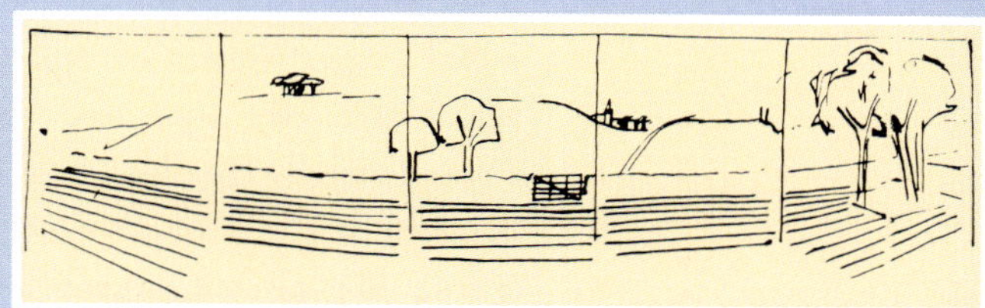

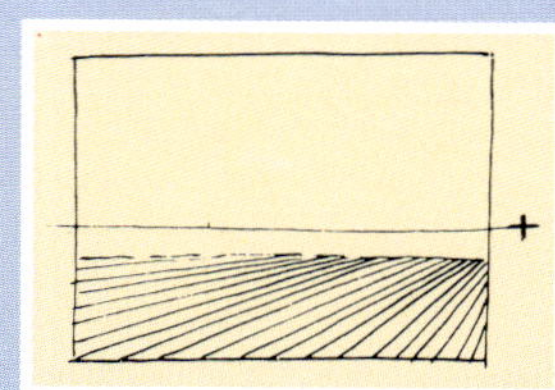

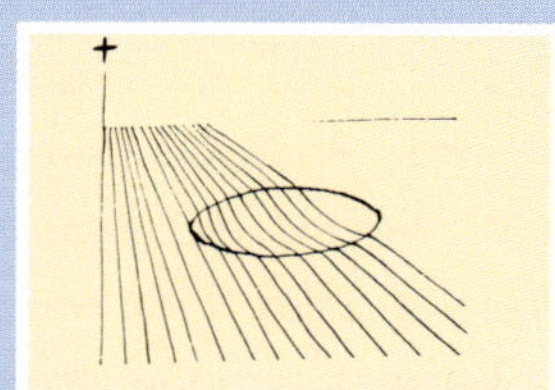

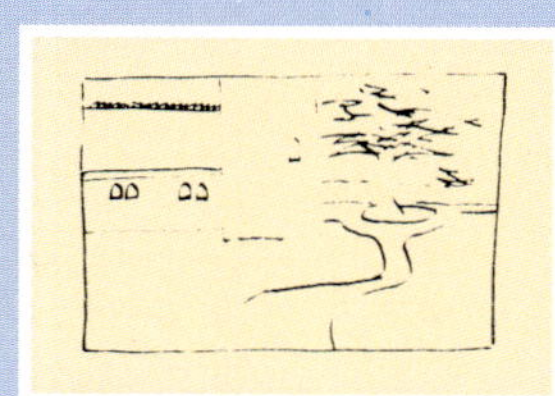

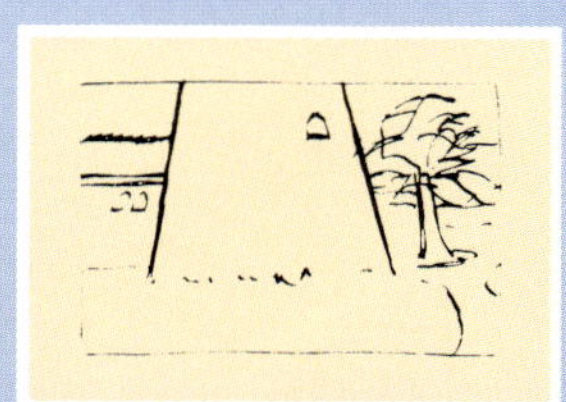

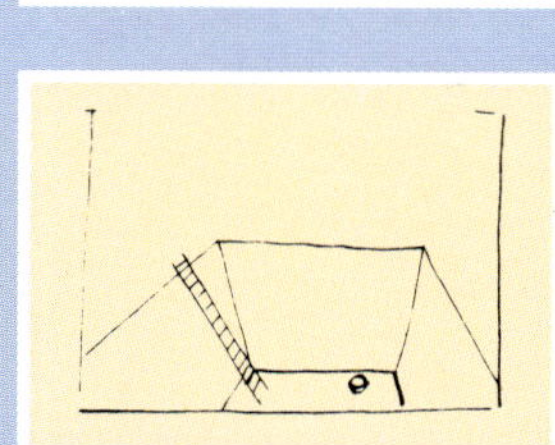

It is a mistake, in my view, to think of color as a separate component of drawing and painting. Understanding color is an integral part of the whole business of learning to see and learning to register what you see. A basic knowledge of color theory is, of course, useful, but time spent observing color in nature is even more rewarding. Cézanne said that painting from direct observation is a way of classifying one's sensations of color. "Drawing and color," he added, "are not separate at all; in so far as you paint you draw. The more the color harmonizes, the more exact the drawing becomes."

Contemporary color theory is founded upon the experiments of Sir Isaac Newton (1642–1727). Newton explained that although sunlight, or white light, is "uncolored," it is made up of seven colored rays: violet, indigo, blue, green, yellow, orange, and red. We see color in objects that reflect and absorb these rays to a greater or lesser degree. The terra-cotta roof of a house in Spain, for example, is a warm, dark-red color at first light, when the sun is low. At midday, however, when the sun is directly overhead, that same roof becomes a pink-orange white. Color theory often gets in the way of how we actually see color—one needs to be able to see beyond the "local" color of objects. The "local" color of an olive tree, for instance, might be green or gray-green; but under strong sunlight the leaves might sparkle like silvered viridian and at dusk become shadowy-black silhouettes. So we need to observe carefully how the effect of light can modify our preconception of the color that an object should be.

An object which reflects all the colored rays of the spectrum appears as white light; an object that absorbs them all appears black. When we talk of light being "absorbed," we are really saying that it is lost. When rays of light are not absorbed, by an object such as a flint wall, for instance, they are reflected in the direction from which they came. The term "refracted" light refers to the phenomenon of light passing through a transparent, or partly transparent body: the light is redirected, or "refracted."

We must realize, therefore, that color is modified by light. It often happens, for example, that traveling along a country lane, we

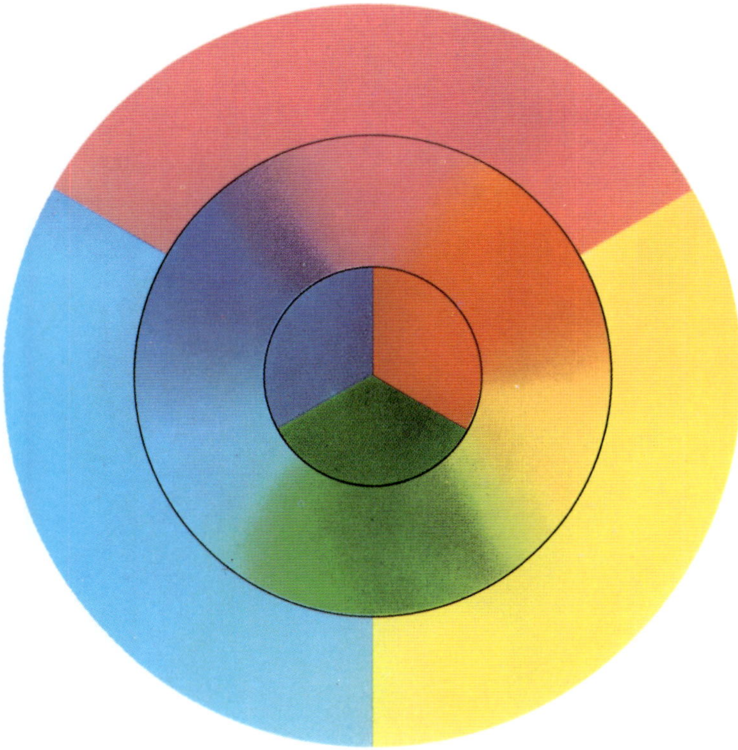

ABOVE: Color wheel: *The inner wheels represent the effect of combining primary colors in the outer wheels.*

RIGHT: *"White light," or uncolored light, is made up of the seven colors of the spectrum. The colors are separated when filtered through a prism.*

see a scene which arouses our interest. Returning with sketchbook and paints a few days later, how disappointing it is to find that same scene transformed, no longer as interesting as it was before. What happens is that our attention is drawn by the way that things appear under certain conditions of light at a particular time of day. We forget that appearances are continually changing—especially in a northern climate.

An artist's palette must be selected from the range of colors available. We need to discover, then, how to express our sensations of color by mixing colors together. The colors produced by mixing can only be an approximation of the transitory effects of light on the colors we see around us. We use color to describe the things we see and to do this effectively we need to be aware of the power of contrast—colors in the light are equivalent to the colors in shadow. We can also use color to make things appear to advance or recede.

LEFT: Color tree: *Colors are divided into different hues. The amount of white or black contained in each color determines its hue. The tree illustrates only the main color variations.*

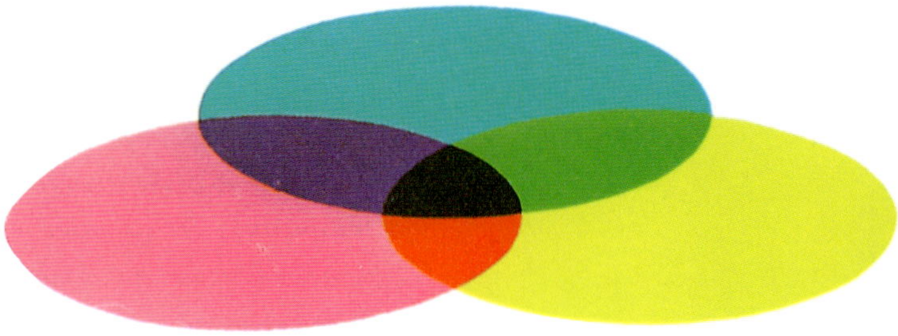

ABOVE LEFT: *Additive primaries. Red, green, and blue are called additive primaries because white light results from combining them. A third color is produced when any two additive primaries are combined.*

ABOVE RIGHT: *Subtractive primaries. The colors produced by combining two additive primaries are called subtractive primaries. Cyan, for example, is made by mixing blue and green. When white light filters through three subtractive primaries it produces black.*

Colors can be divided into two categories, warm and cool. An excellent exercise for any painter is to mix a range of grays which are cool (blue-grays) and also a range of warm grays (red-grays). The range should be quite extensive. Then proceed to paint your subject—still life, landscape, or whatever—using this range of colors only. In this way you will learn very effectively how to work without relying on primary colors or strong contrasts.

The three primary colors are red, yellow, and blue; all other colors are formed from the primaries. The three secondary colors are made from the mixture of two primaries; they are green (blue and yellow), violet (red and blue), and orange (yellow and red). The shade of a secondary color varies according to the proportions in which the two primary colors are mixed together. Green, for instance, can tend toward blue or yellow. Complementary colors are those colors that can be paired on the color circle—red is the complement of green, yellow of blue, and so on.

COLOR AND LIGHT

ABOVE: *In this painting the contrast between the dark and light tree trunks has been emphasized by the use of very thin paint. The solid foliage of the evergreens draws attention to the slenderness of the foreground trunks.*

Color can be a very complex subject indeed—whole books have been written on color theory. Such theory is beyond the scope of this book, and in any case would be more likely to be a hindrance than a help to an inexperienced painter, but there are some basic guidelines which will help you to make a picture work, and there are also some terms which you will need to understand.

Color has two main qualities, tone and intensity, the first being the darkness or lightness of a particular color and the second being its brightness. If you take a black-and-white photograph of a landscape composed entirely of greens, you will see that some appear darker than others—proving that a single color can have dark tones and light tones. In the same landscape, some of the greens will be brighter and more vibrant than others—in other words, more intense.

Colors that are opposite one another on the color wheel, such as red and green, yellow and violet, are called *complementary colors*. These can be used in a deliberate way to balance and "spark off" one another; for example, a small area of bright red in a landscape could be used to enhance and intensify a large expanse of green. The Op Art painters of the 1960s used complementary colors in a highly intellectual way: by juxtaposing complementaries of the same hue and tone they created restless, "jumping" effects.

Colors are basically either "warm" or "cool," and the warm ones will tend to "advance," or push themselves to the front of a painting, while the cool ones will recede. In general, the warm colors are the reds, yellows, bright yellow-greens, and oranges, while cool ones are the blues and colors with blue in them, such as blue-green. Some blues, however, are warmer than others, and some reds are cooler than others. You can see this by placing ultramarine or cerulean blue (both quite warm) next to Prussian or Antwerp blue (both cool), and

alizarin crimson (cool) next to cadmium red (warm).

You can make use of the "advancing" and "retreating" qualities of warm and cool colors in modeling forms and in creating a sense of space and depth. In portrait painting, for example, use warm colors for the prominent areas such as the nose, chin, and cheekbones, and cool colors for receding or shadowed areas such as underneath the chin. In landscapes, use warm colors in the foreground and cool, bluish tones in the background to emphasize the feeling of receding space.

There is no color without light, and the direction, quality and intensity of light constantly changes and modifies colors. This fact became almost an obsession with the Impressionist painter Claude Monet; he painted many studies of the same subject—a group of haystacks—at different times of the day in order to understand and analyze these changes. You can see the effects very easily for yourself if you look at any scene—the view from a window or a corner of the garden—first on a cloudy morning and then in low evening sunlight. In the evening everything will suddenly become golden and a brick wall which might have appeared a drab brown in the morning may now be a bright hue of orange or pink.

Light is vital to a painting, whether a landscape or a still life or portrait study, and the way it falls defines the shape of objects and determines their color. Both photographers and painters of landscape know that the high midday sun is their enemy, as it creates dense patches of shadow and drains the landscape of color and definition. A portrait or still life can also look flat, dead and colorless if lit directly from above, while a side light can suddenly bring it to life, creating exciting shadow areas of purple or green and vivid, sparkling highlights.

ABOVE AND TOP: *The line drawing of two racing yachts is the first stage in developing a pencil drawing to a finished state. A full range of tonal possibilities has been used to create the atmospheric depth of a gathering thunderstorm.*

COLOR AND ITS SURROUNDINGS

Complementary colors are those that lie opposite one another in the color circle. Here is the way in which complementaries work in contrast with one another. They make an interesting point about the way we respond to groupings of colors, and it is absolutely essential for designers to know what they consist of for future use.

Examples of primaries and secondaries consist of: yellow, violet, blue, orange, red, green. And in all these pairs primaries are always apparent—hence the necessity of mixing them together to make secondaries in the early stages. One gets to understand them better by doing so.

These colors are opposite yet require each other: they produce a vividness when adjacent, yet annihilate each other when mixed to produce a dark gray (useful as the basis for a neutral background, or underpainting to work on).

Another useful peculiarity of contrasting complementaries is that, though opposite, they have the remarkable ability to appear perfectly harmonious. This makes using them an agreeable pictorial device for enhancing both paintings and designs. By utilizing the complementary chart, you have the beginnings of ready-made color schemes that can be easily carried out with acrylic.

In the top row of squares, move through yellow, orange, red, to violet, and the bottom row from violet, blue, green, back to yellow. Begin with the primaries and secondaries directly over their opposite, and place the immediate tones and tints in between in their correct order. The gradations of green should be placed under the appropriate gradations of violet above.

As an additional exercise, painting your own color circle will give valuable experience in trying out colors straight from the tube without any mixing at all. Alternatively the secondaries can be mixed from the primaries to observe how possible it is to do so successfully.

Another simple experiment is to try painting on a colored underpainting. Usually you begin on a white surface. Painting on a colored surface opens up a great number of possibilities, too many to start with, perhaps.

ABOVE RIGHT: *This chart shows the primary colors, yellow, blue, and red with their contrasting complementaries, violet, orange, and green, respectively.*

ABOVE LEFT: *A similar complementary contrast chart incorporating intermediate tones and tints.*

how colors interact

Cool colors tend to recede while warm colors advance

Identical red squares are changed by surrounding colors

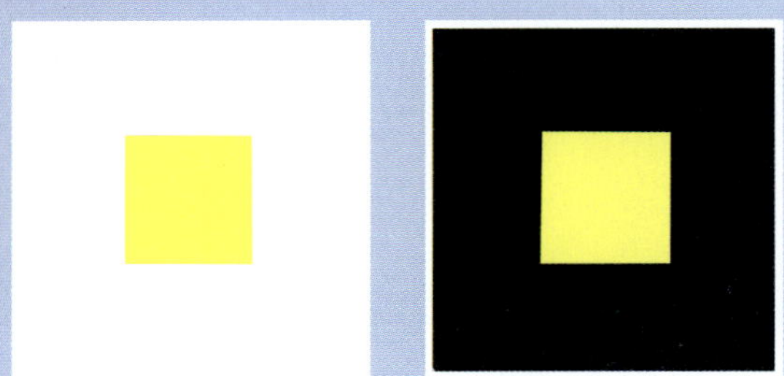

A yellow square looks bigger on white than on black

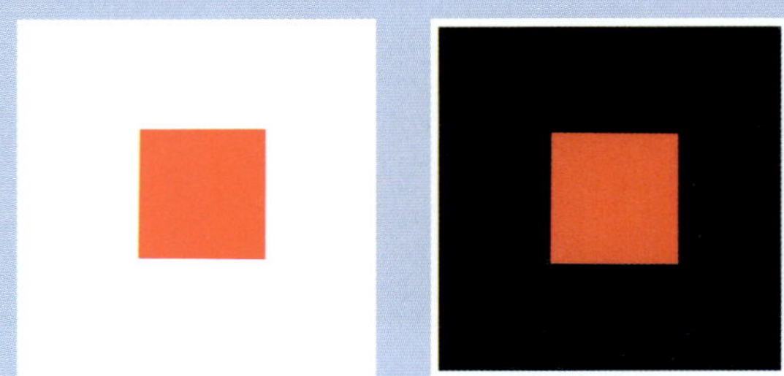

A red square looks smaller on white than on black

exercise

SETTING THE RIGHT TONE

The very first experience with mixing can be with just white and black, before trying out the other colors. It is slightly easier to judge tones and tints of gray than the tones and tints of primaries and secondaries. This exercise is basic to all the color-mixing exercises. It will incorporate mixing, applying, and experiencing the visual impact of tone, tint, and hue.

Mixtures should be well integrated, on the palette, with a knife, and with enough fluidity to allow the brush to make a good, clean stroke.

For the kind of grid that will suit this exercise best, use six squares, about ½ inch in size, which can be conveniently filled with variegated tones of paint from light to dark, and from dark to light.

Method 1 Add black to white, to make a series of grays, from the palest to the darkest tints, in six steps. The gray of medium strength should occur in the center of the scale.

Method 2 Reverse the process by adding white to black.

This exercise can now be repeated with all the colors, one by one, included in the palette, utilizing Method 1 to make tones, and Method 2 to make tints.

Points to remember, observe and develop:

1 These exercises are fundamental. There is no need to paint them carefully, if your natural inclination is to paint them freely. The practice should be as enjoyable as possible. The only proviso is that care should be taken in the mixing of the paint, so that each change of tone, in its respective square, is as clear as possible.

2 There are no rules and no end product to cause worry. The main point is that when trying any new color, do it this way before using it for whatever purpose you have in mind.

3 The aim of this exercise is to sharpen sensitivity, and give valuable experience not only in mixing color, but to see what the color looks like when mixed.

4 The exercises can be carried out in any order; size is optional, but for the best results, white paper or cardboard is recommended, primed or unprimed. For a primed white surface one thin coat is sufficient.

5 The grid may be varied to accommodate more tones and tints, and more colors. As a variation, the tones and tints may be further mixed horizontally as well as vertically.

6 As an alternative exercise the mixing may be carried out without using white. The colors can be lightened by the addition of water to make them more transparent. This is the same technique as is used in painting with watercolors. It is a useful exercise, but needs more care than in using opaque acrylic, as the washes are more difficult to control. However, whatever result is obtained, practice in using color this way is valuable, if only to experience the differences between using opaque and transparent color. As a further experiment the exercise can be carried out on different surfaces (as with watercolor) with both primed and unprimed paper.

7 Painting can be done with knife or brush. Try experimenting with them all, at some time or other, and become familiar with them at every available opportunity. This is the true meaning of practice.

8 Once confidence in mixing is acquired, any other acrylic color may be tried out—the umbers, siennas, ochers, as well as the cadmiums, blues, and greens mentioned earlier.

LEFT: *The grid with separate tones.*

ABOVE: *The horizontal and vertical grid.*

SPECIAL WASHES—WATERCOLOR AND ACRYLICS

COMPLEX EDGES

Sometimes a wash must be laid against a complicated edge, for example, a group of roofs and chimneys with an intricate outline. The wash must then start from the edge rather than end at it, which may necessitate turning the board sideways or upside down. When dampening the paper before putting on the wash take care to dampen only up to this edge, otherwise the wash will flow into the areas to be reserved.

This kind of technical problem highlights the need for initial planning—the success of a painting may hinge on the precise way a certain area has been outlined by reserving. Another method for dealing with intricate shapes is to stop out the parts to be reserved with masking fluid.

GRADATED AND VARIEGATED WASHES

Colors in nature are seldom totally flat or one solid hue. It is often desirable, therefore, to lay a gradated wash, which becomes darker or lighter at the top or bottom or changes from one color to another. For a gradated wash, simply mix more water with the paint to make each successive strip lighter, or more pigment to darken them.

For a variegated wash, mix up the two or more colors to be used, dampen the paper as usual, and then lay on the colors so that they blend into one another. The effect of such a wash cannot be worked out precisely in advance, even with practice—you should be prepared for a happy (or unhappy) accident. As with a flat wash, never make corrections while the paint is still wet.

BELOW LEFT: *Prussian blue and alizarin crimson have been allowed to run into one another, just as they would with a wash of only one color. Such effects are impossible to control accurately; the artist must be prepared for an element of "happy incident."*

BELOW CENTER: *Laying one wash on top of another often gives textural variety as well as intensifying the color. Notice that the bottom band, a pale wash of Payne's gray, is quite even, while the one at the top, a third application of the same wash, shows distinct brush marks.*

BELOW RIGHT: *The possibilities of working wet-into-wet may be explored by producing this kind of doodle in a matter of minutes. The wet-into-wet technique is often used in the early stages of a painting, or for the background, more precise work being done at a later stage or in another area of the painting.*

ABOVE: *To lay a flat acrylic wash, prepare plenty of paint. Use a wide, flat brush and run the strokes in one direction only. Each stroke should slightly overlap the one before.*

ACRYLIC WASHES

Washes used in watercolor painting are perhaps the most difficult to control, and are probably one of the most difficult processes to master. Controlling them is a never-failing source of anxiety for some watercolorists, because if a wash goes wrong it cannot be put right, and so the work loses its point and purpose. Washes, even with acrylic, can be ruined, but because of the nature of the paint itself, you can use whiting-out and put it right again.

Although acrylic can be used like watercolor, it must be clearly understood that acrylic washes function differently from watercolor washes. The main difference is the paint composition itself, for though the pigments may be identical, the binders are not. Watercolors can be diluted so thinly that they have hardly any body at all. The gum binders are capable of holding the pigments together despite overthinning. Acrylic, on the other hand, has a binder that imparts weight and substance to the paint which must be considered, especially when overthinning the paint, and it cannot be ignored without breaking down its inherent qualities. A useful measure to adopt is always to add a good few drops of the acrylic medium when diluting acrylic paint for washes, as a precaution. It will keep the wash from looking thin and lifeless, and will add a sparkle that ordinary watercolor sometimes lacks.

dry-brush with watercolor

Dry-brush work is an excellent method of suggesting texture, such as that of grass or a corn field, but it becomes monotonous if used too much in one painting. Here a number of similar colors have been used over a pale underlying wash to give tonal variation.

EXPERIMENT 1—FLAT WASH

- *Squeeze out ½ in of paint into a clean container.*
- *Add water to dilute, mix well to make sure that there are no lumps of undissolved paint as this will ruin a wash.*
- *Add some acrylic medium last—about a teaspoon will do.*
- *With a large brush spread the wash down the paper or cardboard, working from the top, to make a flat wash. Whatever happens, do not touch the wash once it has been applied. Let the color find its own level.*
- *The application can be carried out upright or on the flat. If upright the wash will run down rather quickly.*

EXPERIMENT 2—GRADATED TONES

Exactly the same as Experiment 1, but in this experiment instead of painting the wash completely in one color, halfway through continue with clean water only and let the color blend into it. This is easy to do with pure acrylic color, provided there is plenty of medium in the wash, and water tension breaker (wetting agent) in the water.

EXPERIMENT 3—MOISTENED PAPER

First cover the paper or cardboard completely with water. Then, before it has properly dried, flood a wash into it as above.

EXPERIMENT 4—ADDING COLOR

This experiment can combine any or all of Experiments 2 and 3. Proceed as above, and before the color has dried flood another color into the wet surface. Usually known as wet-in-wet and can create subtle changes in color.

EXPERIMENT 5—OVERLAY

This is exactly like glazing. Proceed as above, but let the color dry out thoroughly. Then apply further washes over the dried paint. In pure watercolor, the paint may pick up, but with acrylic this can never happen.

EXPERIMENT 6—ANIMATED BRUSHSTROKES

For this experiment, use an ample amount of acrylic medium with the paint and, when well mixed, the wash can be applied, letting the brush play its part by animating the wash with brushstrokes. Hog's-hairs can be used profitably for this experiment.

Washes are one kind of effect that looks well without under- or overpainting, hence their popularity for immediate statements, especially for figurative work like landscape painting where, being outdoors in all kinds of weather, speed and spontaneity are vital.

ABOVE: *Experiment 2. To achieve a gradated effect, work quickly, adding water to the paint in increasing quantities with each successive band of color.*

ABOVE: *Experiment 4. To produce this wet-in-wet, the artist began with a graded wash of cobalt blue and added a graded wash of lemon yellow.*

ABOVE: *Experiment 3. Single color wet-in-wet wash, made by covering the support with a layer of water and allowing a wash of color to flood into it.*

overlay

ABOVE: *Lay the palest colors first, so that the light reflects off the white paper.*

ABOVE: *It is vital to allow one color to dry completely before applying the next one.*

ABOVE: *The artist applies a thin wash of Hooker's green over the first color. Where the two washes cross, a third hue is produced.*

LEFT: *The use of animated strokes with a hog's-hair brush produces a very active texture.*

As has been mentioned, there are many different ways of applying oil paint to create particular effects. Some of these are used almost unconsciously, when the painting seems to demand a particular approach, while others are the result of careful planning.

The method called *scumbling* comes into the first category and simply means applying semi-opaque paint on top of another dry or semi-dry area of colour in an irregular way. Part of the layer below will show through, so that a "broken" color and texture is created. This can be very effective for particular parts of a painting, such as skies, rocks, tree trunks, fabric, and so on. Anything can be used for putting on scumbled paint—stiff brushes, a rag, or even the fingers—and the paint can be dragged, smudged or stippled.

Areas of irregular texture can be made by laying a flat area of color in opaque paint and then "blotting" it, when semi-dry, with nonabsorbent paper such as pages from a glossy magazine. As you peel back the paper, it drags at the surface layer of paint and creates a stippled texture. This technique is called *frottage*.

A way of creating another kind of texture is *impasto*, in which the paint is laid on thickly, often with a palette knife. In the past, artists such as Rembrandt combined impasto with areas of delicate brushwork, pointing up the differences in texture between, for example, flesh and clothing. Today many artists use impasto as a technique on its own, building up heavy layers of paint to make a raised and densely textured surface. Special painting mediums are available which increase the bulk of the paint and some artists even mix paint with sand for a rough, grainy surface.

Interesting effects can be achieved by drawing or scratching into a layer of wet oil paint to reveal another color beneath or sometimes the white ground of the canvas. The implement used can be anything pointed, such as the end of the brush handle or a knitting needle. This method is called *sgraffito*.

ABOVE: *A thin layer of transparent red paint is being laid over a dry layer of yellow. This is the technique called glazing, which gives an effect quite unlike that of one layer of thicker paint, as the color below reflects back through the glaze, giving additional brilliance.*

BELOW: *The photograph shows colors being blended into one another by working wet-into-wet.*

RIGHT: *This small painting was done by the* alla prima *method, with the paint used quite thickly and put down rapidly with little subsequent alteration.*

BELOW RIGHT: *The paint surface here is an important part of the painting, the broken patches and restless texture of the thickly applied color enhancing the vividness of the subject. The paint was applied with a knife alone, and the detail* (LEFT), *clearly shows how different is the effect from that of traditional brush painting.*

TOP: *The still life was given sparkle as well as additional definition by the use of the sgraffito technique.*

ABOVE LEFT: *Here scumbling was used to suggest the texture of the chalk cliffs. The paint was scrubbed on with a brush over dry paint below, and in places was worked in with the fingers. The foreground was put on rather dry.*

A technique that comes into the deliberate planning category is *glazing*, in which thin, transparent paint is laid over an area of already dry paint. Layers of glazes can be built up one over the other to create effects akin to the deep glow of wood that has been lovingly polished—but glazing is not a quick method as each layer must dry before the next is applied. Many of the rich, glowing colors used by artists of the past, such as Titian, were produced by laying thin glazes of brilliant color over an underpainting, and the luminous quality of the landscapes painted by J. M. W. Turner (1775–1851) are the result of layers of glazing over thick, pale impastos.

PASTEL COMBINATIONS

The composition for the drawing below is essentially very basic—a seated figure positioned by a window, with a table, a bowl of fruit and flowers. It is a drawing that demonstrates how a single light source influences the tonality and mood of the picture. The particular placement of the figure is important; the light filtering through the window catches the edge of the form, and the other elements of the composition nearest to the window. Without this sense of modeling, without the gradations from light to dark, the composition would appear flat and reduced to two-dimensional pattern. We use shading with short strokes of pastel to create a sense of solidity and to convey the feeling of three-dimensional form on a two-dimensional surface. The atmospheric mood is induced by softly blending colors together either with a finger or with a paper torchon.

1 Sharpening pastels. *Pastels can be given a sharp edge when rubbed gently onto a sheet of sandpaper.*

2 *Oil pastels are much firmer than chalk pastels and can be sharpened with a knife.*

1

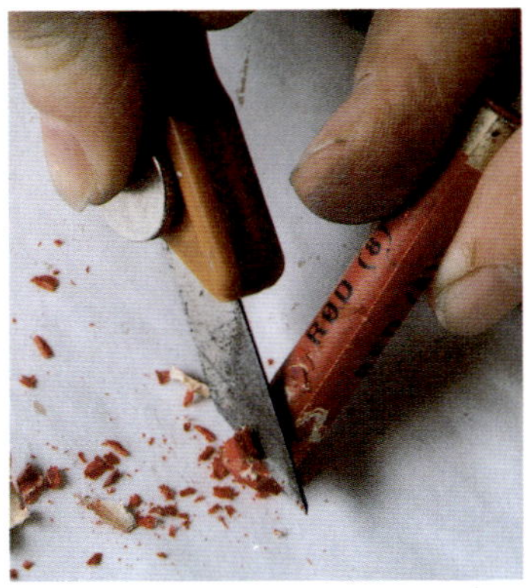

2

1 *The main structure of the drawing is carried out in a single mid-tone color.*

2 *Yellow, blue, and red are added to establish the main divisions of tone and color.*

3 *The contrast between the outside view and the darker interior is heightened by using Prussian blue.*

4 *All the colors are blended together with softer tones in the shadows to evoke a certain mood and atmosphere in the drawing.*

Many watercolorists use masking fluid and masking tape for reserving areas of white paper. Masking fluid, which is specially made for the purpose, is a kind of liquid rubber sold in small bottles and applied with a brush. Purists disdain to use it, but their scorn is baseless. Very attractive and exciting effects, quite different from those produced by the classic method of laying washes around an area, can be gained by it. Stopping out with masking fluid is a method of painting in "negative;" the precise and subtle shades made by the brush remain when the liquid is removed.

The paper must be quite dry before the fluid is applied, and the fluid itself must be allowed to dry before a wash is laid on top. Once the wash has dried, the fluid can be rubbed off with a finger or a soft eraser, leaving the white area, which can be modified and worked

RIGHT: *Sharp, clean lines and highlights can be made by scraping into dry paint with a scalpel or other sharp knife. Take care not to damage the paper by pressing too hard.*

FAR RIGHT: *Watercolor has been used in conjunction with pastel to give liveliness and textural contrast to this painting. Both the building itself and the dark tree on the left are in pure watercolor, while the foreground grass is pure pastel. The sky is a combination of the two. Pastel combines well with watercolor, and a painting such as this often benefits from a "non-purist" approach.*

into if required. Masking fluid should never be left on the paper for longer than necessary, and care must be taken to wash the brushes immediately, otherwise fluid will harden in the hairs and ruin them. Masking fluid is not suitable for all papers, especially ones with a rough surface.

Masking tape is particularly useful for straight-edged areas, such as the light-catching side of a building or the edge of a window-sill. There is no reason why all painting should be done freehand; just as few people can draw a circle without recourse to compasses, few people can paint a really straight line without splashing paint over the edge. Masking tape enables you to use the paint freely without worrying about spoiling the area to be reserved.

Yet another way of keeping the paint away from the paper is to use wax in what is called the resist method, like that used in batik fabrics. This differs from the previous techniques in being permanent; once the wax is on the paper it cannot be removed except by laborious scraping with a razor blade. The paint, moreover, will lie on top of the wax to some extent (this varies according to the paper used), leaving a slightly textured surface. The effect can be very attractive, particularly for flowers or fabrics. An ordinary household candle can be used, or a white wax crayon for finer lines.

The best method of creating fine, delicate highlights when a painting is nearly complete is to scrape into the paint with a sharp point, of a scalpel, say, so that the white paper is revealed. Very fine lines can be drawn in this way to suggest a blade of grass or a flower stem catching the light in the foreground of a landscape.

HATCHING AND STIPPLING

Hatching is a very old and basic means for gradating tones on white paper with something as dense and impenetrable as pen and ink. Gradating tones with a pencil is much easier, as most of us will have experienced before now, and painted washes are perhaps one of the simplest and best means of achieving it in the most subtle and effective way. When painting expanded from simple washes to the more complex paints like gouache, tempera, and fresco, the technique that was adopted was that of hatching, which reached its full development in the fourteenth and fifteenth centuries, before the introduction of oil paint rendered it obsolete. Oil paint could render gradated tones so much more realistically than hatching with tempera—but at a cost. The qualities of texture and color that hatching brought were sorely missed, until renewed interest in water-based painting revived the method. Acrylic, being one of these, is ideally suited to hatching.

Hatching consists of the criss-crossing of hundreds of small lines over each other to produce a rich variegated tone. The more these fine lines are hatched the more dense the tone becomes. Many

ABOVE: *Hatching using ink. By varying the density of the lines, a wide variety of tones is achieved. Freely drawn lines look more lively than perfectly straight, mechanical lines.*

RIGHT: *An old, splayed brush was used to create this slightly rough, hatched texture in acrylic. The underlying color glows through the overpainting to great effect.*

drawings by the old masters were done this way, and so inevitably became the basis of the way they painted. When one examines a fourteenth- or fifteenth-century tempera panel, it will be seen to be made up of hundreds of tiny strokes of color, sometimes going around the forms, to accentuate the solidity, sometimes across the forms to show the play of light and dark.

In painting with a hatching technique, the open network of lines means that not only are the tones gradated, but the underpainting can filter through as well, thus enhancing both tone and color at the same time—another reason why, perhaps, tempera painting has a brilliance that oil painting seems to lack over the centuries.

Hatching with acrylic will involve small sable brushes (0, 00, or 1) as well as thin paint, which can be either transparent or opaque, or even a mixture of both. But it must not be too thick, or the hatching will lose its delicacy, and be more difficult to manipulate.

STIPPLING

Stippling is somewhat like hatching in that it is the building up of tone with hundreds of tiny marks. But with hatching, the marks are strokes of the brush—long, short, thin or thick—whereas with stippling, dabs are made with the point or end of the brush.

If sables are used for stippling, it is wiser to use the older, more worn-out brushes, as stippling can be very hard on them unless used with a very gentle kind of stipple, which is not easy to do as the dabbing action is a forceful one. As with hatching, the process is a painstaking one. The overpainting of hundreds of tiny dots one on the other gives a pleasing effect, and the tonal gradations are even more delicate than with hatching. However, it is unnecessary to cover the work completely with stippling. You can confine it to the parts with a more telling effect.

Georges Seurat, the pointillist painter, who took Impressionism one stage further, stippled his tones and tints of pure color, without mixing them, throughout the painting. The intention was to let the eye do the mixing. Unfortunately, his paintings were not carried out in acrylic, as they hadn't been invented at that time—but there is no reason why acrylics shouldn't be tried in this manner, provided the stippling has some kind of color system as a foundation for the design, or that the stippling is consistent in its marks throughout the work.

Experiment with stippling in the same way as hatching. The paint can be thicker than with hatching, if desired, and stippling can also be carried out with materials other than brushes: sponges, wads of paper, toothbrushes, even fingertips will do as an alternative. As with hatching, the aim should be to keep the dabs as separate as possible to achieve the maximum effect. The dabs should be as crisp as possible, though piled up over each other; they should not smear or smudge into each other. As with hatching, allow any underpainting to filter through if possible.

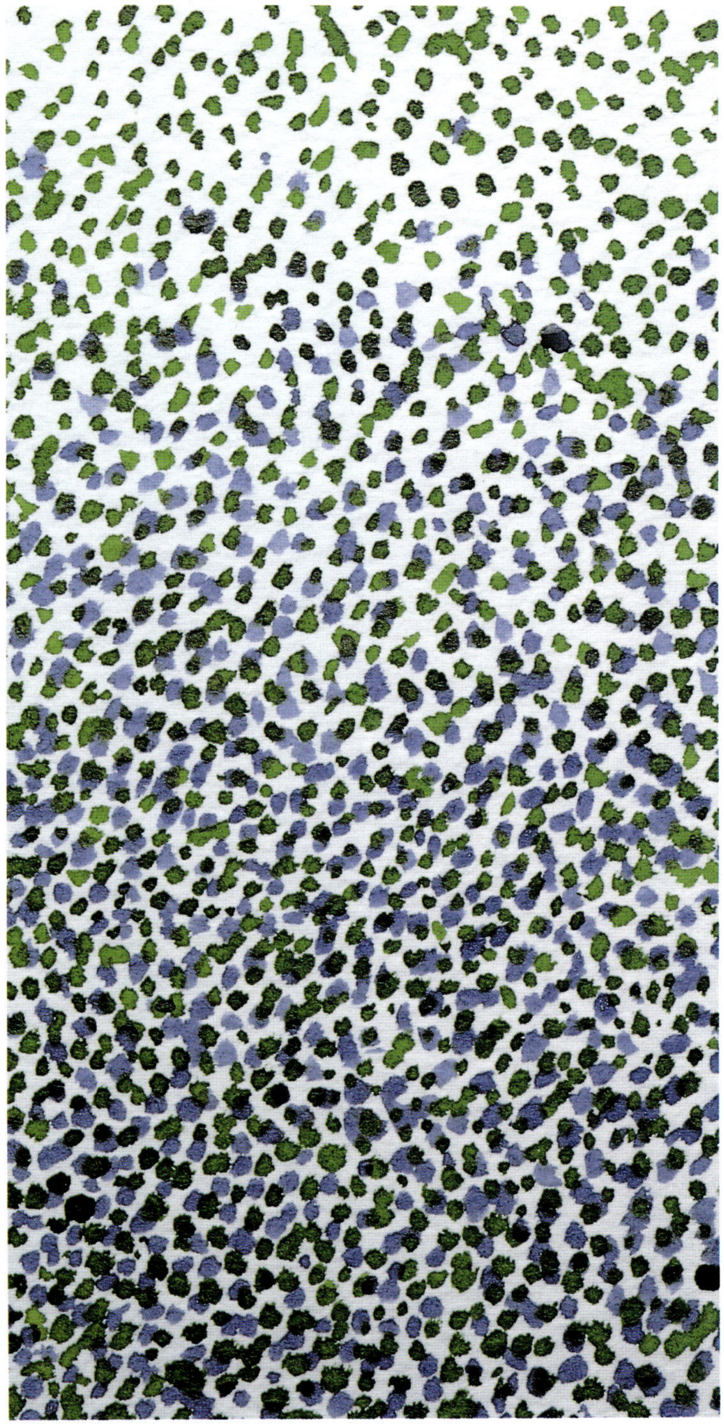

experiment in hatching

Draw a small grid of 1-in squares. About four will suffice. Try filling them with a variety of hatching as follows:

1 *cross hatching with one color,*

2 *cross hatching from dark to light,*

3 *cross hatching from the center outward,*

4 *cross hatching from the outside inward.*

Vary the hatching with both transient and opaque lines, and short and long, thick and thin strokes, to create as much variety of texture as possible.

ABOVE: *The effect is an area of colors that appears lighter and brighter than the equivalent color applied in a flat wash.*

LEFT: *Stippling with a brush is carried out by holding the brush at right angles to the painting surface, and repeatedly touching the tip to the surface.*

COMPOSING A PICTURE—INTRODUCTION

CHOOSING A SUBJECT

Many people seem to feel that, just as there are "proper" ways of going about a painting, there are also "proper" subjects. This is quite untrue; as we have seen, there is no way of applying oil paint that is more correct than another, nor is there any one subject that makes a better painting than another. Nudes, still lifes, flowers, and landscapes are all types of painting hallowed by long tradition, but many artists have made fine paintings of just the corner of a room, a wall with a few flowers against it or a single tree. Vincent Van Gogh made deeply moving and expressive still lifes from such subjects as a pair of peasant's boots or a pile of books on a table.

Still life did not exist as a painting subject until the Dutch artists of the seventeenth century "invented" it. Nor was landscape, except as a background to a figure or group of figures, acceptable until the late eighteenth and early nineteenth centuries. In the past, the subject of a painting was largely dictated by the demands of patrons, but we have no such restrictions.

It should be said, however, that some subjects are more difficult than others, and it can be discouraging to find you have set yourself a task which your experience is not equal to. Portraits, for example,

Domestic interiors have been a favorite subject with artists since the Dutch seventeenth-century masters. These two paintings, Van Gogh's Yellow Chair (LEFT) *and Gwen John's* A Corner of the Artist's Room in Paris, (RIGHT) *although totally different in their treatment and handling of color and paint, both give a strong feeling of serenity, just as the Dutch paintings did.*

are particularly difficult. You have to cope with so many problems: how to render the color of flesh, the texture planes of the face and, finally, how to "get a likeness." If your interests do lie in this direction, you could start with a self-portrait, as in this way you will have total control over your "sitter" and can work at your own speed without feeling rushed and flustered. You will know your own face well already.

Still lifes, flowers, and landscapes all provide good starting points, depending on your particular interests. Subjects for still lifes can be found in most people's homes or the nearest vegetable or flower shop, and you can choose your own arrangement, light it in any way you want and take your time over it. In the case of landscape, if the weather is not suitable for outdoor painting, or if you feel shy about it, you could start by working from a photograph (but beware of trying to "copy" it in exact detail) or you could paint the view from a window.

FAR LEFT: *If the corner chosen to align the drawing—marked "A"—has been correctly positioned, you should be able to achieve a result with a reasonable amount of accuracy.*

LEFT: *This pencil study of a candy jar concentrates on the reflections in the glass, but the basic drawing is no more complicated than the basic study of the boxes.*

A SENSE OF SPACE

Scale and perspective are really the same thing. Perspective is often thought of, incorrectly, as the mathematical theory much used by architects to render a three-dimensional visualization of a proposed building project. This mathematical theory is indeed one form of perspective which is dealt with more thoroughly elsewhere in this book, but linear perspective is only a mathematical device to be able to work out in a logical manner the relative size of objects as they recede into the distance. For the artist, accurate observation of the relative sizes of objects already deals with most of the problems of perspective and scale. Mechanical perspective is often used by beginners because their perception of scale needs the prop of an authoritative theory to convince them that what they are seeing is correct.

This is something that has already been discussed. You know that all the cows in a field are more or less the same size. The problem you have with drawing them in scale—that is, so that the ones farthest away are the smallest—is that your pre-knowledge tells you that they are the same size. The reverse can also happen. You know a stand of bulrushes in the foreground is much smaller than the cow in the adjacent field but try as you may, you find it difficult to believe that visually three quarters of a cow can be obscured from your view by one single bulrush. Your mind tells you to draw the cow bigger. With accurate observation you should be able to believe the visual information that your eyes are receiving. Perspective is a sense of scale, or the size of an object relative to other objects on the picture plane, and their size relative to the size of the picture plane.

BALANCE AND RHYTHM

When an artist produces a painting from visual notes (sketchbook studies made from direct observation) he is putting together, or "composing," a pictorial statement. It is this act of putting things together, satisfactorily, that makes a well-composed painting.

Every time an artist produces a drawing or painting—a portrait, figure study, landscape, still life, or whatever subject is in view—he is consciously, or unconsciously, composing. There are painters whose work follows very closely the classical rules of composition, and others who work more intuitively. One is more conscious of formal composition in a Degas pastel, say, than in an oil painting by Bonnard. Much depends on what the artist is trying to say—studies of the ballet, with groups of dancers on stage, require considered placement in the composition. A casual glimpse of some domestic scene can be less formal.

A painting can be placed historically by its compositional values. Early religious paintings were usually composed symmetrically to support rich decoration and pattern. Renaissance painters discovered a new feeling for space, created by the introduction of perspective. Classical modes of composition reached near-perfection in the work of Poussin and Claude. The French Impressionists adopted a more random approach to composition inspired by snapshot photography.

RIGHT: Beach at Trouville: *Claude Monet (1840–1926). This painting has a strong sense of design; the characteristic shape of the umbrellas serves to provide a link from one side of the composition to the other. Monet's sense of visual judgment was so acute, that he was able to place the elements in his compositions intuitively, rather than by relying on mathematical formulas. The placement of the chair roughly relates to the Golden Section, and prevents the composition becoming too symmetrical.*

ABOVE: *The compositions of Piero della Francesca (c.1420–1492) are usually founded upon an intricate mathematical division of space. In his* Baptism of Christ, *the verticals of the figures and trees harmonize with the implied circle which has a dove at its center. At the same time, the stream in the foreground leads the eye into the heart of the landscape.*

FAR RIGHT: Coming from evening church: *Samuel Palmer. This simply composed painting of a procession of figures from the church to a woodland path is strongly symbolic. The arched branches of the trees create a vignette, and the moon and church steeple provide visual equivalents to the figures in the foreground. By using closely painted tones, Palmer was able to evoke a sense of mood and atmosphere.*

The way that a picture is composed will largely be determined by the subject. Landscape is indeterminate and requires a firm organization to make the various parts of the composition jell. Selection and visual judgment are critical, since one can deal with only a comparatively small area of the total scene in view. With a still-life painter, on the other hand, one can physically pick up and arrange each component, so that the process of composing begins before one starts to draw.

The classical concept of composition is based on the logical arrangement of pictorial elements. Line, shape, and color are organized in such a way that they work together in the design as a whole. Underlying all the work of classically composed painting is a firm linear structure, which is sometimes simple, sometimes complex. No matter how rich and varied the surface qualities of the painting are, everything is held together by the linear structure of the composition. This structure is sometimes called the painter's "secret" geometry, because the final painting usually conceals much of the underlying drawing. Some painters—Degas is one of them—allows us to see the process of their compositional ideas, by a skilful interaction between the linear and surface aspects of their paintings.

The division of space known as the Golden Section is perhaps the best known system of proportion in pictorial composition. The simplest method of finding the Golden Section in any given rectangle is to take a sheet of paper of the size one is working to and fold it in half three times in succession (do this for both the length and breadth of the paper). The folds will divide the paper into eight equal parts, from which a 3:5 ratio can be determined. (Alternative ratios might be 2:3, 5:8 or 8:13.) In the work of artists such as Piero della Francesca, the vertical division of the Golden Section is used to determine the placement of the central figure of Christ. Similarly, in the work of other painters, it is used to place the most important element in the composition. As we develop our powers of observation, however, we sometimes unconsciously place the most significant vertical element in our drawing on that same division in the painting. In landscape the horizon presents a natural division of the total area of the painting. In lowland areas, where the sky is dominant, the horizon will be quite low, as in the work of Rembrandt and other Dutch painters. Where there are hills and mountains, the horizon might be placed high in the composition to give emphasis to rising forms.

There are certain compositional conventions which appear time and time again in "picturesque" paintings: rivers and paths which lead the eye from foreground to significant objects in the distance; trees with masses of foliage on one side with glimpses of the distant horizon bathed in sunlight; and so on. When one is producing a landscape painting from direct observation one has the advantage of being able to leave out anything one might consider excessive to the composition as a whole. And it is this fact which distinguishes the work of the beginner from the more experienced painter. When we first start to draw from direct observation, we put everything in, but with experience we learn to be more selective—to imply, rather than overstate.

Tonal contrast plays an important part in composition. The balance of light and dark shapes connects the various parts of a drawing or painting. One might begin by using just three or four tones from light to dark. Don't be confused by color and tone; if we

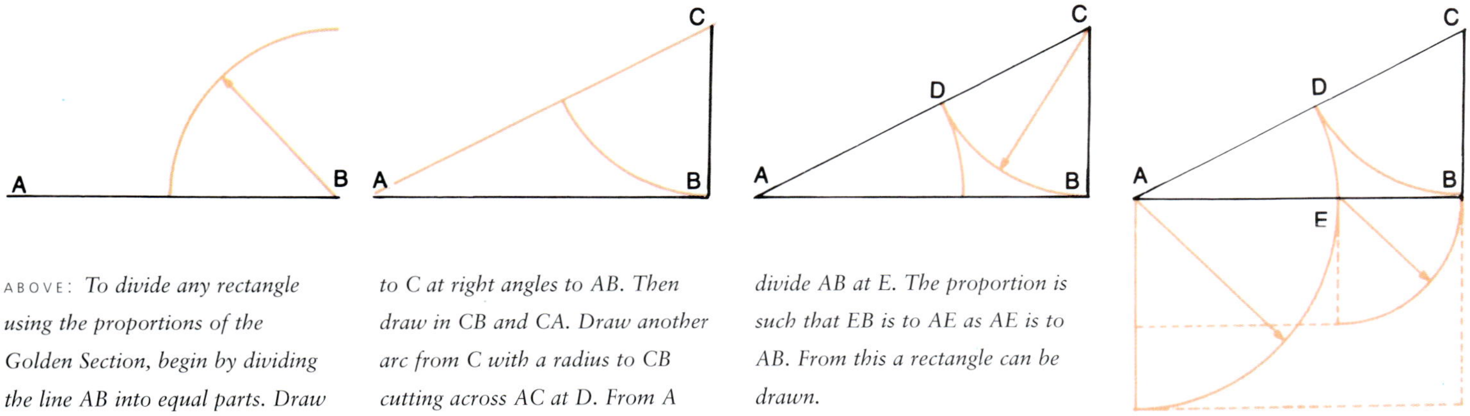

ABOVE: *To divide any rectangle using the proportions of the Golden Section, begin by dividing the line AB into equal parts. Draw an arc from B midway between AB to C at right angles to AB. Then draw in CB and CA. Draw another arc from C with a radius to CB cutting across AC at D. From A draw an arc with a radius AD to divide AB at E. The proportion is such that EB is to AE as AE is to AB. From this a rectangle can be drawn.*

ABOVE: Still life with pitcher: *Paul Cézanne. Even when left unfinished, Cézanne's paintings and drawings have a completeness about them—every brush mark serves a purpose. Cézanne allowed the white ground of the canvas to form an integral part of the total composition. The artist also took great care in the actual placement of the objects before he began painting a still life.*

look at a black and white photograph of a colorful painting, the tones representing each color allow us to "read" the image, because we are able to distinguish the light and dark shapes. A painting can often fail because of a lack of tonal unity. Some painters solve this problem by using color almost monochromatically. In the pastoral paintings of Samuel Palmer, for instance, there are gradations of yellow ochers to dark sombre browns from which the whites glow.

Composition is not concerned simply with static shapes. Rhythm and movement are the life of a painting. Even seemingly static subjects, such as seascapes and portraits, are dependent on a sense of movement. For even though a figure may be sitting perfectly still, a drawing or painting should suggest that the sitter is capable of movement. The still life by Paul Cézanne, for example, is full of interlocking rhythms which make the painting anything but "still." His use of complementary colors gives the contours of the drawing a vibrancy.

It is in the work of Van Gogh, however, that one becomes acutely aware of the disturbing conflicting rhythms that reveal the artist's personality.

ABOVE: *When painting on the spot, making a preliminary sketch is a good way to sort out your ideas before committing yourself to paint. It is essential to be sure of the most important elements of a landscape. Resist the temptation to put everything in just because it is there.*

RIGHT: *The finished watercolor painting benefits from the "editing" process provided by the sketch. The elements of the composition have been established, and remain more or less in place. Most importantly, the rhythm of the composition was maintained.*

Lighting plays a vital part in the arrangement of a still life, flower painting or portrait, and a subject can change quite dramatically according to the way it is lit. Back lighting (TOP LEFT) *can be very effective for flowers, as the light will shine through the petals in places, giving a brilliant sparkle, with the front foliage and vase appearing very dark. Front lighting* (ABOVE) *tends to make any subject seem flat and dull, while side or diagonal lighting* (ABOVE AND BELOW RIGHT) *will define the forms more clearly.*

CHOOSING A SHAPE AND SIZE

This may seem trivial, but in fact both shape and size have an important part to play in the composition and treatment of a painting. A panoramic landscape, for instance, may suggest a wide horizontal shape which will enable you to show the broad sweep of the land as well as giving a sense of peace and tranquillity. A single tree might call for a narrow vertical painting, while a still life with a lot of objects in it could suggest a rather square one.

Size is a very personal matter: some artists work on vast canvases too big to fit in most living rooms, while others produce tiny, detailed work on supports no larger than the average photograph. If you are working at home you are unlikely to want to work on a very large scale, and it is not usually a good idea to start very small. A good starting size is about 20 x 16 in, a standard one in which you can buy both boards and canvases.

Painting is rather like handwriting—people with large writing feel constricted if for any reason they are forced to write small, and if your "natural" size for painting is much larger than the support you have chosen you will soon find out, as your painting will seem to spread of its own volition beyond the edges. Until you have established a size which suits you, it is wise to use an inexpensive support, such as a piece of primed paper or cardboard, oil sketching paper, or "canvas board." Hardboard is not recommended for early attempts as it has a slippery surface which can give a messy and unmanageable paint surface.

ABOVE: *The subject of this simple still life was the artist's collection of assorted bottles, with the fruit used as a balance to the colors and texture of the glass. The lighting was entirely natural, simply the side light coming in through a window, but the objects were set up with care so that the shadows fell pleasingly.*

RIGHT: *Although still life and flower arrangements need not be elaborate, some thought is needed in the initial setting up if the foreground and background are not to become dull and featureless. Thumbnail sketches and polaroid photographs are useful aids in setting up an arrangement.*

These drawings show the different elements of a still life arranged in a variety of ways. A symmetrical arrangement (FAR LEFT) *tends to be monotonous, but the arrangement, with the flat plane of the table angled away from the eye and a more varied grouping of the fruit* (MIDDLE)*, has more visual interest. The drawing of the flower and fruit with draperies* (LEFT) *provides more linear contrasts and a busier background.*

avoiding discouragement

If your painting goes wrong at an early stage you are bound to feel depressed and discouraged. Various suggestions are given here which will help you to avoid or overcome the more common problems.

TINTING THE GROUND

Starting to paint on a glaring expanse of white canvas can be quite daunting, but even more important is the fact that a white surface is also "dishonest," as it prevents you from judging the tones and colors correctly. There is very little pure white in nature, as white, like any other color, is always modified by the light or shadow falling on it. Also, no color exists in a particular way except in relation to the colors surrounding it. Thus, if you start a flower painting by putting down a bold brushstroke of pure cadmium red on a white canvas it will almost certainly be wrong, as the red you are seeing is actually given its quality by its relationship to the background, which may be neutral or even dark.

A method often used by artists is to tint the canvas in a neutral color, usually a warm brown or gray, before starting the painting. This can be done either by mixing pigment in with the primer or by putting a wash of oil paint, such as raw umber, heavily diluted with turpentine, over the white ground. Acrylic paint can also be used for this since it dries much faster than oil paint, and you could buy a single tube just for this purpose. But remember that acrylic paint should not be used over an oil ground; oil can be used over acrylic, but acrylic cannot be used over oil.

PREPARATION

Always start with an adequate drawing or underpainting in order to place the main design elements in the way you want them. Even a simple subject such as bowl of fruit can go very wrong if you fail to judge correctly the size of the fruit in relation to the bowl, or the bowl in relation to the table it is standing on. You may be impatient to start on the real business—the laying on of paint—but it does pay to take your time at this stage, for it will avoid a lot of frustration later.

KEEPING THE PICTURE MOVING

Try to avoid working in detail on one part of the painting at the expense of others. This approach can lead to a disjointed-looking painting, since you are more likely to tire of it half-way through. Generally, it is better to work on all parts of the canvas at once, so that you have a better idea of how one part relates to another in color, tone, and texture.

Some artists, such as the English painter Stanley Spencer (1891–1959), successfully reversed this process by starting with a careful and detailed pencil drawing and then painting area by area. There is theoretically nothing wrong with working in this way, but an inexperienced painter is unlikely to have the very clear vision of the finished painting which is required for such an approach.

In general, it is easiest to build up oil paint light over dark, as white is the most opaque color; so keep to dark and middle tones in the early stages, working up gradually to the light and bright tones and colors. Always try to see the background as part of the painting, not just as an unimportant area; even a plain white wall has colors in it, and a totally flat background can be used as a shape, to form part of the composition. Avoid getting bogged down in detail too early; fine lines, such as the stems of flowers or small facial details in a portrait, are best left until last.

ABOVE: The natural inclination when painting subjects like trees is to try and get everything in, but in this painting the artist has allowed the foreground trees to "bust" out of the frame, giving a stronger and more exciting effect.

DEFINING THE COMPOSITION

The word "composition" has a slightly alarming ring to it—it sounds as though it might be an intellectual exercise quite beyond the capabilities of the ordinary person. This really is not so: composing a painting is mainly a question of selecting, arranging and rearranging, just as you might do when deciding on the decor for a room or when taking a photograph. A large, complex painting with numerous people and objects in it does, of course, need some thought, otherwise there may be too much activity in one part of the picture and not enough in another. But even here, it is less a matter of following a prescribed set of rules than of working out the balance of the various shapes, as in the case of planning a room—no one would put all the furniture crowded together on one side and leave the rest empty.

A "good composition" is one in which there is no jarring note, the colors and shapes are well balanced, and the picture as a whole seems to sit easily within its frame or outer borders. Even a simple head-and-shoulders portrait is composed, and a vital part of composition is selection—what you put in and what you leave out. In the case of a portrait you will need to establish whether the person should be seated, and if so on what, whether you want to include the chair, whether you want the hands to form part of the composition, and

ABOVE: *As the tree is moved to different positions on the picture plane, the composition of the picture is radically changed. Although it is an identical drawing in each case, the composition of each example is quite different, thus illustrating the fact that although the subject matter can be important in making an interesting drawing, it is not necessarily the most important. It is more important that the position of the subject matter within the four sides of the picture plane will make an interesting composition.*

whether you want to use something in the background, for example part of a window frame, to balance the figure.

If you are painting a landscape you may think composition is not involved, that you are just painting what you see, but you will have chosen a particular view, just as you would when taking a photograph, and in choosing it you will have gone at least some way toward composing it. You may then find that you want to exaggerate or rearrange some feature in the foreground, such as a rock or a tree, to provide extra interest, or alter the bend of a path to lead the eye into the picture.

There are some basic errors which should be avoided if possible. In general it is not a good idea to divide a landscape horizontally into two equal halves—the land and the sky—as the result will usually be monotonous. A line, such as a path or fence, should not lead directly out of the picture unless balanced by another line which leads the eye back into it. A still life or portrait should not be divided in half vertically, while a flower painting is unlikely to be pleasing to the eye if the flower arrangement is placed too far down in the picture area, too far to one side, or very small in the middle, with a large expanse of featureless background.

In the case of interiors, portraits, still lifes, and flowers, backgrounds can be used as a device to balance the main elements of the composition. Use part of a piece of furniture behind a seated figure, for example, or a subtly patterned wallpaper which echoes or contrasts with the main shapes and colors in the figure. In landscape painting the sky is a vital part of the composition, and should always be given as much care and thought as the rest of the painting.

Even if you are working quickly, it is often helpful to make some drawings, known as thumbnail sketches (though they need not be small) before you start on the painting. These may consist of just a few roughly drawn lines to establish how the main shapes can be placed, or they may help you to work out the tonal pattern of the composition.

THE FINAL CHOICES

Every painter, working in whatever medium, needs to understand the basic rules of the craft, even if sometimes only to break them. The underlying principles of such things as composition, perspective, and drawing itself, apply to all kinds of painting. The novice, who needs to plan his paintings especially carefully, should have a firm grasp of them from the beginning.

Whether you are painting outdoors or indoors, whether your chosen subject is a landscape, a group of buildings, a portrait, or a single flower in a vase, you need to have a clear idea of what the main elements are and of how you will place them on the paper before you begin to paint. Painting a landscape outside requires you to decide where the view is to begin and end, where to place the horizon, whether to emphasize or alter features in the foreground, and so on. For a portrait, still life, or flower painting you must decide how much to show, the proportion of the figure or flower in relation to the background, the general color scheme and the balance of lights and darks. Composition and selection thus go hand in hand: an artist first selects which aspects of the subject are important and then composes the picture by placing them in a certain way.

There are well-tested mathematical rules for "good composition." The ancient Greeks, for instance, devised the system known as the

BELOW: *Painters of the Renaissance usually planned the composition of a painting on a geometric grid structure. This example, by Piero della Francesca, is based on a triangle, a common compositional device which is still much used, as are circles and rectangles. The drawing on the right shows how other triangles can be discerned within the main one formed by the figures.*

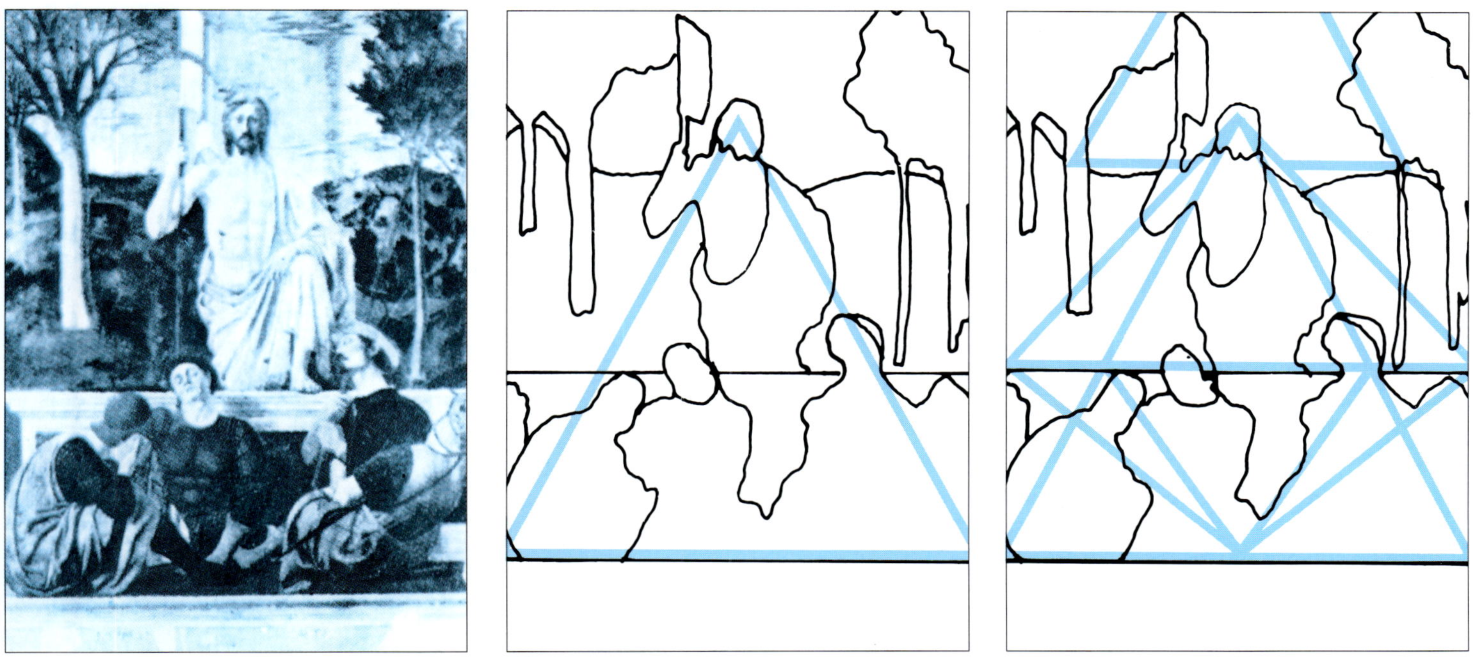

LEFT: *Converging lines in landscapes are often used to lead the viewer's eye to the focal point, in this case the buildings. Unusually, the artist has divided the picture into two nearly equal parts, the land and the sky; but monotony has been avoided by allowing the buildings and trees to break into the skyline and by dividing the foreground by the broken line of white road in the middle distance.*

Golden Section (or Golden Mean), in which the area of the painting is divided by a line in such a way that the smaller part is to the larger what the larger is to the whole. This ensures that the picture plane is divided in a balanced and symmetrical way, and countless artists have made use of the principle. The triangle is another basis for composition (many paintings are based on the framework of a single triangle) as is a series of intersecting geometric shapes such as squares, rectangles and circles.

It is unlikely that someone sitting down to an outdoor watercolor sketch will need a full knowledge of such principles, but there are some simple and practical ones that should be borne in mind. Basically, a good composition is one in which there are no jarring elements; all the parts of the picture balance one another in a pleasing way, and the viewer's eye is led into the picture rather than out of it. Whatever the subject, it is almost never advisable to divide the painting into two equal halves, such as sea and land, or tabletop and background in a still life. The result is at once monotonous and disjointed. The viewer's eye should not be led to one part of the painting to the exclusion of others, but there should usually be a "focal point." For example, a group of buildings in a landscape can be used simply as a counterpoint to other elements, such as trees and hills, or they may be what interests you most about the scene, with the trees, hills, and foreground used as a "backdrop." The buildings need not be large, nor placed directly in the center of the picture (this is not normally advisable); what matters is that the eye should be consistently led to them as the focal point. Compositional devices often used to lead the eye in this way are the curving lines of a path, stream, plowed field or fence, along which the viewer's eye must travel. Such lines should never lead out of the picture unless for a deliberately sought effect.

The focal point of a portrait is almost always the face, the eyes in particular for a front or three-quarter view, and care must be taken not to detract from it by placing too much emphasis on other elements, such as the background, or the hands. Hands and clothing are often treated in a sketchy way so that they do not assume too much importance. A figure or face should be placed in a well-considered and deliberate way against the background to create a feeling of harmony and balance. There should not be too much space at the top. Nor, usually, should the subject be placed squarely in the middle of the picture, though a central position can sometimes be effective.

Backgrounds are part of a portrait painting, as are skies in landscapes, even when they are quite plain and muted in color. If a picture is placed against a stark white background, the white areas will have their own shapes and thus make their contribution to the balance of the painting. Such flat areas are known as "negative space." A more decorative background, such as a boldly patterned wallpaper or still life of a vase of flowers on a table, can be used to complement the main subject, just as the colors in the sky or the direction of clouds do in a landscape.

Many artists use viewing frames to help them work out a satisfactory composition, and some also use polaroid cameras for indoor work, taking several shots of a portrait or still life until they find a

LEFT: *At first sight this appears to be a rapidly executed, spontaneous sketch, as indeed it is; but its composition has been sufficiently worked out to present a pleasing unity as well as a strong feeling of life and movement. The lights and darks are well balanced, the colors are harmonious, and the eye is led into the picture by the gently curving path with its pattern of shadows. This kind of planning is often instinctive; some people have a natural feel for a good composition, while others have to rely on theory and hard work.*

satisfactory arrangement. A viewing frame is simply a piece of cardboard with an oblong hole cut in it (a good size of aperture is 4½ x 6 in, which is held up at about arm's length to work out the best placing of the subject. It is particularly useful for on-the-spot landscape work, as it is very difficult to assess large landscape subjects without some form of framing device. Making small, quick sketches, often referred to as thumbnail sketches, is another good way to work out a composition. A rough scribble, even a few lines, will often provide a clear idea of how the main shapes should be placed within the picture area, and can be an exceptionally useful aid in getting the shapes and proportions of the composition right from the start.

SKETCHBOOKS AND REFERENCE MATERIALS

Painting is about looking at things—a good painter is constantly assessing objects and scenes with a view to translating them into paintings. This kind of analytical vision is largely a matter of habit and training—the more interested in painting you are the closer you will look and the more you will see—but few people have perfect visual memories, and for this reason artists often make visual references to use later on. Normally these take the form of sketches, and art students are always urged to carry sketchbooks at all times. Even a small, rough pencil sketch, sometimes with notes made about the quality of the light and the colors in the scene, can be turned into a complete landscape painting, or sometimes several sketches are made for different parts of a planned painting. For instance, a view of boats in a harbor might call for a rough overall sketch and some additional, more detailed drawings of individual boats.

It is certainly a good idea to carry a sketchbook—it is good practice if nothing else—but it takes some degree of skill to produce drawings which are good enough to provide all the information you may need and it takes experience to know what it is you actually want to make such "notes" about. Photographs are now much used for this purpose, either as alternatives to sketches or as additions to them, and some artists even use picture postcards, either to suggest a theme for a painting or to remind them of some forgotten detail. They are also very useful for portrait painting, since few people are

BELOW: *These thumbnail sketches, of female figures in various poses against different backgrounds, illustrate the way in which some artists try out possible compositions for paintings. Such drawings, which can be done quite quickly and need be little more than scribbles, are an excellent means of working out the arrangement of the main shapes and the balance of lights and darks.*

LEFT: *Different artists have different methods of making sketches, according to their individual style and what particular aspect of a scene they want to note and remember. Some do detailed drawings in pen and ink or pen and wash, some make rough pencil sketches with color notes, while others use oil paint, which is an excellent sketching medium because it can be applied so quickly.*

able to stay in one position long enough for a complete painting to be done.

However, photographs should be used with caution, and treated as aids to painting rather than models to copy. Straight copies of photographs, either of landscapes or people, can look very dull and dead, missing either the sparkle of the original scene or the character of the person. If you are using photographs for landscape painting, try to use several rather than just one, combining elements from each. Make a rough sketch from them and work from this rather than direct from the photographs. For portraits, they are generally used as a backup, with the initial stages of the painting being done from life. The photographs can then be used for details, such as hands and clothing, with perhaps another live sitting for the final stage.

The great advantage of photographs is that they can capture fleeting moments and impressions, such as the light falling in a certain way on a stretch of water, the eerie purple and gold light before a storm, children playing, or a cat asleep in a patch of sunlight. The disadvantage is that they do not actually tell the truth: the camera distorts perspective, flattens color and fudges detail. When you want a clear visual description of some small, but vital, part of a subject, you find only a vague blur. A sketch, even a less than brilliant one, would probably have been more useful, because you would have been forced to look hard at the subject and thus have gained more understanding of it.

masking sketch

The artist has made several sketches of the same subject and is now working out the best way to turn them into a painting. A pair of L-shaped pieces of board in a neutral mid-tone are used to isolate various parts of the drawings, a device which can also be used with a photographic reference.

RIGHT: Sketchbook. *Firmly bound sketchbooks are used a great deal by artists who build up studio paintings from sketched notes made elsewhere, especially outdoors. Such books are durable and can provide a permanent record of objects and scenes recorded over many years.*

USING A SKETCHBOOK

Every artist needs to get into the habit of drawing frequently from observation. A sketchbook is rather like a writer's notebook; one is able to put down everyday incidents, color notes, figure studies, and ideas for composition. The sketchbook can be small enough to fit into a coat pocket, or large enough to record a fairly large landscape scene. Quite often, the artist's most interesting work will be found in his sketchbook; the small sketchbooks used by John Constable, for instance, reveal a wealth of intimate detail in terms of cloud studies, the effect of light on the landscape, and details of artefacts, such as farm wagons, all of which he used as reference for his larger paintings.

Most drawing media are suitable for quick sketches; selection really depends on personal choice. The speed at which charcoal can be used with little pressure perhaps has a certain advantage for the beginner.

developing the sketch

1 *The artist begins a drawing of a building, having first decided on a particular viewpoint.*

2 *He establishes the main vertical and horizontal elements in the drawing first.*

3 *Local color is added with colored pencils.*

4 *The building appears to be more solid as the drawing develops tonally.*

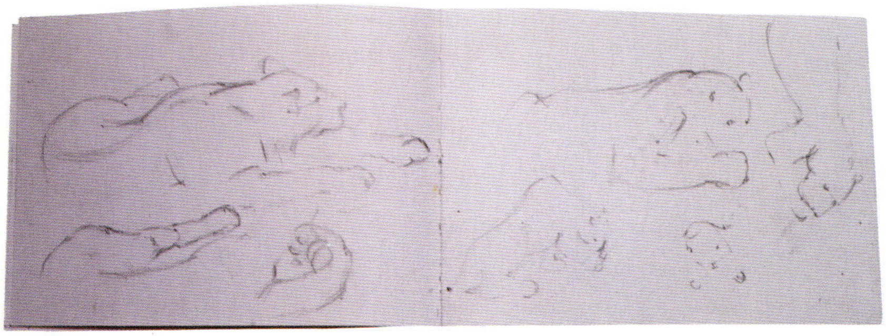

TOP: *Pencil studies of leopards and lions.*

RIGHT: *This drawing on pale yellow cartridge paper in pen and gouache was made from the small sketch in the bottom right hand page of the sketchbook. The sketch was reversed by taking a tracing and transposing the image onto the paper.*

LEFT: *Sketchbook study: William Turner. A rapid notation in pastel using a black chalk to reinforce the low horizon.*

LEFT: *This pencil study is a good example of multi-point perspective. All the elements make for complication; the rising steps on one side and the lane moving away downhill on the other, and the fact that none of the buildings are square to one another, make it very difficult for the beginner to work out all the various vanishing points. The viewing frame shoould be used to understand the relationship of all the elements.*

BELOW: *Sketchbook studies: it is no hardship to take your sketchbook with you, practically wherever you go. It will provide excellent practice in developing your visual awarenesss and a valuable source of material for more finished works developed later. Are these sketches complete? That is, of course, up to the artist.*

from sketch to painting

The central theme of this picture is the brightly colored fruit trees sparkling in the sunshine, contrasted against the slanting shadows of the street below.

The painting is based on a small sketch, rapidly executed while the artist was on holiday in the Mediterranean. Over the years he has amassed a large collection of sketches like these, which he does not regard as "finished drawings" but rather as records of interesting scenes or objects, which can be used later, either as foundations for complete paintings done later in the studio, or as fragments to be inserted into other compositions.

The habit of always carrying a sketchbook is an invaluable one, particularly when traveling abroad. You may be just "passing through" a place, and yet a scene or objects may present themselves as ideal subjects for a painting. A sketch can be done in minutes, and provides enough information about the subject to allow you to make a painting at a later date. A photograph may also help, but with a sketch you can make a more personal statement, isolating and emphasizing those elements which particularly appeal to you. A photograph is much less selective, and besides, there is no guarantee that it will turn out as you expected!

Because acrylic is adhesive, the paint can be mixed with other substances such as sand or grit and thus interesting textural effects can be obtained. In this painting the artist has mixed ordinary builder's sand with the paint in order to capture the rough sandy surface of the stone wall.

1 *This small sketch was made several months prior to the painting, yet it gives the artist enough to kindle his imagination and memory because it includes written color notes and details about the play of light and shadow.*

2 *The artist begins by transferring the image on to a primed canvas in black paint applied with a sable brush.*

3 *Changing to a bristle brush, the artist blocks in the dark tones of the tree trunk and leaves.*

4 *The artist mixes ordinary builder's sand with the paint to capture the rough, sandy texture of the wall. Only a little sand is necessary, otherwise the effect can look too crude and there is a danger of overloading the paint.*

5 *The artist has created a highly personal interpretation of the scene, which is much more exciting than a mere photographic copy. Because the scene is viewed from the shade of a sidewalk café, there is a frame of shadow around the picture which helps to focus the eye upon the brilliantly sunlit street. Although the colors are bright, they are nevertheless harmonious; yellows, greens, and earth colors have been skilfully woven throughout.*

Although watercolors cannot be altered so drastically or so often as paintings in any of the opaque media, changes are possible. It is a mistake to abandon a picture because a first wash has not gone on quite right.

The first thing to remember is that a wash which looks too dark or too vivid on a sheet of otherwise white paper will dry much lighter and may look quite pale when surrounded by other colors. If the first wash looks wrong, let it dry. If you are still quite sure it is not what you intended, sponge it out with a clean sponge and clear water. This may leave a slight stain on the paper, depending on the paper used and the color itself (some colors stain the paper, like a dye, while others do not) but when dry it will be too faint to spoil the new wash. When a wash has flooded, sponge it out immediately without waiting for it to dry; flooding cannot be entirely remedied, though it can sometimes create an interesting effect, even if not originally planned.

One of the most common faults is accidentally to take a wash over the edge of an area to be reserved. There are three ways of dealing with this, depending on the size of the area and the type of edge desired. If the wash is pale and the area to be reserved is a broad and imprecise shape, such as a stone in the foreground of a landscape, you can simply sponge out the excess paint with a small sponge or cotton wool damped in clean water. A soft edge will be left. For a more intricate shape, or one requiring a sharp, clear edge, you may have to scrape the paint away (after it is dry) with a razor blade or scalpel, the former for broad areas, the latter for small ones. Hold the blade flat on the paper so that the corners do not dig in and scrape gently. The same method can be used to lighten an area or to create texture by removing a top layer of paint. The third rescue technique —to apply Chinese white with a fine brush—should be used only when the painting is otherwise complete; if the white is allowed to mix with other colors it will muddy them and spoil the translucency.

A wash that has "gone wrong" (LEFT) *and flooded has been worked in to create a sky effect not originally planned* (RIGHT). *One of the attractions of watercolor is that new uses of the medium are often supported by "mistakes."*

The small blots and smudges that often occur when you take a loaded brush over a painting or rest your hand on a still-damp area can also be razored out when dry. If a splash of paint or dirty water falls on the painting, quickly soak up the excess with a twist of tissue or a cotton bud, let it dry and then razor it out gently. If you are intending to apply more paint to the area, rub it down lightly with a soft eraser to smooth the surface, which will have been slightly roughened by using the eraser.

Even professionals, of course, sometimes find that a painting has gone so wrong that small corrections will not suffice, or has become so clogged with paint that further work is impossible. If this happens you can, of course, throw it away. But you can also wash out the whole painting, or large parts of it, by putting the paper under running water and sponging the surface. Leave it on its board if you have stretched it. A slight stain may be left, but this can be an advantage as the faint shadow will serve as a drawing for the next attempt. A whole sky or foreground can be removed in this way, while leaving intact those areas with which you are satisfied.

OIL REMEDIES

Even paintings by professionals go wrong, but the beauty of oil paint is that they can so easily be altered. If you suddenly notice that your drawing is incorrect and that you have quite misunderstood a shape or color, the best course is not to try to overpaint, but to scrape off the area with a palette knife and then repaint it. You may even decide to scrape down the whole painting and start more or less from scratch—this is often more satisfactory than trying to alter each individual area only to find that something is still not right. If you find that the surface of the painting has become so overloaded with paint that you are just churning it up by continuing to add layers, there is a useful method, invented by a painting teacher called Henry Tonks and named *tonking* after him. This is done by laying a sheet of absorbent paper, such as newspaper, over the painting, rubbing it gently and removing it; this takes off the top layer of paint, and leaves you with something similar to a colored underpainting.

chapter III

PROJECTS

There is no "right" subject for a drawing or painting, but there are tried and tested compositional areas that have attracted artists for centuries: Landscapes, Buildings, Nature, Still Life, and the Human Figure. Basic principles underlie the approach to any of these areas, and some of them are best suited to a particular medium. The step-by-step projects in the following pages show how working artists approach each area, offering you the chance to study their techniques and to try your own hand at a similar composition.

LANDSCAPES, SEASCAPES, *and* SKIES

BASIC PRINCIPLES

Landscape is the preferred subject matter as an introduction to painting and drawing. This is very understandable because it combines so many pleasures. There is not only practice in drawing but there is the added delight of being in the countryside "communing with nature." Landscape as subject matter is less exacting for the beginner than, say, portraiture, and a pleasing and satisfying result can be achieved quite early on. These successes should add greatly to the beginner's self-confidence and enable him or her to tackle more complex subjects in a less tentative way.

ABOVE: *A mine in winter: pencil and conté. The angularity of the machinery is complemented by the clarity and detail of the trees, hills and wall.*

In Europe there is a long tradition of landscape painting and drawing, although it became recognized as an independent art form in the seventeenth century. Before that time most landscapes were backgrounds in compositions where figures or groups of figures played the most important role. The evolution of the landscape as an independent art form did not happen overnight, moreover, but developed from paintings often depicting a group of figures in an idyllic pastoral setting with Greek temples, castles, or ruins, setting the scene firmly in an Arcadian past.

The kind of painting now recognized immediately in a modern sense as landscape art is a northern European innovation practiced in particular by a seventeenth-century Dutch school of artists. In these paintings the subject matter is contemporary with the time the painting or drawing was made. It is not an idealized landscape. It is one in which the clouds can rain and the sun can be scorching hot; a landscape that is instantly recognizable today even though such pictures were painted three hundred or more years ago. This style and attitude toward landscape painting has been kept alive particularly in Britain, the US, and the rest of the English-speaking world and elsewhere in Europe by a succession of artists throughout the generations to the present day.

Two of the most revered exponents of landscape painting, John Constable and J.M.W. Turner, are familiar names to many people whether they have any interest in art or not. Almost everybody has heard of them. The present-day view of Constable's work is somewhat different from the view he himself and his contemporaries held. We tend to see these artists' works as representations of a countryside pictured in an idyllic past. To Constable and his contemporaries they were a view of rural life as it actually was in the eighteenth century and early nineteenth century. There is a tendency among amateur artists now to look for similar subject matter—for example, thatched cottages and water mills—and to leave out of their paintings any modern intrusion, such as power cables, tractors and vapor trails from jet aircraft. Such features are excluded often in the misguided notion that Constable would not have put them in. Obviously he could not because they were not there in his day. If they had been, both Constable and Turner would have included them in their paintings as they would have been an integral part of the contemporary landscape—and legitimate subject matter.

Imagine the discussion and argument that the building of a railway viaduct must have caused among those used to horsedrawn transport in Victorian rural England. "Such brick monstrosities are a blot on the landscape!" Yet Turner, very much a painter of his contemporary world, willingly included them in his great range of subjects, and through his acceptance of these new phenomena in the landscape in such paintings as *Rain, Steam and Speed*, and *Snowstorm*, he made these modern features perfectly acceptable as subject matter for great art.

ABOVE: *A detailed sketchbook study of a pine tree; the hatching describes the spiny foliage very effectively.*

BELOW: *In this charcoal study, both linear and atmospheric perspective are incorporated. The linear perspective of the ruts in the track is reinforced by the line of the secondary growth of the hedge on the left. The lightening of tones from the foreground to the background—atmospheric perspective—is quite obvious.*

ABOVE AND RIGHT: *If you intend to take a drawing to a finished state it is most useful to have a sketching stool and easel. Although not absolutely essential, it is more comfortable. Position yourself in such a way that you can see that part of the landscape that you wish to draw, also your drawing, without moving your head too much. You are looking at a landscape through an imaginary picture plane which you are then transposing onto paper. Try to avoid having direct sunlight on your paper, as the glare can be very tiring on the eyes.*

It is not necessary to live in an area of outstanding natural beauty to produce successfully a landscape drawing. There are numerous examples of interesting paintings and drawings of industrial canals, gas and petroleum plants, major road overpasses, and suburban back gardens. Try to draw those things that are familiar to you and are around you. By working in your immediate environment you will make a drawing which in its own way will be as relevant an observation of our world as Constable and Turner made of theirs. Try not to leave out those things in the scene that do not fit your notion of the perfect landscape. A drawing of a stand of trees flanking the drive of an inner-city park drawn without the high-rise buildings, lamp posts, and other street furniture says less about our contemporary landscape than if they were included.

This attitude should also be applied in the countryside. It is extremely rare to find a farmyard which has an old barn that has not had built adjacent to it a modern concrete pig unit or tractor shed. The machinery about the yard will not be a handcrafted wooden hay wain but more likely a construction in bright red tubular steel with fat rubber tires.

ABOVE: *The Venetian painter, Titian, is not known to have painted an independent landscape, and in this painting,* Sacred and Profane Love *(1516) we have a typical example of how landscapes were used as backdrops to the main subjects. If these landscapes are looked at independently it will be seen that they are a well-observed study from nature, but they cannot be considered as independent paintings. During the Renaissance the landscapes in the backgrounds of paintings were often used to show scenes of secular life. On the left-hand side of this painting a rider at full gallop at sunset is hoping to reach the town before nightfall and curfew. On the right-hand side, two horsemen are engaged in a hunt and a shepherd is gathering his sheep ready for the night vigil. These two landscapes are not celebrations of nature, but are used as a setting for human activities.*

RIGHT: *A beginner's attempt at watercolor by the direct method. This entails no preparatory drawing, and therefore great skill and confidence are required to work directly with the brush. This example has become slightly confused, and under normal circumstances it is recommended that the beginner makes preparatory drawings.*

LEFT: *A watercolor of stones at Avebury. The cool tones express the clarity of daylight and the calm grandeur of this ancient monument.*

PRACTICAL HINTS FOR OUTDOOR PAINTING

Once landscape had become an "official" subject for painters, working outdoors directly from nature became increasingly common, the more so after the French Impressionists set the example. It is not now so popular. Photographers lining up to record a beauty spot are a more usual sight than artists doing so. It is, however, an excellent discipline, which forces you to look hard at a subject and make rapid decisions about how to treat it and lends immediacy and spontaneity to the work itself.

Watercolor is a light and portable medium, ideally suited to outdoor work. But on-the-spot painting, whatever the medium, always presents problems. Chief among them is the weather. You may have to contend with blazing heat which dries the paint as soon as it is laid down, freezing winds which numb your hands, sudden showers which blotch your best efforts or wash them away altogether, and changing light which confuses you and makes you doubt your initial drawing and composition. If the weather looks unpredictable, take extra clothes (a pair of old gloves with the fingers cut off the painting hand are a help in winter), a plastic bag or carrier large enough to hold your board in case of rain, and anything else you can think of for your comfort, such as a vacuum flask of coffee and a radio. If the sun is bright try to sit in a shaded place; otherwise the light will bounce back at you off the white paper, which makes it difficult or sometimes impossible to see what you are doing. If you are embarrassed by the comments of passers-by, a personal stereo serves as an efficient insulation device. Some people also find it an aid to concentration, though others do not. Always take sufficient water and receptacles to put it in, and restrict your palette to as few colors as possible.

Choose a subject that genuinely interests you rather than one you feel you "ought" to paint, even if it is only a backyard or local park. If you are familiar with a particular area you will probably already have a subject, or several subjects, in mind. On vacation in an unfamiliar place, try to assess a subject in advance by carrying out a preliminary reconnaissance rather than dashing straight out with your paints. Finally, try to work as quickly as you can without rushing, so that the first important stages of the painting are as complete as they can be before the light changes. If necessary make a start on one day and complete the work on another. Seascapes are especially difficult, since the color of the sea can change drastically as and when the light of the sky changes—for example, from dark indigo to bright blue-green, or from blue to hues of red—in a matter of minutes. It is often advisable to make several quick color sketches and then work indoors from them.

COMPOSING A LANDSCAPE DRAWING

A convenient way to start drawing a landscape is to view the landscape through a viewing frame; this certainly helps to choose the best pictorial composition. For the beginner the frame is an essential piece of equipment. It is not absolutely vital to have a folding easel or a stool, but if a study is going to be made to a near-finished state outside it can be very tiring to stand in one place holding a sketchbook.

Start by drawing a rectangle on your paper. This is to represent the picture plane as seen through the viewing frame. Decide where you are going to start, and with a 4B pencil make a continuous line drawing of the scene in front of you that you have selected through your viewing frame, going around the main outline of all the features.

Do not at this stage get involved in any detail because that could interfere with the overall structure and composition of the drawing. Once all the large features are drawn, add lines designating all the large areas that are in shadow. If you intend to use the drawing as a basis for a watercolor, you will probably have sufficient information for it at this stage.

If, however, you intend to take the drawing to the state of a finished work there and then, start working greater detail into areas in the middle ground, so that the drawing begins to develop a sense of three-dimensional space.

BELOW LEFT: Carrick Ferry*: Paul Sandby. This picture demonstrates the matt surface resultant from the use of body color.*

BELOW RIGHT: *Seascapes seen through different viewing frames.*

RIGHT AND BELOW: *You can see that by altering the position of the picture plane the composition of this painting is altered. In photography every time you point your camera in a slightly different direction at the same landscape you are altering the camera's picture plane and you will therefore take a different photograph. The artist's eye, when working in a representational manner, is reacting to the landscape in a similar way to the camera. The simplest frame (below) will help you to decide upon the most stimulating picture plane for any scene.*

Now start to outline the areas which are in deeper shadow within the already drawn area of shadow. Shade both these areas again. Now concentrate in greater detail on those areas of the composition that·you have decided to make the focal point. If the focal point of your composition is in the middle distance, again, do not over-embellish. Successful drawings may depend far more on what is suggested to be there than what actually is. Always leave room in your composition for the imagination of the viewer. If the drawing is overdetailed, the viewer is not encouraged to do more than scan, for all the information that is required for the viewer to understand what he or she is looking at is immediately apparent. If the middle ground is overdeveloped, it also makes it impossible to do anything with finer-detailed work on the immediate foreground.

To attempt to bring the whole composition to a high degree of finish, as many beginners do, may result in the drawing just looking incredibly flat and cluttered with too much visual information, so that it may even become difficult to see the overall intention of your original concept. Remember that your mind perceives far more detail than is physically possible to record in your drawing. Select those elements of the composition that are visually most useful to you.

CAPTURING CLOUDS

In a landscape painting, sky and land should always be seen together and in relation to one another, since the particular light cast by the sky—varying according to the amount of cloud cover and the position of the sun—has a direct influence on the colors and tones of the land below. Also, the shapes and colors of clouds can be used as an important part of a composition, perhaps to act as a counterfoil to some feature of the foreground or to echo a shape or color in the middle distance.

Watercolor lends itself very well to sky painting, since by working wet into wet, effects can often be produced which resemble those seen in skies. Care must be taken, however, not to allow too many hard edges to form or the soft, rounded appearance of the clouds will be lost. Here the artist has kept the paint quite loose and fluid, using the brush to draw the cloud shapes and laying one wash over another to build up the forms. He has worked all over the painting at the same time, repeating some of the warm pinky-browns of the foreground and middle distance in the clouds themselves, so that the painting has a feeling of unity, with no artificial division between sky and land. The horizon has been placed quite low, as the sky is the main focus of interest.

1 *The artist started with some pencil lines to indicate the position of the horizon and the diagonal line of the river. He then began to lay wet washes on the sky and distant hills, using the brush as a drawing implement to describe the shapes of the clouds.*

1

2 *The artist continued to build up wet washes, keeping the middle ground fairly light at this stage, and repeating the warm pink tones on the undersides of the clouds.*

3 *The hills on the left have now been deepened in tone, so that they separate themselves from the more distant hills behind. At the same time further modeling has been added to the clouds by building up the mid-tones with Payne's gray, warm blue-gray, and pink.*

2

3

MATERIALS USED

- **Support:** pre-stretched watercolor paper *(10 x 14 in)*
- **Brushes and other equipment:** Nos. 12, 8, and 4 soft brushes, cotton buds
- **Colors:** ultramarine, cobalt blue, olive green, burnt sienna, cadmium yellow, alizarin crimson, Payne's gray

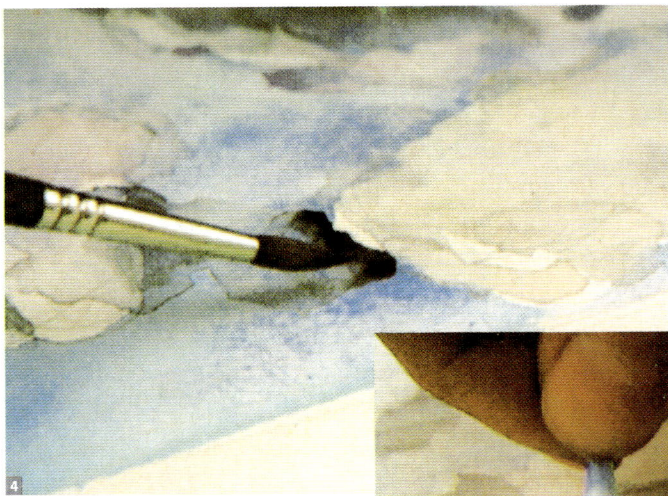

4 *Here the artist is seen working wet into wet, adding small touches of Payne's gray to parts of the clouds. Notice how the fine lines which have formed in places where the paint has flooded have been cleverly exploited to give a crisp look to the clouds.*

5 *Sponges and cotton buds are particularly useful for a painting like this, as they can be used to soften edges, as here, or to draw paler shapes into an existing wash.*

6 *The final touches, which have brought the whole painting together, were to add some definition to the foreground and to increase the intensity of the blue above the clouds, so that the darker tones of land and sky are pleasingly well-balanced.*

using gum arabic

Gum arabic is the medium that binds the pigments in watercolor. A dilute form is also very useful. It adds richness and texture to watercolor and, because it acts as a kind of varnish, keeps the colors very bright. The artist started by painting the hedge with pure watercolor. He then mixed dilute gum arabic with the paint and you can see how much denser the color is. He added more texture to the foliage of the trees by sprinkling it with water, creating splattered areas of lighter color which suggest the pattern of light on leaves. He then blotted the wet area and more of the color lifted off.

ABOVE: *A study in pencil and watercolor wash; here the brush has been used with great skill as a drawing instrument.*

GUM ARABIC

Gum arabic is the medium with which the pigments in watercolor are bound together. This is a misnomer today, as all the acacia trees in the Middle East from which the gum was taken have now died; the water springs which fed them having dried up. Most of the gum now comes from Senegal and South America. Different pigments are manufactured with varying amounts of gum arabic, and behave differently when they are applied. It is useful to have some gum on hand, so it can be added when needed. Only the experienced watercolorist will notice the minute differences between colors mixed with smaller or larger amounts of gum, or gum of varied qualities, but recognition of them can stimulate experiment. Small quantities of sugar or glycerine can be added to give the paint more body and to delay the drying time.

DOWN TO EARTH

The landscape of Italy, and the region of Tuscany in particular, has long been favored by artists. A small farmhouse, nestling between cypress trees on a hillside, provides the subject for this painting. The artist must first select his viewpoint, and this might mean walking around the subject to view it from different angles and different levels. The farmhouse itself provides the main interest, and everything in the painting appears to radiate from it. The pink stucco of the building contrasts with the olive-green color of the surrounding trees and vines. The tall verticals of the cypress trees draw attention to the center of the composition.

1 *The landscape is drawn lightly in a soft pencil. Washes of color are added very sparingly with a No. 6 sable hair brush.*

2 *The details such as windows and contours are more sharply defined with a No. 3 sable hair brush. Washes are overlaid in certain areas with a broader brush to bring the tones closer together.*

3 *A harmony is established in terms of the color relationships and in the related parts of the composition.*

project

LANDSCAPE WITH PALM TREES *(oils)*

A photograph provided the main reference for this painting, and in this case it was quite adequate, as the shapes are all quite bold and clearly defined. However, the photography is noticeably dull in comparison with the painting, which reflects the artist's interests and ideas in a highly personal way. The paint has been used in a way which creates its own excitement and drama, enhancing the spikiness of the trees in the foreground and the angularity of the cypresses.

One of the most striking features of the painting is the sense of depth and recession which the artist has managed to convey through the use of aerial perspective. The mountain in the background is painted in pale shades of gray with rather thin paint, while the foreground has much more tonal contrast, and the paint has been applied very boldly, with vigorous brushstrokes. Another device used to increase the feeling of space was to allow the main vertical shapes, the palm trees, to go out of the frame at the top and bottom of the picture, thus bringing them forward so that they exist on what is usually referred to as the "picture plane," while the cypresses are clearly further back in space, in the middle distance.

2 *The foliage was added when the paint for the sky was fairly dry, and a painting knife was used to flick on the paint. This gave an effect unlike any that could be achieved with a brush. It needs a sure hand to use a painting knife with confidence and ease.*

1 *A rough pencil drawing was done on the canvas, after which the painting was begun with very diluted paint, each area being developed at the same time. Using paint thinned with turpentine and just a little linseed oil enabled the main shapes to be blocked in quite quickly. At this stage all the main areas had been blocked in and the canvas was completely covered, but the shapes were as yet treated only as broad, flat areas, and the foliage at the top right-hand side had not been treated at all.*

MATERIALS USED

- **Support:** ready-primed canvas board *(30 x 24 in)*
- **Brushes:** bristle numbers 6 to 12 in both flats and rounds together with soft synthetic brushes for the finer details and a medium-sized painting knife
- **Colors:** titanium white, ivory black, yellow ocher, alizarin crimson, raw umber, Prussian blue, Hooker's green, and the painting mediums were linseed oil and turpentine

The composition itself has departed from that in the photograph in seemingly minor, but actually vitally important, ways. The uncomfortable central placing of the two trees in the photograph has been changed to place the tall tree slightly further to the right, with the front tree to the left so that it balances the cypresses, while the tree at the far right has been brought just far enough into the picture for it to read as a tree rather than as an anonymous and rather dull shape. The detail of the middle distance has been considerably simplified, and the foliage at the top left given a more definite and pleasing overall shape. When working from photographs, always allow yourself to change the composition in whatever ways you feel will benefit the painting, even if you have taken the photograph specially with a particular painting in mind.

The paint itself has been applied in a way which creates an interesting surface, an important aspect of any painting. A variety of brushes was used to create a range of textural effects; thick paint was drawn into with the handle of a brush and scraped into with a knife (the technique known as *sgraffito*), and paint was flicked on with a painting knife to suggest foliage and the bark of the palm tree in the foreground. The palette itself was limited to only six colors plus white, an unusually small selection which has nevertheless produced a lively and varied color scheme.

3 *Paint was smudged on with the fingers and a small piece of rag in places where a soft effect was desired. The foliage was further defined by using a soft brush to work thick paint on top of the still-wet layer below. This is called "working wet into wet;" the top layer will pick up some of the paint from the layer below, an effect which is exploited deliberately in paintings such as this.*

4 *Texture was added to the tall tree and the mountain was defined with cool, pale grays to increase the sense of space (cool colors recede, while warm ones come forward). The cypress trees just in front of the mountain were added, being just suggested with one brushstroke each, working wet into wet so that the green was modified by being allowed to pick up some of the underlying gray.*

The painting shows the bold shapes of the trees and is far more expressive than the photograph it depicts.

BUILDINGS *and* TOWNS

BASIC PRINCIPLES

Although paintings that take a building or a group of buildings as their subject are usually regarded as a branch of landscape painting, it is more practical to regard architectural painting and drawing as a separate subject. It presents its own problems, not the least of them being the intricacies of perspective. Obviously not all paintings of buildings need be as accurate and precise as an architect's drawings—this is seldom desirable—but a painting of a house, church or ruin is similar to a portrait. It is that particular building you want to paint, because you are attracted to its shape, color, or atmosphere. It is therefore important to get the proportions and perspective right, just as you would the features of a face.

ABOVE: *Turner was a master of every kind of painting he turned his hand to, and he could portray the intricate details of a building with the same skill and sensitivity that he brought to atmospheric landscapes. This detail from his* Study of Tintern Abbey *shows a combination of the topographical draftsman's precision and the painter's eye for mood, tone and color.*

THE TOPOGRAPHICAL TRADITION

Before the time of the great watercolor landscape painters of the later eighteenth and early nineteenth centuries, watercolor had been used mainly for quick sketches and topographical drawings, that is, precise visual records of landscapes or buildings. Many such drawings and paintings were intended as the basis for engravings or etchings, and were not really painterly in approach, color being used in flat washes to supplement a linear drawing, often in pen and ink. In the nineteenth century interest in buildings was stimulated by the comparative ease of travel to foreign parts. Crumbling medieval ruins, Roman remains and picturesque streets in old towns became favorite subjects for artists. By then, too, the use of watercolor had become much more inventive, and artists were concerned with conveying the feeling and atmosphere of buildings, not simply recording their outward appearance and superficial details as an architect or draftsman would. Paintings such as Bonington's *Castelbarco Tomb* and Turner's *Tintern Abbey* are accurate records of the buildings, but they are also full of life and vigor, thus combining the topographical tradition with that of poetic landscape.

Artists in the twentieth century have tended to look at the city in an expressionist and abstract manner. A cool, analytical, perspective study of a city street can often miss the essential quality of vibrance, noise and excitement that the city expresses to those who live in it. Expressionist drawings may not be accurate representations of the city, but they may poignantly and emotively convey a sense of urban vibrance. John Martin's watercolor drawing of the Singer building, painted in 1921, has a greater sense of turmoil of the metropolitan street scene than an ordinary perspective drawing or a photograph

RIGHT: *Use of the squared screen can be of great assistance both in landscape and townscape drawing as a device for finding interesting angles of composition. It can also eliminate the complicated use of multipoint perspective. The artist is working from the squared screen onto squared paper.*

LEFT: *Churches can be a good architectural subject for the beginner, because they are sometimes situated where a lengthy study can be undertaken without too much disturbance. The drawing in sepia conté crayon is typical of a beginner's approach. An attempt has been made to depict the building in a clear and concise manner. The result is not outstanding, either in composition or drawing technique, although it is quite competent. It has little interest in itself to anyone who is not familiar with this particular church.*

could ever convey. A work like this is conceived pictorially on more than one level. Compare the work of Canaletto, Lowry, Utrillo and Burra to discover the four main approaches to townscape. Many of the expressionist works of the twentieth century take this multi-point view in one work.

It would often be impractical or very difficult to approach drawing a townscape in the same manner as drawing a landscape; there is not least the difficulty of trying to set up an easel and stool in a busy shopping street, and it is the tackling of such a subject surrounded by physical complications that brings a full realization to the beginner of the usefulness of a sketchbook.

PRACTICAL HINTS

Some knowledge of perspective is needed to make a building look solid and convincing, but the most important factor is close and careful observation, which leads to a good foundation drawing. Try to work directly from the subject itself wherever possible: photographs, which distort the perspective, are not the ideal source of reference for architectural subjects. A photograph taken with a standard instant camera, which usually has a wide-angle lens (35–45mm focal length) will cause a tall building to look much shorter and wider; and any details in shadow, such as the top of a wall under the eaves of a roof, will probably be indistinguishable.

Watercolorists of the past sometimes paid a draftsman to make a preliminary drawing for them. They would simply put on the color! Most of us, however, have to do our own donkey-work, and with a complicated subject it can take time. Fortunately, the drawing can be done on one day (and can take as long as necessary, since changing light does not matter very much at this stage) and the actual painting on another, or even indoors. A photograph might then be used as a reference for the color only.

A small ruler is a useful addition to your usual drawing kit as it

ABOVE: *With the use of a squared screen the artist found a more interesting and unusual aspect of the same church. This pencil study was started on a late Fall evening and finished later in the studio. The artist exploited the fact that the sun was low on the horizon on the left-hand side, bathing the tower in a pink glow of light and plunging the body of the church into deep shadow. The last of the sun catches the tombstones in the foreground and sets them brilliantly against the dark shadows. With the early moon in the right-hand corner, this pastel study is given an eerie melancholy; a marked contrast to the pedestrian study of the other side of the church.*

can be used to check angles, verticals and horizontals by holding it up at arm's length and to draw guidelines on the paper. There is no reason why all drawing should be done freehand; the rather mechanical-looking lines given by ruling will be obscured once the paint is laid on. Proportions can be measured by the pencil-and-thumb method, and all such measurements should be constantly checked and reassessed as the work progresses.

Once the painting itself is begun, you can work in a much freer manner, altering small details to improve the composition. But architecture generally calls for a more methodical approach than landscape. Lines usually need to be crisp and clear. So allow each wash to dry before putting on the next, turning the board sideways or upside down, if need be, to fill in each area.

When the first washes have been laid on, texture, such as that of brickwork or stone, can be suggested and small, precise details can be added carefully with a fine brush. Final touches are often added with a pencil or pen and ink to give a crisp definition to the painting, but they must be handled carefully. A heavy, black line can destroy the delicacy of a painting.

USING ACRYLICS TO ADVANTAGE

These days, many of us dwell in towns and cities, and are often far removed from the traditional subjects of the landscape painter: hills, valleys, rivers, coastlines, and so on. The city does, however, offer exciting opportunities for those artists who are prepared to seek out more unusual subjects.

One of the most accessible subjects we have is the view from our own window. A high window, in particular, offers an excellent vantage point and can be just as exhilarating as looking at a view from a mountaintop. The geometric shapes of buildings and rooftops, for example, can afford the opportunity to create bold, dynamic compositions in which shapes, colors, and patterns are greatly emphasized.

The particular view illustrated in this painting is a fine example of how an artist with a searching eye can find a certain beauty in even the most commonplace subject. Out of a cluttered jumble of buildings and rooftops, he has created a calm and ordered composition in which roughly half the canvas is given to empty sky and the other half to lively geometric patterns.

1 *The subject is complicated, and the artist starts by making a drawing in which he simplifies the tones and colors.*

3 *The middle tones are blocked in next, using Payne's gray and a No. 3 sable brush.*

2 *A fairly detailed outline drawing is made on the support. The artist begins by blocking in the darkest areas using a mixture of black and raw umber, well diluted.*

4 *The artist now begins to add colors over the original dark tones, using mixtures of white, yellow ocher, cadmium red, and burnt sienna.*

5 *The painting is now developing into an interesting pattern of abstract shapes and colors.*

6 *This detail reveals the thinness of the paint, and how simply the blocks of color are applied.*

MATERIALS USED

- **Support:** hardboard primed with latex *(22 x 26 in)*
- **Brushes:** No. 6 sable, No. 10 synthetic fiber
- **Colors:** Payne's gray, ivory black, cadmium yellow, yellow ocher, cadmium red, burnt sienna, raw umber, titanium white

7

7 *The artist adds details using rich reds and beiges mixed from Payne's gray, yellow ocher, and white.*

8 *In the final painting the sky has been added with a flat wash of cerulean blue mixed with titanium white, toned down with a thin glaze of raw umber. The artist has resisted the temptation to fill the picture with too much detail; the large, empty space of the sky provides an exciting contrast with the clutter of roofs beneath.*

8

LEFT: North East corner of Piazza San Marco: *Antonio Canaletto. Canaletto is one of the great masters of linear perspective and many of his works have a photographic accuracy. He often worked to achieve this accuracy with a "camera obscura." This was a drawing aid very popular with typographical artists that accompanied many gentlemen on the Grand Tour of Europe. It works in a similar way to a single lens reflex camera, but instead of the image being projected onto a sheet of film it is projected onto a sheet of paper or glass and the image is then transposed with a pencil. Although a knowledge of perspective is useful, it is by no means essential when drawing the contemporary urban environment.*

RIGHT: The Pond: *L. S. Lowry. Lowry's approach to townscape differs from Canaletto, in that the city acts as the environment for the ant-like inhabitants that Lowry makes the main theme of his paintings; he makes little attempt to glorify the buildings of the city. The Canaletto concentrates on the beauty of architecture, and the inhabitants play a secondary role. The aerial view in this painting enables the viewer to embrace a wide panorama. It is a very personal approach to perspective which does not offer any one dominant center of activity.*

project

CHURCH IN FRANCE *(Watercolors)*

Buildings present special problems to the artist, especially the watercolorist, and they demand a fairly precise and planned method of approach. In a painting such as this, where the church is the *raison d'être* of the picture rather than being just one feature in a landscape, the perspective must be convincing, the lines sharp and clear, and some suggestion made of the texture and quality of the masonry.

This artist has worked in a very deliberate way, starting with a careful outline drawing made with a sharp pencil and ruler to map out the main areas, so that he is sure where to place his first wash. He then put on a series of flat washes, the first one being laid over the sky area and the second, very pale, over the building itself. Next he began to consider the best way of suggesting the stonework, and decided on masking fluid, applied in slightly uneven brushstrokes. When this was dry he washed over the top with brownish gray paint

1 and 2 In a subject like this a careful outline drawing is essential. Once the drawing was complete the artist laid an almost flat wash over the sky and then a paler one over the building. These established his base mid-tones, enabling him to gauge the tonal strength of the steeple.

3 The steeple was painted and allowed to dry, after which masking fluid was put on to areas of the masonry, not as a flat wash but as individual brushstrokes. Brownish paint was washed over this when dry so that it sank into the areas between the brushstrokes.

5 *Here the spattering technique is being used to give further texture to the walls. It is sometimes necessary to mask off surrounding areas so that they do not get splashed, but this artist makes use of the method quite often, and is confident of his ability to control the paint.*

6 *At this stage only the foreground, with the dark trees and bright grass, remain unpainted. The artist worked the painting piece by piece, as he found that having no overlapping layers of paint gave a crisper definition, but it is not a method recommended for beginners.*

4 *Here the masking fluid is being rubbed off with a finger, leaving the irregular lines of dark paint to suggest the edges of the stones. This is a more effective method than painting in the lines, and gives a much more natural look because the technique is a very slightly "random" one.*

and then removed the fluid, leaving lines of paint between and around the original brushstrokes. Further texture was applied at a later stage by the spattering method, and crisp lines were given to details, such as the face and hands of the clock, by drawing with a sharp pencil. The whole painting has a pleasing crispness, produced by the very sharply defined areas of light and dark; no attempt has been made to blend the paint in the shadow areas, and very distinct tonal contrasts have been used—in the small round tree in front of the church, for example. The artist has also avoided the temptation to put in too much detail, which might have reduced the impact and made the picture look fussy and untidy. The tiled roof consists simply of a flat wash; although there is just enough variation in the sky to avoid a mechanical look, no attempt has been made to paint actual clouds.

7 *Here the hands and face of the clock are being carefully drawn in with a very sharp pencil over the original pale wash.*

8 *Further texture is given to the stonework by rubbing a candle over the paint. Candles or wax crayon can also be used as a resist method, like masking fluid, in which case they are applied before a final paint layer.*

MATERIALS USED

- **Support:** pre-stretched 200 lb Bockingford paper
- **Brushes:** Nos. 2, 7, and 9 sables and a 1-in bristle brush for spattering
- **Additional equipment:** masking fluid, a candle, and gum water
- **Colors:** cobalt blue, sap green, yellow ocher, raw umber, brown madder alizarin, Payne's gray, and ivory black

9 *The mid-tones of the grass have now been laid in, providing a foil to the red-brown of the tiled roof.*

10 *The artist now works carefully on the shadow side of the tree, using a fine brush and very dense dark-green paint.*

The final touches were to darken the left-hand tree and paint in the straight, dark shadow in the foreground. Two small trees were also added in the shadow area at the bottom of the church.

NATURE *and* ANIMALS

BASIC PRINCIPLES

From the sixteenth century onward watercolor became a favored medium for botanical illustration, which, with the great upsurge of interest in describing and cataloging plants and flowers, was very much in demand. Just as it did for architecture, the medium proved ideal for the detailed and delicate work demanded by such subjects.

NATURAL-HISTORY PAINTING

In the early years of the sixteenth century Dürer pioneered the use of watercolor with body color for botanical subjects, and such works as *The Great Piece of Turf* and *Young Hare*, faithful renderings of nature, laid the basis for a tradition of botanical and natural-history painting which has continued down to the present day.

RIGHT: *This watercolor study of waterlilies, by Marc Winer, was painted on the spot, with much use of the wet-into-wet technique. The artist allowed some colors to run into one another in a semi-random way, sometimes creating hard edges, sometimes more gentle transitions, an effective way to suggest the soft wetness of the leaves and flowers floating in water.*

practical hints

Flowers and plants always make attractive subjects and present no particular problems other than the usual one of getting the drawing right. However, many people frequently buy a bunch of flowers and paint them at home, but do not think of going out to paint them in their natural environment. There is nothing at all wrong with the still-life approach. Countless superb paintings have been done of plants and flowers indoors. But painting or drawing on the spot is an excellent way of observing nature, and the plants or flowers do tend to look more at home in their natural setting.

Animals and birds present much graver problems to the would-be wild-life painter. They simply will not sit still. For most professional wild-life artists, birds or animals are a life-long passion, and they have often made a long study of their chosen subject from books and museums before beginning to sketch and observe from nature. A family pet, however, can often be prevailed upon to stay in one place for long enough to be sketched—especially if it has just had a good meal—and photographs can sometimes be used in combination with sketches as the basis for a painting. Anyone who decides to make animals or birds his subject should try to observe them as often and as closely as possible, both in movement and in repose. You may think you know exactly what your dog or cat looks like, but if you try to draw it from memory you will soon realize the limits of your knowledge.

In the eighteenth and nineteenth centuries the majority of natural-history painters and illustrators made their initial watercolors as bases for engravings. Some, notably the famous French flower painter, Pierre-Joseph Redouté (1759–1840), mastered the art of engraving, the techniques of which in turn influenced styles of painting. In America natural-history painting in watercolor reached new heights with the marvelous bird paintings of John James Audubon (1785–1851), paintings which became familiar to a wide public through the hand-colored engravings done from them. These works, although they are in the illustrative tradition of accurate observation, are now regarded as art rather than illustration (there is really no dividing line between the two) and change hands at staggering prices.

Watercolor is still much used for precise botanical and natural-history illustration, but it has also come into its own as a medium for depicting nature, particularly flowers, in a more painterly way, either in its natural environment or in the studio as still life.

The painting of waterlilies shows how superbly the medium can be used to give a feeling of life and immediacy: the waterlilies could almost be opening before your eyes.

ABOVE: *The White Tiger of the West guards the seventh-century tomb of Princess Yung Tai in China; at once naturalistic (if not anatomically accurate) and symbolic of strength and imperial dignity, the flowing, single brushstrokes of the image are perfectly executed.*

ABOVE: *Sketchbook studies of camels.*

ANIMALS

Animals as subject matter for the visual arts have a longer history than any other subject. The first images drawn by the human race depicted the animals that were hunted for survival: the prehistoric cave drawings at Niaux (Ariège), in France, are some of the best preserved examples. Lions, tigers, and hippopotamus were frequent subjects for wall paintings in ancient Egypt and for relief carvings in ancient Syria. There are numerous Greek and Roman examples of animal images in mosaic, bas-relief and sculpture. There is no period in art when animals have not played a major role.

In modern times, with the widespread use of mechanical transportation and with fewer people working on the land, everyday contact with animals has become more distant than at any other time in human history, so that first-hand experience of animals for many Western people comprises the particular relationship between man and his domestic pets.

Art has tended to reflect this change in social conditions with the result that many animals tend to be represented in art as cuddly and lovable, and the images are full of sentimentality. Even wild and savage animals observed at a zoo are often depicted as having all the ferocity of a large domestic cat. This has tended to turn animal representation into a secondary art form considered only fit as images

RIGHT: *An eland painted by San Bushmen of South Africa; note how large the animal is in comparison to the human figures. The eland was not merely an important source of food, but was also imbued with particular magical powers. Its relative size reflects its overwhelming importance to the artist. The white is powdered clay mixed with plant juice; the red is hematite with ox blood.*

BELOW: *Contemporary drawings of wild animals are usually drawn in a zoo environment. The animals often retain their natural dignity as this drawing amply expresses, but the full vigor of a wild beast's ferocity can rarely if ever be experienced by urban man.*

LEFT: *Pen, watercolor and pastel drawing of two rhinos; this drawing was made from a series of rapid sketchbook studies drawn at the zoo.*

RIGHT: *A quick assessment of the movement of birds is necessary if they are to be drawn in their natural habitat. It is vital when using this line and wash technique not to concentrate on the detail of the surroundings at the expense of the birds; all too tempting, especially for the beginner, because the terrain is static.*

for greetings cards. Our contemporary approach to this genre of painting is a far cry from the savagery and excitement depicted with such clarity in such works as the Syrian bas-relief of the lion hunt in the British Museum, London. It is not surprising that we find it difficult to draw animals with the directness with which our forebears saw them, for our sensibilities to and our relationship with the animal kingdom has changed so much.

William Blake, the eighteenth-century poet, engraver, and pamphleteer, might give us an indication of an approach to visual images of the animal kingdom more appropriate to today. His stunning engraving of a tiger with eyes burning bright to illustrate his poem, *The Tyger* depicts a primitive savage—but on reading the poem it is equally possible to come to the conclusion that the content is more about the conscious and unconscious savagery of humankind and that the tiger is used as a metaphor for the human condition. "*What immortal hand or eye/Dare frame thy frightful symmetry*" is a relevant question for today's artists, so isolated from the animal kingdom.

It is perhaps by taking this philosophical attitude to drawing the animal kingdom—portraying animals as a metaphor for the human character and condition—that it might be possible to break away from the sentimental imagery so often depicted. We are all familiar

with animals being used as metaphor and in caricature by the political cartoonist, where the assumed character of a particular animal takes on the features of a person in the public eye. Many animals are associated with particular human traits—the courage of a lion, the infidelity of a monkey, the stupidity of a donkey, the wisdom of an owl, and a baying pack of jackals are commonly used as metaphorical images—and they have a long history of mythological (and religious) association.

ABOVE: *Dürer's marvelous brush drawing of a young hare is one of the best known of all animal drawings. It is remarkable in the detail of its observation; every hair has been faithfully recorded. In the hands of a lesser artist this degree of detail could make for a lifeless drawing, but the hare is obviously an alert, living creature.*

This painting demonstrates very well how in the right hands watercolor can be an ideal medium for capturing the rich colors and strong, yet intricate, forms of flowers and foliage. The starting-point was a single bloom in a garden trough, but the artist has transformed the rather ordinary subject seen in the photograph into a highly dramatic painting with a strong element of abstract pattern. He has reduced the background to an area of dark neutral color, which allows the shapes of the leaves to stand out in bold contrast, but he has given it interest by varying the tonal contrasts while using only one color. He has done this by allowing the paint and water to mix

1 The colors were built up gradually from very light to very dark, and the first step was to apply dilute washes of green and red to the leaves and flower head.

2 The leaves were then darkened in places and touches of cerulean blue added to the flower head with a No. 2 sable brush.

3 Once the main shapes of the leaves and flower had been established, the artist began to paint the background, using a mixture of Payne's gray and cerulean blue and judging the tones very carefully. Assessing the strength of a dark wash takes practice, as watercolor appears much lighter when it is dry.

4 Next the artist began to darken the tones on some of the leaves, mixing the Payne's gray used for the background with cadmium green. Using only a small selection of colors helps to give coherent unity to a painting.

5 Payne's gray was again used, this time pure, to paint the fine, delicate lines formed by the stems and veins of the leaves. A No. 2 sable brush gave the fine brushmarks needed for this work.

6 *The general leaf shapes were produced with a very wet green wash. The paint was then drawn out, while still wet, into thin strands to create the leaf stems.*

MATERIALS USED

- **Support:** pre-stretched watercolor paper with a Not surface *(18 x 23 in)*
- **Brushes:** Nos. 10, 6 and 2 sables and a small household brush for the background
- **Colors:** vermilion, yellow ocher, cadmium green, Payne's gray, cerulean blue, and black

unevenly, and even form blobs in places, and by scrubbing the paint with a stiff household brush.

Although no preliminary drawing was done, the artist had a very clear idea of the composition before he began to paint; the positioning of the flowers against the background is a vital element in the effect of the painting. The leaves have been slightly cropped by the frame on both sides, thereby bringing the flowers and leaves toward the picture plane. The almost horizontal band of lighter color in the foreground, suggesting the garden trough, adds to this effect, firmly "mooring" the plant in the front of the picture. It is interesting to compare the finished painting with the penultimate stage, in which the flower appears to float in space.

7 *The red of the flower head had to be as vivid as possible, and the depth of color was achieved by laying deep washes of vermilion over paler ones in which a little blue had been added. Note how the artist has varied the intensity of the colors and left small lines of a lighter tone showing through to suggest the shapes of the petals.*

HORSES AND DOGS—PERENNIAL FAVORITES

Acrylic is a popular painting medium with animal artists. Its rapid drying time means that artists do not have to struggle home with a wet canvas after a day's work in the field. In addition, its versatility means that it can be used to render a wide range of textures, from the softness of fur to the clean, sharp lines of a bird's feathers.

The artist has been painting animals all his life and so has an extensive knowledge of their anatomy, appearance and characteristics. This painting was developed from two separate drawings of the horse and the dog, made at different times and then combined into a picture that derives as much from imagination as from fact. It is a good idea to keep a sketchbook with you at all times, so you can make drawings of things that interest you and which can later be incorporated into your paintings.

As is often the practice with acrylics, the artist here has used a combination of transparent and opaque techniques. This combination of thin washes and opaque color creates a range of textures which reflect the quality of the surfaces they describe. The finished result resembles both transparent watercolor and body color, because very little thick paint has been used and only fine sable brushes have been employed.

MATERIALS USED

- **Support:** cartridge paper *(18 x 23 in)*
- **Brushes:** No. 6 sable
- **Colors:** raw umber, burnt sienna, bright green, cadmium yellow, cadmium red, cobalt blue, ivory black, titanium white

1 *One of the drawings that became the basis of the horse in the painting—though in reverse.*

2 *The artist makes a detailed drawing of the subject with a 3H pencil. He then applies a very dilute wash of burnt sienna over all the parts of the horse which will be brown.*

3 *The background and foreground are washed in with very pale tints of blue and green.*

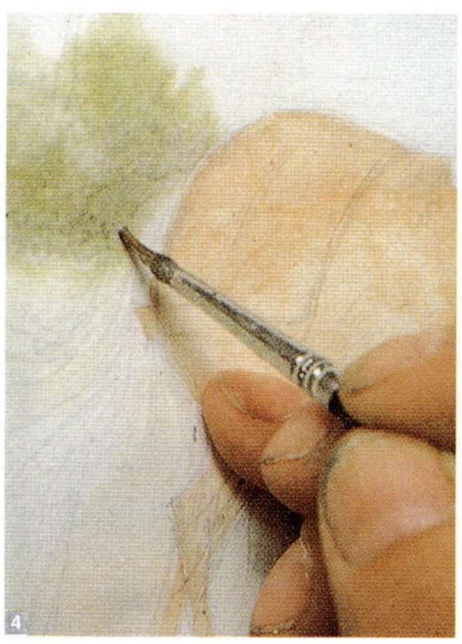

4 *To create an impression of mistiness in the foliage, the artist wets the paper in that area and allows the colors—raw umber and bright green—to blend so that they diffuse with soft edges.*

5 *The trees are treated in a similar way, but more opaque paint is added for the fir trees. When the background washes are dry the artist works on the horse, using a series of transparent washes.*

6 *The artist works on one of the trees, stippling opaque color over a pale underwash to build up texture and form in the foliage.*

7 *With the broader areas now established, the artist starts on the finer details. Here he is using a fine brush and thick white paint for the horse's mane.*

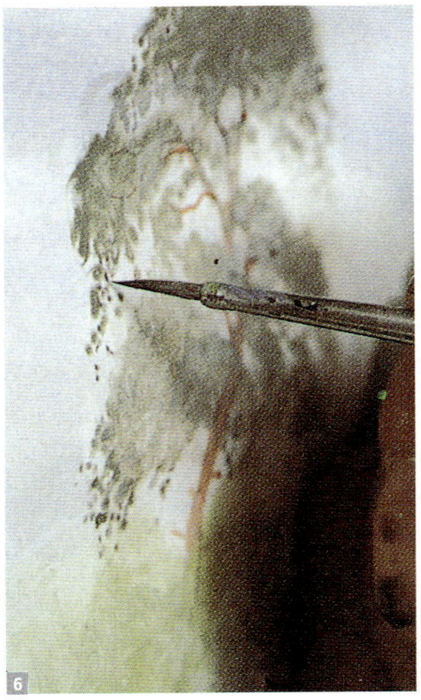

6

7

8 *For the grass the artist uses bright green and a No. 6 sable brush, adding raw umber and white in the shadow areas.*

9 *This detail shows how the artist works around the shape of the dog.*

8

9

10 *The final painting. Only in the latter stages does the artist add the finer details. The dog's coat, and the characteristic plumes of hair on the horse's legs, are added using thin white paint, and then the harness and chains are added with black, red, yellow, and white. The lesson we learn from this painting is that it is better to begin broadly and only finalize our work, adding in the detail, in the latter stages. Working from large to small, and from light to dark, is the ideal way to control a painting.*

10

TROPICAL FISH *(watercolors)*

It can be difficult to find natural-history subjects that remain still for long enough to be observed and studied by the artist, but fish in a tank almost beg to be looked at and admired, and although they are always on the move, at least they do not move very far. Many wildlife artists make a particular branch of the animal world their own, often because of a life-long interest. This artist has studied fish very closely, and has made a great many drawings of them over the years.

The painting was done from a series of drawings and from past observations of the structure and colors of the fish. It makes use of both the wet-into-wet technique, in which new color is applied to a wash before it is dry, and the wet-into-dry technique, in which wet washes are laid over dry ones so that they overlap in places. The hard and soft edges formed in this way create the illusion of rippling water, a very important element in the painting. The background washes had to be applied extremely carefully and accurately so that they did not spoil the crisp edges of the fishes' bodies and fins. A careful drawing was made before any paint was put on.

Although people often think of watercolors as pale and delicate, the colors can be made as vivid as you like, simply by being less diluted. In places the artist has used the paint almost pure to create bright and glowing effects. She has also used complementary colors to good effect: the bright oranges of the fish are accentuated by the complementary greenish-browns in the background.

1 *This sketch is just one of many that the artist has made in the past and uses as reference for her paintings.*

2 *Having made a careful drawing on her stretched paper with a sharp pencil, the artist began by painting in the shapes of the fish with a mixture of cadmium orange and cadmium yellow pale. The colors and tones were varied to show the lights and darks of the bodies as well as the individual differences between the fish. Some of the broader details were drawn into the bodies before the first wash was dry, giving a soft effect.*

3 The background color was a mixture of black and lemon yellow, which gives a warmer color than blue and yellow. When laying the wash the artist took special care to work precisely and accurately between and around the fins and bodies in order to preserve the clean, crisp lines that are such a vital feature of the painting.

3

4

5

MATERIALS USED

- **Support:** pre-stretched watercolor paper with a Not surface *(14 x 20 in)*
- **Brushes:** Nos. 7, 5, 3 anc 00 sable
- **Colors:** cadmium red, cadmium orange, cadmium yellow pale, lemon yellow, yellow ocher, sap green, Payne's gray and black, plus a little Chinese white

6

6 A very fine sable brush was used to paint the delicate details of the scales, and touches of white were added in places. When doing detailed work in the center of a painting, make sure the area below is quite dry or you may ruin the painting by smudging it.

4 When the broad area of the background has been laid in with deliberately uneven washes to suggest ripples, the painting was allowed to dry. Further layers of color were then added, so that the water became darker around the fish and lighter at the top, where the proportion of yellow to black was increased.

5 Here the artist is painting the leaves with a fine brush in a very strong lemon yellow, barely diluted. This covers the original pale wash and is slightly modified by it.

Final touches deepened and enriched the colors of the fins and tails and gave definition to the foreground, hitherto left as an area of water. Opaque paint (Chinese white) was mixed with the watercolour to produce grays and ochers, which were used to pick out the pebbles. Opaque paint should be used sparingly and only in the final stages, but it is extremely useful for touches such as these.

STILL LIFE

BASIC PRINCIPLES

Still life as its name implies, simply means a composition of objects which are not moving and which are incapable of doing so, they are usually arranged on a table or could be a collection of furniture objects; the French call it "dead life" (*nature morte*).

The subjects can be whatever you like, but traditionally the objects in a still-life group are in some way associated with each other—a vase of flowers with fruit, a selection of vegetables with cooking vessels or implements, and sometimes a dead fish, game, or fowl with a goblet of wine, perhaps, or a bunch of parsley. (Culinary still lifes are less popular nowadays, possibly because they run the risk of looking like the cover of a cookery book.) Good paintings can be made from quite homely subjects. Vincent Van Gogh (1853–1890) made a wonderful and moving still life from nothing but a pile of books on a table.

BELOW: *Cézanne used still life to explore the relationships of forms and their interaction on various spatial planes. He usually worked in oils, but* Still Life with Chair, Bottles and Apples *shows his understanding of watercolor.*

RIGHT: *William Henry Hunt produced charming portraits as well as genre subjects, using his paint rather dry to depict colors and textures with great accuracy.* Plums *is an unusual approach to still life, as it has an outdoor setting but it was almost certainly done in the studio from sketches.*

Most artists have painted still lifes at one time or another, and several, notably Jan Vermeer (1632–1675), included them in their figure paintings. In the seventeenth century a group of Dutch artists became obsessed with still life to the exclusion of all other subjects, and vied with one another to produce ever more lavish portrayals of tabletops gleaming with edible produce, rare porcelain and golden goblets. In many of these, tiny insects are visible among the foliage, blood drips from the mouths of freshly killed hares or rabbits, and bunches of grapes shine with tiny droplets of moisture, every object painted with breathtaking skill.

Because the subject of a still-life painting can be entirely controlled by the artist, as can its arrangement and lighting, still lifes present an unusual opportunity for exploring ideas and experimenting with color and composition. the greatest master of the still life, Paul Cézanne (1839–1906), found that the form allowed him to concentrate on such fundamental problems as form and space and the paradox of transferring the three-dimensional world to a two-dimensional surface.

The ability to control the subject of a still life means that you can take as much time as you like to work out the composition and complete the preliminary drawing, and you can practice painting techniques at leisure, trying out new ones as you feel inspired. Oddly, watercolor was seldom used in the past for still lifes other than flower paintings, but it is now becoming extremely popular.

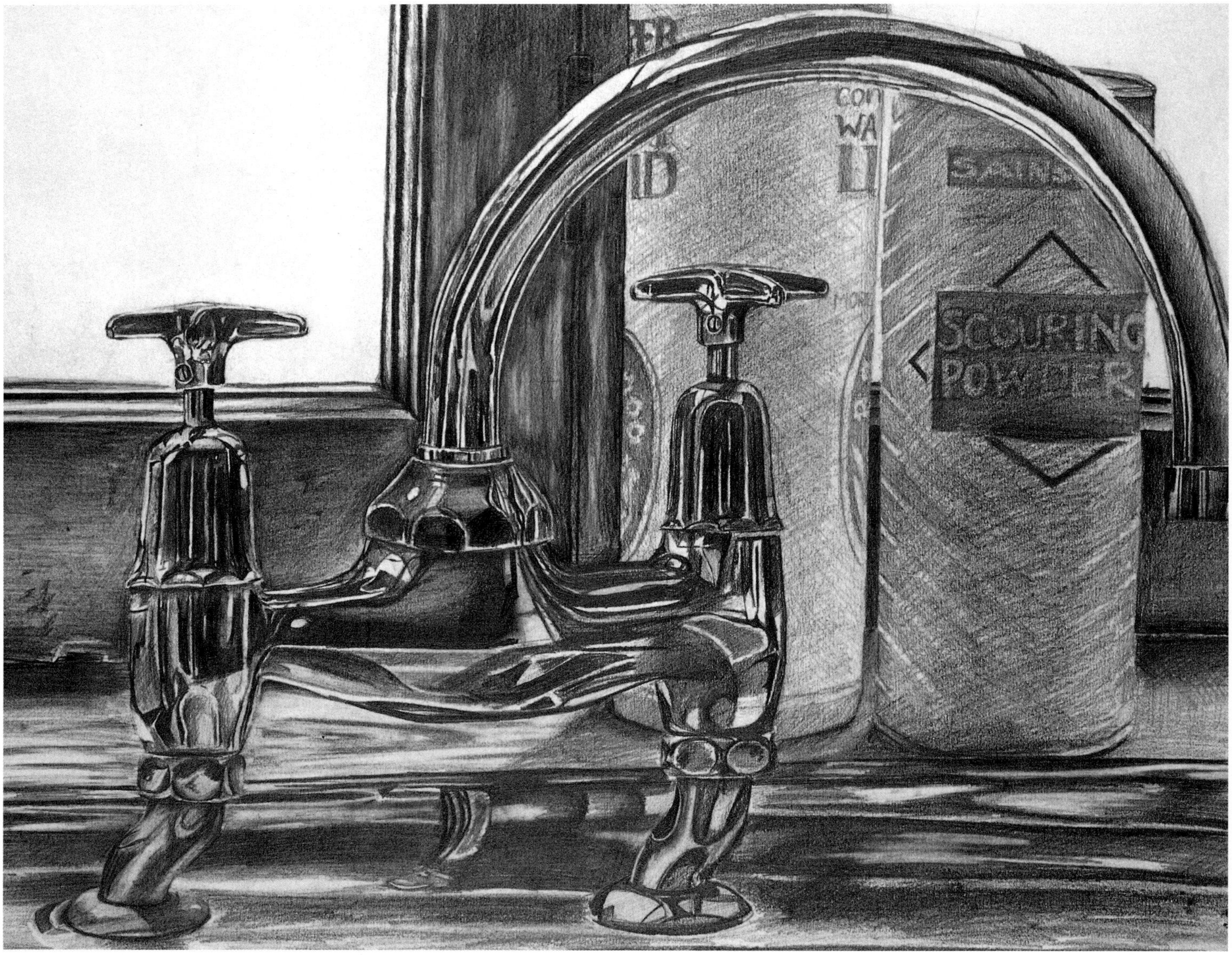

ABOVE: *This pencil study shows the influence of Baroque still life painting in a modern study. The complexity of the reflections is rendered in a manner that shows the student's skill and competence in tackling a highly polished and complex reflected surface.*

SETTING UP A STILL LIFE

There are no specific problems in painting a still life or flower piece once it has been set up. The real challenge is arranging it, and this may take some time—plopping an assortment of objects down on a table will not give you a good painting. The wisest rule to follow at first is to keep the composition simple. The more objects you have the more difficult it is to arrange them in a harmonious way. It is also best to have a theme of some kind: if the various objects are too different in kind they will look uneasy together.

Start with something you like, a bowl of fruit on a patterned tablecloth, perhaps, or a pot plant, and keep arranging and rearranging until you are satisfied that you have achieved a good balance of shapes and colors. Drapery is often used to balance and complement the main subject, and it is useful to have a selection of fabrics or tablecloths on hand for this purpose. Many artists make small sketches or diagrams to work out whether a vertical line is needed in the background, or a tabletop shown as a diagonal in the foreground. Finally, when you are fairly sure that the arrangement will do, look at it through a viewing frame to assess how well it will fill the space allotted to it. Move the frame around so that you can assess several possibilities. Often you may find that allowing one of the objects to run out of the picture actually helps the composition.

Lighting is also very important. It defines the forms, heightens the colors and casts shadows which can become a vital component in the composition. If you are working by natural light other than a north light, it will, of course, change as the day wears on. This may not matter very much so long as you decide where the shadows are to be at the outset and do not keep trying to change them; but often it is more satisfactory to use artificial light. This solution sometimes brings its own problem, however, since if you are painting flowers or fruit they will wilt more quickly. You may simply have to decide which is the lesser evil.

As an exercise, collect together four or five household objects that are no longer required for everyday use. Give them a coating of white emulsion paint so that they all appear to be made of plaster. The whiteness of the objects will help you to see the effect light has in causing shadows. Set up your still life in a convenient corner, and with the aid of an adjustable lamp, direct light from one specific direction onto these now white but familiar shapes. Keep your drawing board as upright as conveniently possible and, remembering the picture-plane concept, outline the pattern of the objects in front of you. Then draw around the shadows. Notice that there are two distinct types of shadow. One is the shadow that is present on the side of objects away from the light source. This is called "actual" shadow and is more difficult to see, particularly on a cylindrical or round object, as the dark side gets progressively darker, and the exact line where the grayness begins is sometimes difficult to see. Because the objects are painted white, however, this should be easier to recognize. A simple way for the beginner to draw the actual shadow is to decide where the darkest part is and shade this as dark as possible. Then decide where the lightest gray is. Divide the area between the lightest shade and the darkest shade into four, and graduate the shading accordingly.

The other type of shadows are "cast" or "projected" shadows. A cast shadow is that area that light cannot get to because there is an object in the way. Because light travels in a straight line, a cast shadow's shape is a version—perhaps a distorted version—of the shape of the object that is casting the shadow. Draw round the cast

LEFT AND BELOW: *In the four photographs we have ordinary domestic objects which have been painted white, and in each photograph the single source of light has been moved, giving each photograph a different two-dimensional pattern of lights and darks. The relative positions of the objects to the camera has not been altered in any of the photographs.*

shadows on your still life and you will notice that there is no variation in the darkness of a cast shadow. If there is, this variation is caused by light reflected off an adjacent object and shining into the shadowed area. Reflected light can be a very useful device and is much used by painters—discussed later.

Without altering the still-life arrangement, change the position of the light, and draw the same subject matter again in the same way. Notice that all the patterns and shapes in your second drawing are very different from those in your first, although you have not moved the objects or altered the position from which you are drawing them. Make further experiments by changing the position of the light source.

Now have another look round your home and find a potential subject that is lit by a table lamp or a single light source. Set yourself up to make a drawing of it. The first thing to notice is that because all the objects in view are not white but their rightful colors it is much harder to see the shadows—although even on a black telephone the lights and darks are still there. The part of the telephone turned away from the light is a blacker black than that part of the telephone turned into the light.

So in drawing as a method of recording, considerable clarity is required. Think of your sketchbook more in terms of a notebook or reference book. For example, if you do a study of a child's bedroom, and then of a child at a different time and probably in a different situation, the drawings in your sketchbook should be sufficiently clear in the information they hold to enable you to combine the two drawings together and make from them an interesting painting or drawing. Professional artists look through their old sketchbooks to find a suitable tree, boat, car, or person, that they need for inclusion in a composition. Unfortunately, the word "sketch" seems to indicate something hurriedly and indecisively drawn.

Try not to restrict your drawings in a sketchbook to scenic compositions. Careful studies of wild flowers, rock formations and all manner of natural forms may be exceedingly useful to you. Also make studies of cars, bicycles, windows, doors, people, and animals. Many people are restricted in the time of the year at which they can draw and paint, and the visual information on flowers gathered at the height of summer can be crucial to the successful completion of a landscape painted or drawn at home in the depths of winter. Flower painting and drawing offers enormous possibilities, and it is often the desire to use color that makes this subject most attractive. However, many beginners' paintings of flowers rely on an exuberant use of color at the expense of form.

Drawing flowers without the use of color might at first seem not to be a very rewarding pursuit. The necessity to concentrate on the form or construction of a flower is, however, well worthwhile. A flower is not a haphazard splash of color but a construction of a series of delicate shapes. A well-handled drawing of roses can give the viewer all the impression of color and delicacy of form. Some varieties of wild flowers, such as the thistle, have a sculptural and pictorial quality that makes them ideal subjects to be drawn as a separate entity and unrelated to other objects. All flowers and plants are very worthwhile to draw because they demand great sensitivity and observation.

A two-dimensional drawing or painting is made up of flat patterns. These patterns can be caused by the shapes of the objects as well as their color. Now to express their shape we know that we can use a line. To give an indication of color, all you can do in drawing is to indicate the lightness or darkness of the color, rendering your drawing as a series of flat tonal shapes. Actual shadow and cast shadow in this instance are seen as a variation of color on the object.

All this information in one drawing has a tendency to flatten out the three-dimensional quality of the objects being seen. To express this quality and create an illusion of depth, it is often an advantage to ignore variations in color, and to restrict your drawing merely to showing the light and dark areas caused by actual and cast shadows, because it is the shadow on an object—and the shadows it casts—that make for the realization in a viewer that the object is round or flat. If this is done successfully, the viewer's mind can "assume" the missing tonal values of color.

BELOW: *The beginner often finds it difficult to recognize potential subject matter, particularly in surroundings which are completely familiar. This pen and ink study of an armchair by a window must be typical of thousands of homes; such a subject can be treated in a variety of ways. Here, the artist has chosen to concentrate on all the different patterns to create a very two-dimensional image.*

ABOVE: *In this strongly rendered charcoal drawing an otherwise uninteresting pile of wood on a workbench has been given the grandeur of architecture by the high contrast of light and dark.*

For this still-life painting, the artist has used an intriguing combination of a modern medium—acrylic—and a traditional oil-painting technique dating back to the days of the old masters, namely, that of developing a detailed underpainting over which transparent glazes of color are applied, layer upon layer, to achieve a translucent and shimmering surface.

Hundreds of years later, the miraculous effects achieved by the masters still fill us with admiration and awe. However, the technique which they used was a slow and laborious one, since each layer of paint had to be left for several days to dry out before the next one could be applied. If a layer of oil paint is applied over an underlayer that is not completely dry, cracking ensues and the painting can be ruined in a very short time.

With the advent of acrylic paints in the 1950s, this problem was at last resolved. Like oil paint, acrylics can be used thickly or in thin

1 *For this still life, the artist chose objects whose soft colors and shiny textures would lend themselves well to the glazing technique.*

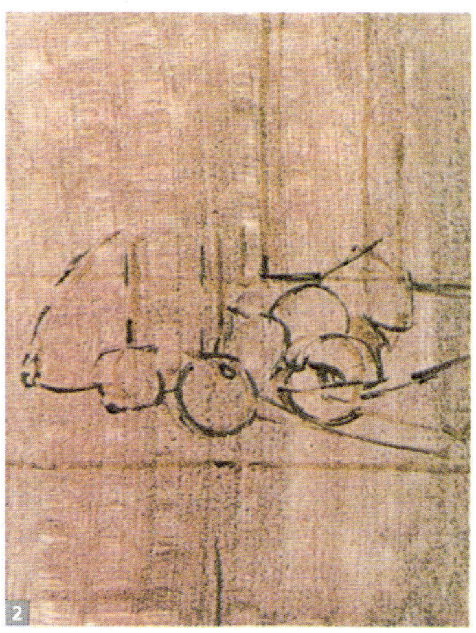

2 *The first step is to tone the canvas with a thin wash of burnt umber, well diluted with water. This sets the tone for the whole painting, and softens the stark white of the canvas. The still-life objects are then indicated with thin black paint and a No. 2 brush.*

3 *Next the artist blocks in the lightest areas of the painting with thin white paint and a No. 10 brush, blending them with a rag.*

4 *Working over the entire surface, the artist blocks in the strong highlight areas with a No. 4 brush and pure white paint, used a little more thickly this time.*

5 *With a No. 2 sable brush, the artist redraws the outlines of the subject in black thinned with water.*

MATERIALS USED

- **Support:** prepared canvas board *(16 x 20 in)*
- **Brushes:** Nos. 2, 4, and 10 sable round oil brushes
- **Colors:** ivory black, burnt umber, cadmium yellow light, yellow ocher, titanium white

6 A dilute mixture of cadmium yellow and white is used for the onions. Then the shadow areas around the onions and the table are strengthened with thin washes of ivory black.

7 A cool tone of white and yellow ocher is now applied with a No. 10 brush and worked well into the surface. Note how the warm underlayer still shines through.

8 With a fine brush and white paint, the artist develops the highlights and reflections in the bottle and the onions.

washes; but, unlike oils, they dry very quickly and repeated layers of color can be built up without any danger of cracking. Acrylics, then, can achieve all that oil paint can, but much more quickly.

Following the traditional method, the artist has here worked on a tinted ground, painting from dark to light with very thin layers of color. Before starting to paint, the artist drew a detailed sketch of the still life. This, coupled with the quick-drying properties of the acrylic paints, allowed him to complete the painting rapidly once begun, as all preliminary planning and decision-making had been finished beforehand.

9 The completed painting has all the vigor of an alla prima *painting, yet it also has a subtlety and delicacy. The dark underpainting ensures a unity in the painting as it permeates all subsequent layers of paint giving an overall warmth.*

1 *The tall, elegant irises are placed against a cool, gray background which complements the cold blues and greens in the arrangement.*

2 *The artist places the subject off-center, to create an interesting visual tension with the space.*

3 *Because the artist intends to build up the picture systematically, the drawing is detailed enough to act as a guide to the placement of each area of tone and color.*

A still-life subject such as a vase of flowers may seem like a simple one, but it is nevertheless very important to plan the composition carefully in order to create a pleasing image.

Because this vase of irises was such a symmetrical shape, it could have produced a stiff, boring picture. But the artist has avoided this problem by lighting the subject from one side to create interesting elongated shadows. He also arranged the subject on the canvas in an interesting way. Rather than place the vase of flowers in the center of the canvas, which would have been the most obvious solution, he chose to place it off-center, where it interacts with the rectangles created by the shelf and the side of an alcove.

Part of the appeal of this painting is in its crisp, clean edges. The artist used masking tape as a stencil in order to achieve the clear-cut characteristics of the highlights and shadows on the vase and the tall leaves.

In painting the subtle colors of the irises, the artist has used oil paint over an acrylic base. Because oil paint is slow-drying, it can be blended to create soft gradations of tone and color—something which cannot be done with acrylics because they dry so fast. Do remember, however, that oil paint can be used over acrylic, but not vice versa. Acrylic paint will not adhere to an underlayer of oil paint, and starts to crack off in a very short time.

4 *The artist begins by painting the flowers. A purple-blue is mixed from ultramarine, white, black, and a little crimson.*

5 *The irises are developed from light to dark, each tone being completed in flat patches of color. White is added to the lighter areas.*

6 The leaves are painted in three tones of green mixed from chromium oxide, ultramarine and white. Light touches of cadmium yellow pale are added to the centers of the irises.

7 The vase is painted with a mixture of emerald, chromium oxide, and raw umber. For the shiny highlights, the artist uses the basic vase color with added white and yellow ocher.

8 The straight edge of the background shadow on the left is achieved with the aid of a ruler. The shadow area is then painted with a mixture of Payne's gray and ultramarine.

9 The background is a pale gray, made from white with touches of black and ultramarine. A slightly darker tone of gray is used for the shadows of the flowers, which are softened and blurred at the edges.

10 The shelf is painted next, using a mixture of raw sienna and white. The dark shadow is mixed from black, white, ultramarine, and raw umber.

11 *The final details of the flowers are completed in oil paint because the color is slow-drying and easier to manipulate. The darks in the flowers are mixed from ultramarine, alizarin crimson, and a touch of white.*

MATERIALS USED

- **Support:** stretched canvas treated with acrylic primer *(30 x 30 in)*
- **Brushes:** No. 3 bristle, No. 4 sable
- **Other equipment:** masking tape, a sharp scalpel, a B pencil
- **Acrylic colors:** napthol crimson, ivory black, cadmium yellow pale, emerald green, chromium oxide, raw umber, yellow oxide, yellow ocher, ultramarine blue, cobalt blue, titanium white
- **Oil colors:** ultramarine blue, alizarin crimson, sap green, chrome green, ivory black, yellow ocher, cadmium yellow, raw umber, titanium white

12 *When the paint is dry, the artist begins work on the crisp shapes of light and shadow on the leaves. He uses masking tape as a stencil, sticking it firmly to the canvas so that no paint can seep under the edges.*

13 *The delicate shapes to be painted are cut out with a sharp scalpel or blade, being careful not to cut the canvas. These shapes are then peeled away.*

14 *Thick oil paint is used to paint the shapes which have been cut out of the stencils.*

16 *Because the style of the picture is so graphic, the artist decides to add texture to the flat background color using a soft pencil.*

15 *When the paint is thoroughly dry, the masking tape is gently peeled off the canvas, revealing the sharp, clean lines of color on the leaves.*

17 *The finished painting has a pleasing sense of harmony and balance. The square canvas is divided into three geometric shapes, whose straight lines provide a contrasting setting for the organic flower forms and their soft shadows cast upon the wall behind. The loose pencil strokes are in complete contrast to the tight composition and precise shapes.*

project
TEA CADDY ON A WINDOW SILL *(oils)*

This small, quietly harmonious painting, has a limited range of colors and simple subject. It also illustrates the way in which color and composition can be used quite deliberately to create mood: here there are no jarring compositional elements and no bright or discordant colors, but the effect is far from dull—just pleasantly peaceful.

Most people have one or two items about their homes that seem to suggest an idea for a painting, and in this case the artist was attracted to the swelling curves of the pot and its decorative motif. In order to highlight these qualities, he chose to make the composition a geometric one, in which the horizontals and verticals of the window frame and shutter act as a foil for the curved and rounded shapes. The composition is very carefully balanced, with the strip of blue-gray in the foreground just slightly narrower than the window

1 and 2 As the composition is so simple, no underdrawing was necessary. Instead, the main elements were quickly blocked in, using thin paint and a sable brush, in more or less the colors that appear in the finished painting.

1

3 At this stage a bristle brush was used, as the paint was rather thicker (though still relatively thin). The blue of the pot was built up using a mixture of ultramarine and white, with white and Payne's gray used for the window sill. Payne's gray is a useful and versatile color, with a slight mauvish tinge. Here it appears quite warm in relation to the deep blue. A mixture of black and white would have given a much less "alive" quality.

2

3

4 *Masking tape was applied to the line which separates the edge of the window frame from the little rectangle of landscape beyond. This allowed the paint to be applied quite freely on the window-frame area.*

5 *The tape was then lifted off, leaving a clean, straight edge. To use this method successfully the paint must be quite thin and at least semi-dry, otherwise the tape, when lifted off, will take the top layer of paint with it.*

sill above, and the rectangle on the right large enough to be "read" as the view through the window but not so large as to dominate the painting. The verticals of the window frame have been carefully planned so that they do not interfere with the dominant shapes of the pot and bowl, and the slanting shadows on the left, which appear in the photograph as very distinct areas of tone, are merely hinted at by a very slightly darker color at the top left.

The paint has been applied very carefully and meticulously, with sable brushes used to build up thin layers, and the support, a fine-grained canvas, was chosen as particularly suitable for this kind of painting. For a picture like this it is important that the straight lines should really be straight—an accidentally slanting vertical line, for example, would provide just the jarring element the artist has been at pains to avoid—so masking tape was used to aid the process. At one time such techniques were considered rather "mechanical," and

6 and 7 At this stage, several thin layers of paint had been built up one over the other, but the details, which give a crisp definition to the finished painting, had not been added. If you look at the finished painting you will see that this delicate diagonal line is actually vital to the composition, leading the eye to the pot and bowl, which are the focal points.

MATERIALS USED

- **Support:** small, ready-primed, fine-grained canvas *12 x 10 in*
- **Brushes:** small sable and a No. 8 round bristle
- **Colors:** titanium white, ivory black, Payne's gray, yellow ocher, cadmium yellow pale, viridian, ultramarine, Prussian blue

frowned upon, but it is extremely difficult to draw a straight line freehand, let alone paint one with a brush, and there is no reason why masking tape or rulers should not be used.

The range of colors used was deliberately very small—just two blues, a green, gray, black, and yellow. It can be a useful discipline to limit your colors in this way, choosing just one or two colors and their complementaries (blue and yellow, as here, or red and green) plus grays and browns. It may cut down your choices, but this can also be an advantage as you will have fewer to make, and you may find that your painting achieves a harmony and unity that it might not have had with a whole range of colors at your disposal. It will also teach you far more about mixing colors than reading a whole book on the subject.

The brickwork was painted in a mixture of Payne's gray, yellow ocher, and white, with viridian and white used for the mini-landscape through the window. Great care must be taken with an area such as this; if the tonal contrast were too great or the colors too bright the landscape would "jump" forward, assuming too much visual importance and conflicting with the foreground. Viridian, being a cool, rather blue green, is useful for receding backgrounds.

PORTRAITURE *and* THE HUMAN FIGURE

BASIC PRINCIPLES

As more and more artists succumb to the charms of watercolor, it is becoming an accepted medium for portraits and figure paintings, hitherto regarded as the province of oils. Its softness and translucence make it ideal for capturing the living qualities of skin and hair, but it needs particularly careful handling in this branch of painting if the surface is not to become muddy and dull. Accurate drawing is also vital, especially for portrait work. Try to draw from life wherever possible and avoid the temptation to put the paint on before the drawing is right.

LEFT: *This portrait,* Blowing Bubbles, *by Elaine Mills, was done from a photograph. The artist wished to capture the child in movement, not in a stiff, artificial-looking pose. A scaled-up drawing made from the photograph was transferred to the painting surface by means of iron-oxide paper. The painting itself was built up in a series of thin washes, the colors kept light and clean throughout. The details of the face were done last, with the point of a No. 2 sable brush.*

RIGHT: *This painting presents a striking contrast to the previous example, both in its technique and in the atmosphere it conveys. The artist was interested in light and color rather than in achieving a likeness of a particular person, and the paint was kept fluid and free, with the minimum of detail, thus enhancing the relaxed mood of the light-flooded figure in the armchair.*

practical hints

Photographs provide a very useful source of reference for portraiture and figure work, particularly if the subject is a figure in motion. Blowing Bubbles *is an example of a painting done almost entirely from a photograph. It is advisable, even so, to work from life wherever possible, and since a watercolor study is not likely to take as long as an oil, it should not be difficult to persuade people to sit.*

Good drawing is essential for human subjects, since a misplaced eye or an ill-drawn hand or foot can completely destroy the harmony of a painting. Never start a painting until you are sure that the drawing is correct; and as you draw, check proportions and measurements constantly. When you are drawing a figure, it often helps to look at the space behind the head or between limbs. If a person is standing with one hand resting on a hip, for instance, the triangle formed between the arm and the body will be a particular shape. Foreshortened limbs, an arm resting on a chair for example, are difficult to get right, but they can usually be checked by using some part of the background as a reference point. You can see at which particular point the arm would be intersected by a vertical line formed by the wall behind, or how the hand lines up with the legs of the chair.

Before you even begin to draw, compose the picture carefully and give thought to both the background and the lighting. The light will define the figure by casting shadows in a certain way, and lighting can also be used to create atmosphere. A figure seen against a window will appear almost in silhouette, the colors deep and merging into one another; a front light will give a hard, flat look, while a strong side light, or one from above, will give drama to the subject by producing strong tonal contrasts.

PAST AND PRESENT APPROACHES

Although artists have always used watercolor or pen-and-wash to make quick studies of faces and figures, there is really no tradition of portraiture in watercolor, and until this century paintings of the figure have also usually been in oil. The reasons for this have nothing to do with any inherent unsuitability of the medium itself. In the past, portraits were the artist's bread and butter—they were seldom done for pure pleasure as they are today—and the sitter who paid to have his image or that of his family hung on his wall wanted a large and imposing painting as well as one that would stand up to the ravages of time. Watercolors, although we have better ways of preserving them now, as well as more permanent pigments, are prone to fade, and the paper can become mildewed and blotched. Figure paintings were also traditionally fairly large, and most artists found that they called for a slower and more deliberate approach than that normally used for watercolors. Nowadays we have a different attitude to such subjects. A rather sketchy and impressionistic treatment of a figure, either clothed or unclothed, is not only acceptable but often desirable, and can suggest light and movement more easily than a more heavily worked painting.

ABOVE: *In this caricature of George Bernard Shaw, those parts of the face and head which indicate character have been exaggerated. The intellectualism is expressed in the large dome-like forehead. The rugged ears and ferocious glare suggest his celebrated acerbity.*

ABOVE: *Pen and ink sketches; the thick black swathes of ink give the figures an appropriate solidity, and the features, although exaggerated, do not quite become caricatured.*

Figure paintings in watercolor became more usual during the nineteenth century, partly as a result of the far-reaching influence of William Blake's symbolic and allegorical paintings. The Pre-Raphaelites and Edward Burne-Jones (1833–1898) pioneered new techniques, such as rubbing in dry color and scratching out. Burne-Jones' watercolors are barely recognizable as such; they have rather the appearance of medieval manuscripts. Another nineteenth-century artist, influenced by the Pre-Raphaelites, though, like Burne-Jones, not actually a member of the Brotherhood, was John Frederick Lewis (1805–1876), whose paintings of Middle Eastern scenes such as *The Harem* glow with jewel-like brilliance. A comparison of *The Harem* with *Girl in Armchair* reveals startling differences in technique. It is difficult to believe that the same medium has been used. Painters such as Lewis used watercolor almost like oil, with the minimum use of washes and much fine-brush work, but his paintings never look tired, as an overworked watercolor easily can. Today there is a tendency to favor the classical, broad-wash technique, but many others are also used, such as dry-brush and stippling, and some artists combine several techniques in one painting.

DEVELOPING A VISUAL MEMORY

Figure drawing and painting obeys the same basic rules of drawing and painting as for any other subject matter: the problem still consists of translating what is three-dimensional onto a two-dimensional surface. But to most beginners, and even to artists of some experience, the problem of drawing the figure appears to be insurmountable. It is often incorrectly thought that the artist requires years of detailed anatomical study and of practice in drawing the figure from life before any satisfactory result can be achieved. This tends to make beginners avoid inclusion of any figure in their drawings and

ABOVE: *A fine pen and ink study by Albrecht Dürer in which the hand and the face are defined by individual lines that follow the direction of the form. This is particularly noticeable under the left eye where the lines echo the curve of the eyeball behind the lower lid. Drawing self portraits, including hands, is one of the most useful exercises for the beginner.*

paintings wherever possible. Children, however, are in no way inhibited when it comes to making a representation of their parents, brothers, sisters, or teachers, and they quite freely make images of people which, although not photographic images, can be stunning observations.

To introduce yourself to drawing the figure, do not at first try to make an accurate representation as you might do in still life. Accuracy of observation is certainly still required, but for drawing the figure the student must begin to develop a visual memory. Unlike still life, the human figure is animated and moving for most of the time, so some system of retaining and then recording the particularities of people is required. The character of a person is seen not only on the face but also in the way in which he or she stands, walks, and moves the arms and head. Someone who is reasonably well known to you can be recognized from behind by the way in which he or she walks.

First practice drawing matchstick figures—but instead of drawing

ABOVE: *A costumed figure drawn in pencil; notice the shape of the collar and the back of the shirt in relation to the neck, and the way in which the collar is being pulled away because the head is leaning forward. The trouser leg is taut at the back where the calf is pushing and the folds are being pulled to the front. The folds round the arm of the shirt clearly show the elbow. This quick study clearly shows that there is a body inside the clothing.*

RIGHT: *This delightful pencil study captures the round softness of the child's face. The form of the cheek has been further enhanced by lighting the subject from the top right-hand corner, and the soft suggestion of shadow under the cheek gives that part of the face a fullness you would expect in such a young child.*

RIGHT: *Self portrait in charcoal; this is never an easy subject to tackle, but it is a marvelous exercise for any student. Try and make your self portrait as interesting as possible by lighting the face in an imaginative way.*

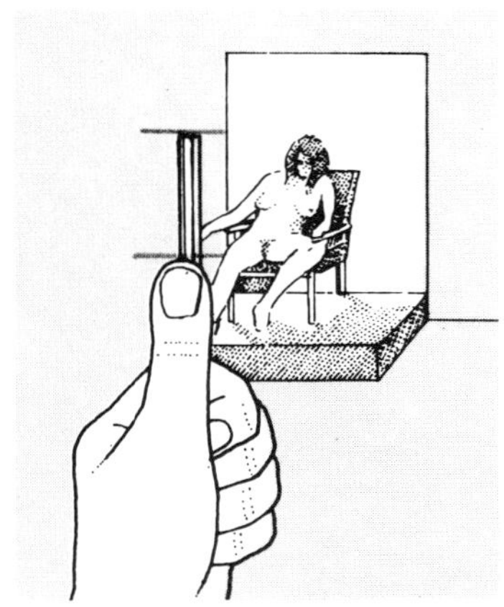

LEFT: *When drawing a figure from life, measurements and angles need constant checking. By holding up a pencil and moving your thumb up and down on it you can check proportions; angling the pencil to follow the line of the body or limb shows you the precise slope, which can be double-checked by relating it to a vertical, such as a chair leg.*

them in a childlike fashion, start considering where the joints of the arms and legs actually are. In this way, by observing people in their everyday activities and translating them into matchstick figures from memory, you will learn two of the most important elements in successful figure drawing. You will extend your visual memory and you will develop an understanding of animation. Artists such as Lowry developed the matchstick figure to a very high level of expression. On close examination of any of his paintings, what at first appears to be a matchstick figure turns out to be a highly animated individual, with very little reference to any particular anatomical feature.

This approach is not dissimilar to that revealed in Aboriginal cave paintings, in which each individual character in the hunt can be seen playing an individual part in the action.

To help understand the way in which a figure is animated, it is useful for most beginners to make themselves a figure out of pipe cleaners and a bit of modeling clay, or obtain an artist's lay figure. By articulating the arms and legs where the joints occur, the figure can be set in a great variety of poses. It is usually obvious if the pose in which you have set the figure is incorrect. When satisfied with the pose, draw the matchstick figure from various angles. In this way, an understanding of how the arms and legs work in conjunction with one another can be appreciated. (You will probably find this exercise more difficult than you thought.)

After some practice, get a friend or member of your family to sit for you in as natural a pose as possible. Take into account non-professional models tend to be a little stiff and formal. Do not expect them to sit totally still for more than about ten minutes at a time, for it can become very uncomfortable and you could lose a potential model (and perhaps a good friend). After all, people are living and moving subjects, and you cannot make them static, like objects in a still life.

Most of our experience of the figure takes place in a fully clothed situation, and it is sometimes difficult for the beginner to appreciate fully that inside a jacket sleeve is an arm, and about half way down the arm an elbow joint, and so on. Yet although it is helpful to draw from a nude model, it is by no means absolutely essential. If a life class or a life model is not immediately available, ask a fully clothed friend to pose—but instead of drawing him or her, articulate your pipe cleaner figure or lay figure into the same pose as your model. With careful observation you will notice that even on a fully clothed figure there are many indications as to where the points of articulation take place. The way in which a trouser leg falls, or the way it folds round the knee of a seated figure, clearly indicates the point of articulation.

The next time you are in a public place, look at the people around you and make some rapid sketches in matchstick form of how the figures are articulated, making particular notes of knees, ankles, elbows, and so on. For these matchstick figures really do work. Remember: the points of articulation must be in the right relationship and proportion to one another.

For the beginner, it should be stressed that the most important areas of anatomy to be studied are the points of articulation, as discussed above. Unless a particular interest is developed in drawing and painting the life figure, a detailed knowledge of anatomy is not really necessary, especially if most of the drawings you intend to do are going to be of the clothed figure. What is important is the interrelationship of the individual parts of the figure that go to make up the whole. Such interrelationships include, for example, the way in which the shoulders fit across the top of the ribcage like a yoke, and how the arms are articulated at the shoulders from the ends of this yoke; how the pelvis is articulated through the waist; and how the spine is a connecting column linking the head, shoulders, ribcage and pelvis. A closer study of how all these interconnecting parts work together can be undertaken by looking at yourself in a mirror. It does not matter how many Latin names for the muscles and bones that you know—in the end, drawing the figure depends on intelligent observation and on ability to translate this observation into two-dimensional form. All a beginner requires is the capacity to perceive what is happening—not an overcomplicated anatomical knowledge of why it is happening.

One area of figure drawing that has a particular appeal to a beginner is portraiture. As an art form, however, the photographer's work has to a large extent taken over the position formerly held by that of the representational portrait painter, and it could be argued that a formally drawn representational portrait has today lost some relevance.

Many modern portraits are very expressionist, verging on the abstract, and in these works the character of the sitter is expressed in non-representational form. However, in this book only representational portraiture is discussed. For the beginner it is more important

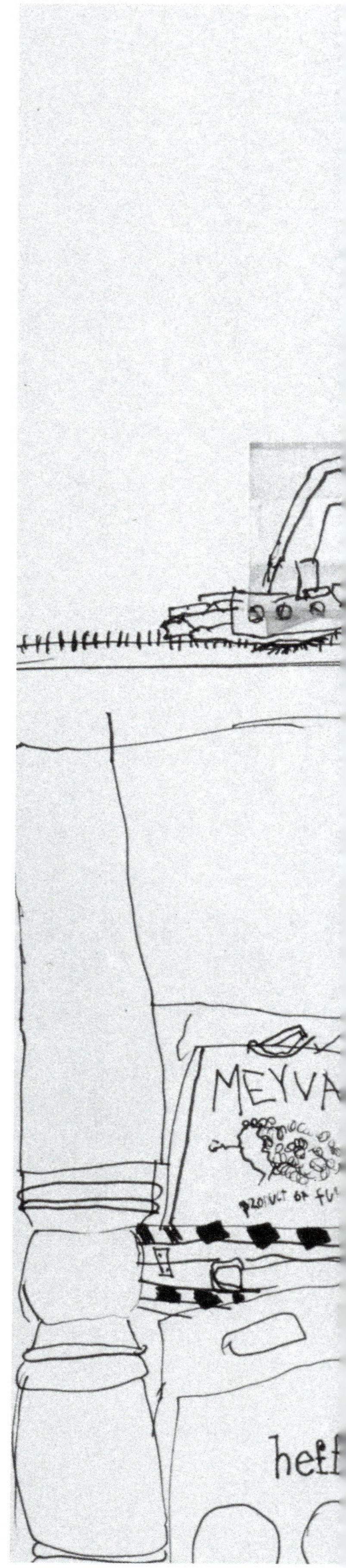

RIGHT: *This uninhibited and delightful pen drawing by a thirteen-year-old of his brother makes few concessions to anatomy but it is expressive of the character of the sitter, even though he is drawn from behind.*

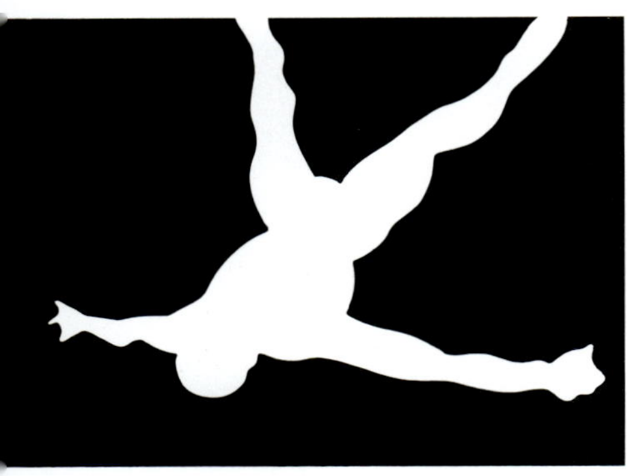

to draw a portrait in a direct and honest manner, searching for the character of the sitter. The peculiarities of an individual's face—the difference between the left eye and the right eye, perhaps, and the realization that they are not identical—are more important to observe than the mere likeness. Even careful observation may not at first produce a truly representational drawing. Do not be overconcerned at this. It is yet again caused by the fact that it is all too easy to place too much importance on the individual elements that make up a face—the mouth, the eyes, the nose, and so on—and it is only a matter of getting these individual parts into their right relationship, and seeing the face and head as a whole.

In a child's drawing, the eyes, nose and mouth are the most important features, and the eyes are often drawn right at the top of the head. Analytical observation proves, however, that a person's eyes are actually situated about half way down the face, and the nose and mouth are both in the lower half. The actual "face" on any head is a relatively small area, but because it is the area we look at and communicate with, the beginner tends to draw the face much larger.

A beginner, starting a portrait, usually first draws an eye, then the other eye, and progressively records all the features. He or she then tries to fit the outline of the head around these features. Instead of starting in this way, make a line drawing of the head, neck and top of the shoulders; then place the other features in their correct overall positions. Observe the proportional distance from the end of the nose

TOP: *A quick conté drawing of a sunbather; notice the direction of the lines under the top of the right arm which indicate the plane that the figure is lying on.*

LEFT: *For the beginner, it is helpful if the image is seen in the simplest possible terms. Try to draw the first statement as simply as possible. With practice, recognition of negative and positive shapes will become automatic.*

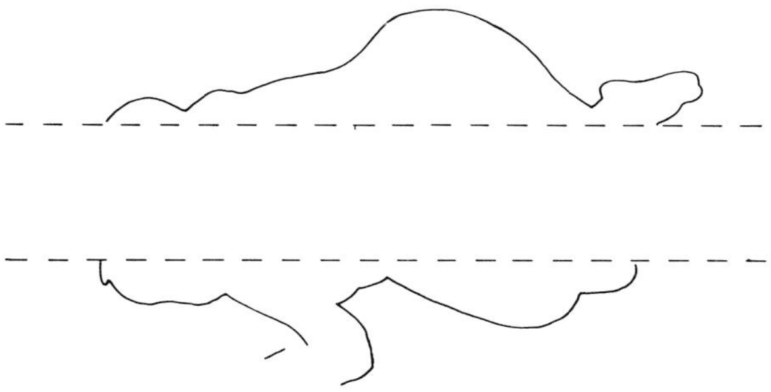

LEFT: *A reclining nude drawn in charcoal; it can be seen that this drawing has gone through several stages of development until a satisfactory contour has been achieved. The whole feeling of the drawing is very sculptural.*

BELOW: *No matter how complex a figure drawing may at first appear, it is always possible to see the figure as a silhouette. Drawing one half and then the other, by arbitrarily dividing the subject at any angle, will help you to develop a sense of this two-dimensional aspect.*

to the eye, and from the nose to the mouth, and represent both accurately. In this way you will notice that the head is quite a large object, and is not made up only of the obvious features. You will also notice that the skin behaves in different ways on different parts of the face. It appears tight and drawn in one part, and loose and flexible in another. The tautness is where the skin is thin and runs over the bones of the forehead, scalp, cheek, chin, and jaw, and those areas that are softer are where the movement of the mouth and eyes take place.

The anatomy of the head very quickly explains its surface structure. This is one area in which some knowledge of anatomy is of real benefit. A well-rendered eye depends to a large extent on an understanding of the workings of the eye. The arrangement of the spheroidal eyeball within its socket ("orbit"), and the muscles that push and pull to enable the folds of skin above, below and each side of the eye to move, can be observed quite clearly on many faces. A study of the mouth is also quite important (it is all too often drawn as though the lips are stuck on and the mouth is just a slit). Again, an intelligent observation with some knowledge of anatomy soon reveals that the mouth is an integral moving part of the whole lower face, and the shape of the mouth is closely related to the size and angle of the jaw and the arrangement of the teeth. (If someone who has false teeth removes them, a great deal of the mouth and jawline seems to collapse.)

Another area that is often poorly observed by the beginner is the neck/head/shoulder relationship. The neck is commonly drawn as a stick with a ball on top, whereas in fact the neck extends to the back of the skull, approximately level with the ears. The neck and shoulders are important in a portrait, even if they are not fully drawn, because they determine the angle and poise of the head. The poise of the head is one of the most important points to help indicate the character of the person being drawn. Few people sit with their head dead upright, as though on military parade. Hair can also be better understood when you realize that, irrespective of how complex the coiffure, the shape is largely determined by the skull underneath. In addition, the way in which the hair grows, or the hairstyle is arranged, can be used as a visual indication of the character of the person, and can be just as vital in portrayals as the eyes and mouth.

LEFT: *Notice the negative space between the legs and between the arm and the torso. Link those spaces with a continuous line round the outer contour of the figure and you will see that this pose can be viewed in quite simple terms. The biggest problem the beginner has to overcome is the feeling of being overwhelmed by the figure in all its individual parts. Concentrate on the positive and negative spaces and the outer contour when drawing the figure.*

Hands can be a very important part of a portrait. The hard, marked, strong-fingered hand of a farm worker can imply a great deal about the character and life of the poser, as can the soft-formed hand of a young girl. Hands do present a number of problems in drawing; most of these are again, however, due to the way in which the hand is perceived. Although each finger has a certain expressiveness and fingers are commonly thought of individually—e.g. index finger, thumb—it is impossible to draw the hand one finger at a time, and it is only when the hand is seen as an overall shape, including the first three or four inches of the lower arm, that it can be successfully tackled. A tree, after all, is easily perceived as an overall shape that is made up of a number of branches because it is thought of as one object. With the hand, the reverse is true. We think of it not as one shape or object but as a combination of individual shapes or objects.

The hand, like the head, is a much larger object than most beginners think. Place the bottom of the palm of your own hand on your chin. You do not have to spread your fingers very widely to cover the majority of your face. But look at any untutored drawing and you will find that the hand is drawn as five very small fingers coming out of the end of the arm. The hand really begins some distance back from the wrist joint.

It is well worth a beginner's time to study the hand. This can be done by using your own hand: with the aid of a mirror the hand can be drawn from a variety of angles. Start by making a line drawing of the whole hand and then drawing into this shape the individual fingers and the spaces in between them. What generally happens when drawing the hand is that you see only two or three of the fingers at one time. Carry on drawing the hand in a variety of positions, concentrating on the whole shape. With a very limited knowledge of the anatomy of the hand, plus intelligent observation, it will not take long before you feel confident including the hand as part of the portrait.

A portrait, then, is much more than just a photographic likeness. Artists have completely under their control those elements of the features they wish to emphasize and those they wish to diminish. This choice is determined by a perception of the character of the sitter and an assessment of which features help to emphasize that interpretation. A portrait can include much more than the main features of eyes, nose, and mouth. Neck, hair, and shoulders play just as important a part in the making of a successful picture.

The features of the model are sharply defined when seen against the plain background of a white wall in the studio. A three-quarter view was selected by the artist standing at an easel 6 feet distant. The model usually rests at half-hour intervals so that the position of arms and hands needs to be marked with chalk. All the materials are within easy reach on a painting table.

1 *The main features of the model are first drawn in lightly with a stick of charcoal.*

2 *Charcoal tends to make color dirty, so that the surface is brushed lightly with a cloth leaving a faint image of the drawing as a guide.*

3 *The contours are painted in a single color—preferably a mid-tone.*

4 *Washes of the same color are laid in to establish the light and dark areas of the painting.*

5 *Flesh tones are added and the dark Prussian blue of the sweater painted in, leaving some of the underdrawing exposed.*

6 *The various planes of the head are restated using a smaller brush.*

7 *A hogs-hair brush is used to define the modeling of the head.*

8 *A bamboo brush with a fine tip is useful for features such as eyes, nose, and mouth. These finish off the portrait, and the sitting lasted only 90 minutes.*

project

SELF PORTRAIT

If you are looking for a convenient model for a portrait painting—someone who is inexpensive, reliable and available at times that suit you—then there is no better subject than yourself. Painting a self-portrait has the added advantage that you don't have to worry about flattering your sitter!

Acrylic paints are an especially suitable medium for self-portraits. Their consistency can be varied to suit a whole range of styles, from loose and impressionistic to tight and realistic, depending on the mood you wish to convey.

Strangely, it is usually difficult to "see" ourselves properly. You may think you know your own face extremely well, but when it comes to painting a portrait it is essential to study your features as if for the very first time. If necessary, make a series of sketches before you begin the actual painting.

When posing for a photograph, many of us tend to look awkward and self-conscious. The same thing can happen with a self-portrait, so try to relax in front of the mirror and select a comfortable pose. It is a good idea to mark the position of the easel, the mirror and your feet so that when you come back to the painting you will be able to take up the position again.

For this self-portrait the artist chose an unusual but effective composition in which his own image is cropped off at the corner. His shadow cast on the wall behind helps to stabilize the composition and adds three-dimensional depth to the image.

1 *The artist begins by making an outline drawing of himself on the canvas, using a B pencil. He then blocks in the main light and shadow areas on the face with broad strokes of burnt sienna, diluted with water for light areas.*

2 *Now the dark tones of the hair, beard and moustache are put in with burnt sienna darkened with cobalt blue.*

3 *This close-up reveals how the artist is building up the broad masses and planes of the face with thin washes of color which indicate the light, medium, and dark tones.*

1

2

3

4

4 *The artist continues to model the face using various tones of earth colors such as burnt sienna, burnt umber, Turner's yellow, brilliant orange, and raw sienna. The eyes are painted with Payne's gray and black, and the mouth with red ocher.*

6 *The details of the shirt and tie are painted with a No. 3 sable brush and cadmium red medium and brilliant orange.*

5 *Now the cast shadow on the wall is brushed in with a 1-in bristle brush and a weak solution of Payne's gray, white, and yellow ocher.*

7 *Washes of ultramarine blue complete the coloring of the shirt. These bright, vibrant colors are deliberately chosen to bring a touch of vitality to the otherwise somber composition.*

8 *The artist now completes the modeling of the head and the facial features. The highlights in the skin tones are added with thin washes of Turner's yellow and white, and white highlights indicate the reflections on the mouth and eyes.*

MATERIALS USED

- **Support:** gesso-primed hardboard *(20 x 16 in)*
- **Brushes:** Nos. 4 and 7 synthetic and a l in bristle brush
- **Colors:** burnt sienna, cobalt blue, Turner's yellow, yellow ocher, brilliant orange, cadmium red medium, ultramarine, Payne's gray, titanium white

The finished portrait. Notice how the unique placement of the figure and the use of clean, white space around it force the viewer's eye into the face of the subject. The strong colors of the shirt and tie contrast with the white of the paper and create a dynamic visual tension.

In this painting the figure is seen in the context of an interior, and the effects of light interested the artist most. Watercolor has been used very loosely in thin washes, with a large amount of paper left uncovered, and the impression of a large, spacious room lit by diffused light has been created with minimal attention to detail. Although the paint has been used mainly pure, the artist also used gouache in the final stages for certain areas such as the blue bed and the smaller highlights on the face and body. Gouache can destroy the quality of a watercolor by giving a matt, dead surface, but here it has been used very skilfully without detriment to the painting.

The composition, with its careful arrangement of lights and darks, is well balanced. The crisp, diagonal lines of the blind contrast with the softer contours of the model, who is placed in silhouette against the white wall. It is the relationship between the figure and the window that gives the painting its interest, and the two are unified by the expanse of bright blue formed by the bed, which is in turn echoed by the cushion and shadow behind the model.

1

2

3

3 The next step was to lay a dark gray-blue wash at the top of the window area, leaving white below so that the light was chaneled through the bottom part of the window. The body was then established with a strong cadmium orange, balanced by the crimson of the skirt and the blue of the bed.

4 The artist continued to work all over the painting, modeling the outstretched leg and adding definition to the face and neck. A strong tint of raw sienna was used for the darker flesh tints in order to echo the orange-brown of the blind and window frame.

1 The artist has deliberately chosen the pose to fit in with a preconceived composition, and he was sufficiently sure of the placing of the main shapes not to need a preliminary pencil drawing. Instead, the main lines and shapes were mapped out with much-diluted watercolor.

2 The tree just visible through the slates of the blind was painted in freely over the orange-brown lines of the blind. The darker lines show through the green wash, giving the shimmering effect of light striking the soft, uneven form of the tree.

4

5 *Although pure watercolor was used for most of the painting, some white gouache was added for the smaller highlights, such as those on the leg and face.*

6 *As a final touch, a deep pink flesh-tint was put on the body, and the area of the bed was strengthened by using a wash of blue gouache with white added. Too much use of gouache with watercolor can destroy its quality, but here it has been used skilfully.*

MATERIALS USED

- **Support:** pre-stretched Arches watercolor paper with a fine grain *(18 x 28 in)*
- **Brushes:** a selection of sables and a small bristle brush
- **Colors:** lemon yellow, cadmium yellow, cadmium orange, cadmium red, alizarin crimson, raw sienna, sap green, cobalt blue and Payne's gray, plus cobalt blue and white gouache

NUDES—THE ULTIMATE CHALLENGE?

Figure painting, like portraiture, presents a great many problems, not the least being that of getting the drawing right. When faced with a complex subject such as this, you will find your task much easier if you make the most important decisions *before* you start work. First, decide which aspect of the subject you are actually interested in and then how you intend to treat it. Some artists will be most concerned with attempting to convey the sheer beauty of the human body and the marvelous and varied colors of flesh and hair, while others will be interested in the pattern that might be created by a figure against a background. Another artist might not be concerned with either color or pattern, and will aim at conveying the dynamic and sculptural qualities of the body, and the way the various planes and shapes relate to one another. Part of this decision will, of course, depend on the model. Some artists' models are beautiful, and cry out to be painted simply as lovely natural forms, while others are less conventionally beautiful but are interesting to a painter in more subtle ways.

This painting shows one particular approach to the subject; here the artist's main concern was not in the body as such, or the colors of the flesh, but in the interplay of shapes and the relationship of lights and darks. While being quite distinctly a "figure painting," it is quite abstract in feeling, with the figure seen as just one element in the composition. The shadows—both that cast by the figure on the

1 *A careful drawing was made with a sharp HB pencil, after which the shadow areas and outlines were strengthened with thinned black paint applied with a small brush. It is important to start with a good underdrawing to establish the composition. At this stage, you need to have a firm idea about how much of the figure you want to show, and how it should be placed in relation to the background.*

2 *As the prime concern of the artist was the relationship of light and dark shapes, he painted in the dark areas first so that they provided a "key" for the rest of the painting, leaving the lighter and brighter areas white at this stage.*

3 *The shadow areas across the body were painted (with burnt sienna) before the flesh was blocked in, and all the other areas were then related to these.*

4 When most of the flesh had been painted, the red-brown area behind the figure was laid on, the color echoing the flesh color but darker in tone. The tonal contrast had to be judged very carefully here, as otherwise the shoulders would have lost all definition.

7 The tones were lightened across the central section 8 and the dark tones strengthened with black and dark blue .

5 The yellow patch, representing the fall of light, was added and then balanced by the small patch of bright red in the foreground.

6 The skin tones were refined in the upper part of the body, and a dark blue shadow laid along the right leg.

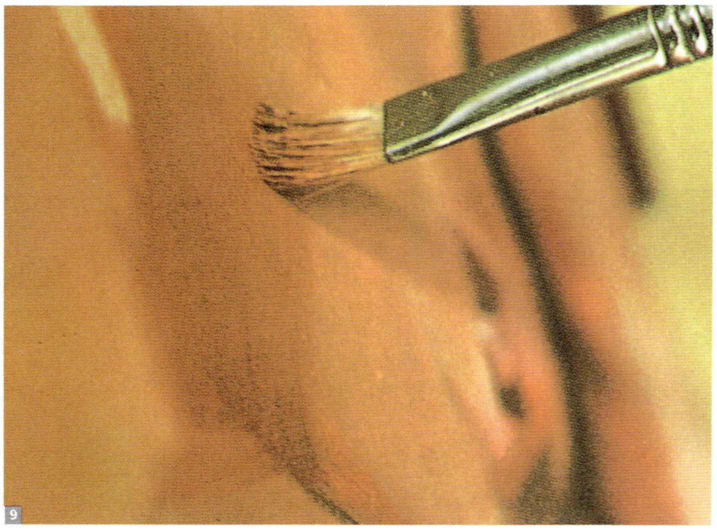

9 *and* 10 *A medium-sized bristle brush was used to blend the shadow areas on the torso into the surrounding lighter colors. Blending must be done with care, or definition will be lost and shapes will appear soft and rounded when they should be sharp.*

MATERIALS USED

- **Support:** cotton duck, stretched and primed *(36 x 20 in)*
- **Brushes:** two No. 6 bristle flats, a No. 6 round sable and a 1 in housepainter's brush for the background areas
- **Colors:** ivory black, titanium white, burnt sienna, raw sienna, raw umber, burnt umber, cadmium yellow, yellow ocher, ultramarine, vermilion. The medium was turpentine

background and that cast on the figure by the window bars—have been given considerable importance, as have the shapes in the background. Another artist, whose preoccupations were different, might have played down these elements, or even excluded some of them, softening the shadows and painting the background as an area of space.

The painting was begun with a careful drawing in pencil, in which the figure was drawn in outline. This is not a method recommended for a beginner, as a drawing such as this, although it looks simple, is the result of years of practice and observation. But a good underdrawing in pencil, charcoal, or thinned paint is important in a complicated subject, as without it you will find yourself having to make endless corrections, which may ruin the composition you were aiming at as well as giving you a clogged and overworked paint surface.

The dark side of the figure was then outlined more distinctly with black paint and a small brush, after which the shadow across the body was painted carefully with burnt sienna. The flesh tones were related to this before the red-brown background, related in turn to the flesh tones, was blocked in. Each area of the painting was worked on more or less separately, the yellow patch of sunlight and the bright red patch in the foreground being added at a late stage. This artist had a very accurate idea of how the finished painting would look and so the method has been successful, but an inexperienced painter would find it hard to work in this way, as it would be difficult to assess the color of the flesh, and the degree of tonal contrast within the body area, against the harsh white of the background.

The highlight areas and facial details were painted with a fine sable brush and a mid-tone was blended between the shadow and highlight areas. Facial details should be left to a late stage in a figure painting, when you are quite sure no alterations have to be made to the drawing and composition.

GLOSSARY

A

Acrylic A polymer based on synthetic resin. Acrylic paint, which is pigment dispersed in acrylic emulsion, dries to a tough, nontoxic flexible film. Acrylic emulsion is used principally as a painting medium, but also as a varnish for acrylic paintings.

Alizarin A synthetic coal-tar dye used in the manufacture of pigments.

Alla prima A method by which a passage of painting is completed with wet pigment in one session.

Amyl acetate Obtained from alcohol, and used as a solvent for some synthetic resins.

Aqueous Applied to painting, refers to media and pigments soluble or suspensible in water.

B

Binder In painting, any medium of some liquidity which forms a paint when mixed with powder pigment.

Bitumen A tarry substance formerly used as an oil color. Now obsolete in painting because of its tendency to crack and darken.

Bloom A white discoloration on the surface of varnish.

Bole A clay, often red, used as a preparatory undercoat for gold leaf.

Bright A flat brush.

Burnishers Tools used for polishing surfaces, such as gold leaf and etching plates.

C

Cadmiums In painting, brilliant and permanent pigments prepared from cadmium sulfate.

Canada balsam See Venice turpentine.

Casein The protein of milk, produced by separation of curd from sour skimmed milk. Dried and mixed with acid, it is used as an adhesive or paint-binder.

Catalysis Effect produced by substance which causes a chemical change in other bodies while remaining itself unchanged. Thus egg will emulsify water and oil by acting as a catalyst.

Chamfer A symmetrical bevel cut in a right-angled edge or corner.

Chiaroscuro Pronounced quality of light and shade in painting.

Chinese ink See Indian ink.

Chinese white See Zinc white.

Cobalt A metal resembling nickel, from which a range of pigments is made.

Composition The arrangements of various elements in painting or drawing, for example, mass, color, tone, contour, etc.

Copal A resin made from fossil trees, used as a varnish and in paint media.

Cover The capacity of a pigment to obscure an underlying surface. Alternatively, its capacity to extend by given volume over a surface.

D

Damar A coniferous resin used as a varnish, and sometimes as part of a mixed medium.

Distemper A water-soluble paint using egg-yolk or glue-size as a binder. Used mostly for flat indoor wall decoration.

Drypoint Method of working directly into a metal engraving surface with a point.

E

Earth colors Pigments made from inert minerals, such as ochers, siennas, and umbers.

Efflorescence Formation of white crystals resulting from penetration of moisture through paint-coated walls—especially brick, tile, or uncoated plaster. Also produced by soluble materials present in the wall itself.

Emulsifier A substance which acts as a catalyst combining oil, water and varnish into media for painting.

Enamel Made from silicate, enamel pigments are applied to metal plates by various techniques, and fused by firing at high temperatures.

Encaustic Technique of painting either by burning in color, such as clay into brick, or by the use of hot wax as a medium.

Etching Using acid to incise a metal plate.

Extender, Extending Material used to increase bulk of pigment: the act of adding such material. Often used in cheaper quality paints. Filler, filling, has the same meaning.

F

Fat (adj) Possessing, as in paints, a high proportion of oil.

Ferrule The metal hair or bristle holder of a brush.

Figurative Literally, containing figures. Used loosely to describe nonabstract painting.

Filbert A conical-shaped brush.

Filler See Extender.

Fixatives Thin varnishes, natural or synthetic, sprayed on drawing media for protection.

Flat A flat-shaped brush.

Foreshortening The effect of perspective in a single object or figure, in which a form appears considerably altered from its normal proportions, as it recedes from the artist's viewpoint.

Fugitive Applied to dyes or paints which are short-lived in color or intensity, due to inherent defects, or the action of natural forces, especially sunlight.

G

Gilding Technique of applying gold/silver or gold leaf to a surface, as for frame decoration, for parts of a painting, or in illuminated manuscripts.

Glair Tempera medium made from white of eggs.

Glaze A transparent film of pigment overlying a lighter surface. See, by contrast, Scumble.

Graphite A form of carbon. Compressed with fine clay, it is used in the manufacture of pencils.

Grisaille A gray underpainting, laid for subsequent color glazing.

Ground The surface preparation of a support on which a painting or drawing is executed. A tinted ground may be laid on white paper to tone down its brilliance.

Grout A mortar used to fill gaps between tiles, etc.

Gum arabic or Gum acacia Hardened sap secreted by acacia trees. Used as a binder for water-soluble pigments.

H

Hatching Graphic technique employing sets of parallel lines to create effect of density or solidity.

Hiding The hiding power of a pigment refers to its opacity.

I

Impasto The thick application of paint or pastel on a surface.

India ink, Indian ink Also Chinese Ink. A dense black ink made from carbon.

Iron oxide Compound from which, in natural or artificial form, many permanent pigments in the yellow and red range are made. See Mars pigments.

J

Japanned Lacquered with a hard resinous varnish.

K

Key (i) In mural painting, the firm wall surface to which paint will adhere without causing crumbling.
(ii) Name sometimes given to wedges for canvas stretchers.

Kolinsky Fur of the Siberian mink, hairs from which are used for the finest "sable" brushes.

L

Lapis lazuli A blue stone from which natural ultramarine pigment is ground. Once widely used, it is now extremely expensive.

Lean (adj) Of paint, possessing little oil in relation to pigment.
Levigation Reduction of material to fine smooth paste or powder.

Lightfastness Ability to resist fading on long exposure to sunlight. Denotes permanence when applied to pigment.

Local color The inherent or self-contained color hue of an object or a surface, without modification by light qualities, atmosphere or proximate contrasting colors. Thus the characteristic local color of a lemon is yellow.

M

Mars pigments Artificial iron oxide pigments, yielding strong tints from yellow through brown to violet.

Masking A technique of retaining the color of the ground in parts of a painting by protecting it with tape or masking fluid while colors are applied over and around the masked areas.

Mastic Gum or resin obtained from certain coniferous trees, used in varnish, employed as a medium and as a picture-protecting surface.

Medium (i) Substance mixed with pigment to form paint, such as oil for oil paints and gum arabic for watercolors.
(ii) In oil painting, mixtures of turpentine, oil, varnish, etc., are added to paint to facilitate its application to the support.

Megilp Mixture of linseed oil and mastic (or turpentine) used as a medium.

Mica Aluminum and other silicate minerals. Found usually in granite, either in scales or crystals.

Mottling Appearance of spots or blotches of color in paint, and on paper.

Mucilage Gum or any viscous substance, derived from plants.

N

Nocturne Painting, usually landscape, made at night.

O

Ochers Natural earths used to make pigments.

Opacity The power of a pigment to cover or obscure the surface to which it is applied.

P

Palette Slab for mixing colors: can be wood, metal, glass, china, marble, plexiglass, or paper. Also denotes range of colors at artist's disposal.
Perspective Systems of representation in drawing and painting which create an impression of depth, solidity, and spatial recession on a flat surface.

Pigment Coloring-matter made either from natural substances, or synthetically, used in paints and dyes.

Plein-air Painting outdoors.

Polymerization Process of molecular change by which acrylic and other synthetic resins are produced, and by which linseed oil is turned into stand oil.

Polymer paints Paints based on acrylic, or other synthetic, resin.

Polyvinyl acetate A synthetic resin used as a medium or varnish.

Porosity Capacity of material, such as brick or plaster, to absorb moisture through minute surface openings.

Q

Quill In drawing and calligraphy, a pen made from a goose's feather.

R

Rabbit skin From which the best quality of glue size is made.

Rebate In framing, step-shaped cut in reverse side of molding to receive edge of canvas, board, etc.

Relief In printing, a raised surface which receives ink.

Resins Substances obtained from coniferous trees, variously used in media and as varnishes. Synthetic resins are now made by polymerization.

Retouching varnish A weak temporary varnish for oil paintings.

Rouge paper Red paper, similar to carbon paper. Used for transferring drawings, the red marks are easily removed.

S

Sable Animal whose hair is used for making fine soft brushes. See Kolinsky.

Sanguine A red chalk drawing medium.

Saponify Turn into soap by decomposition with alkali.

Scumble To apply a thin, often broken, layer of paint over a darker layer, so modifying the underlying paint. A technique developed by the Venetian School. See, by contrast, Glaze.

Sgraffito Method in which a line is produced by scratching through one pigmented surface to reveal another.

Shellac Resinous substance secreted by the lac-insect. It is melted into plates and used in the preparation of varnish.

Silicon Common element, whose compounds—sand, quartz (silica), clay, asbestos, and glass—possess inert properties, making them highly suitable for inclusion in a painting medium.

Silverpoint A drawing point made of silver, which is used on a gesso-coated surface.

Size Gelatinous solution, such as rabbit skin glue, used to prepare surface of support for priming and painting.

Stipple Drawing or engraving method employing series of dots rather than lines.

Stylus A pointed instrument used to grave into a softer surface.

Support The term applied to the material which provides the surface on which a painting or drawing is executed, for example, canvas, cardboard, or paper.

Swatch Manufacturer's sample of range of cloths, fabrics or paper.

T

Tempera, Temper Painting processes or media involving an emulsion of oil and water. Normally refers to an egg emulsion.

Tenebroso Style of painting relying on marked contrast between light and shade.

Terra In painting, earth from which pigment can be made, as in Terra vert (Terre verte).

Thixotropic The capacity of fluids to decrease in stiffness when stirred. Such fluids are produced as oil-painting media and are included in oil primers. They tend to be fast-drying.

Titanium An oxide used as a white pigment of great permanency and covering power. Usually extended with other whites to improve its brushing and drying properties.

Tone In painting and drawing, tone is the measure of light and dark as on a scale of gradations between black and white.

Tooth Degree of roughness or coarseness in texture of paper or canvas allowing paint film to grip surface.

Torchon or Tortillon A rolled paper stump, or stomp, used for drawing with powdered pigment such as charcoal.

Toxicity Degree or state of poison in a material. Toxic paints include: Flake white (White lead), whose dry pigment should never be handled, and Naples yellow.

Tragacanth White or reddish gum derived from herbs. Used as a water-soluble binder.

Transfer paper Paper coated with a tint, usually powder, for transferring a drawing to another surface.

U

Ultramarine Blue pigment made from ground lapis lazuli. Rarely used because it is extremely expensive. French ultramarine is an artificial substitute.

V

Value Of colors and tints, the tonal position in the range from white through gray to black.

Vellum Fine parchment, originally calf-skin, used traditionally for manuscript.

Venice turpentine Canada balsam, an oil resin or balsam obtained from conifers.

Viscosity The stickiness of fluids; their resistance to flow proportional to pressure applied.

W

Wax Used in painting as a binder. Either beeswax, vegetable wax, or synthetic wax.

Wedges Small, triangular pieces of wood, driven into the interlocking corners of wooden stretchers to produce tension on canvas support. Also called keys.

Wet-into-wet The application of fresh paint to a surface which is still wet, which allows a subtle blending and fusion of colors.

Whiting Ground and dried chalk used in plate-cleaning and in the preparation of gesso.

Y

Yellowing A tendency on the part of binding media to turn in tint toward yellow. Most liable to occur when linseed oil is included.

Z

Zinc white White formed from zinc oxide, giving pure cool cover. In oil it needs much medium, and has some tendency to crack. In watercolor known as Chinese white.

Zinnober green Another name for Chrome green.

MANUFACTURERS AND SUPPLIERS

U.S.

Alvin & Co. Inc.,
Box 188, Windsor, Conn.
06095; 2418 Teagarden St,
San Leandro, CA. 94577.

Arthur Brown & Bro. Inc.,
2 W. 46th St, New York,
NY. 10036.

Connoisseur Studio,
Box 7187, Louisville,
KY. 40207.

Dahle (USA),
6 Benson Road, Oxford,
CT. 06483.

Duro Art Supply Co. Inc.,
1832 Juneway Terrace,
Chicago, IL. 60626.

Faber Castell Corp.,
41 Dickerson St, Newark,
NJ. 07107.

Gramercy Corp.,
1145 A. W. Custer Place,
Denver, CO. 80223.

M. Grumbacher Inc.,
460 West 34th St,
NY. 10001.

Loew-Correll Inc.,
131 W. Rugby Avenue,
Palisades Park, NJ. 07650.

The Morilla Co. Inc.,
43–01 21st St, Long Island City,
NY. 11101.

Permanent Pigments Inc.,
2700 Highland Avenue,
Cincinnati, OH. 45212.

F. Weber Co.,
Wayne & Windrim Aves,
Philadelphia, PA. 19144.

Winsor & Newton Inc.,
555 Winsor Drive, Secaucus,
NJ. 07094.

Yasutomo & Co.,
24 California St, San Francisco,
CA. 94111.

CANADA

Artist Gallery,
3350 Fairview Street,
Burlington, Ont. L7N 3L5.

Mona Lisa Art Salon Ltd.,
1518 7th Street, SW Calgary, Alberta
T2R 1A7.

Pro-Graphics Ltd.,
6019 4th Street, SE Calgary,
Alberta T2H 2A5.

The Art Store,
10054 108th Street,
Edmonton, Alberta T5J 3S7.

Rapid Blueprint Inc.,
P.O. Box 306, 35 King William Street,
Hamilton, Ont. L8N 3G5.

Hunt Canada International,
5940 Ambler Drive,
Mississauga, Ont.
L4W 2N3.

Maritime Graphic Arts Ltd.,
1730 Granville Street,
Halifax, Nova Scotia,
B3J 1X5.

Wallack's Ltd.,
231 Bank Street, Ottawa, Ont.

Norcal Reprographics Ltd.,
1180 Winnipeg Street,
Regina, Saskatchewan,
S4R 1J6.

M. Francis Kelly Ltd.,
P.O. Box 5715, 5c Golf
Avenue, St. Johns,
Newfoundland, A1C 5W8.

Curry's Art Store Ltd.,
756 Yonge Street, Toronto,
Ont. M4Y 2B9.

Loomis & Toles Company Ltd.,
963 Eglington Avenue E.,
Toronto, Ont. M4G 4B5.

Lynrich Arts Enterprises Ltd.,
64 Gerrard Street E,
Toronto, Ont. M5B 1G5.

Selectone Paints Ltd.,
39 Gail Grove,
Toronto, Ont. M9M 1M5.

Hansen's Art Supplies,
1130 Robson Street,
Vancouver, B.C. V6E 1B2.

Maxwell Artists Materials Ltd.,
601 West Cordova Street,
Vancouver, B.C. V6B 1G1.

Island Blueprint Co. Ltd.,
905F, Fort Street, Victoria, B.C.
V8V 3K3.

Fraser Art Supplies Ltd.,
414 Graham Avenue,
Winnipeg, Manitoba,
R3C 0L8.

Lewis Art Supplies,
1438 Erin Street, Winnipeg,
Manitoba, R3E 2S8.

Demco Manufacturing Inc.,
1660 Route 209, Franklin Center,
Quebec, J0S 1E0.

U.K.

Acorn Art Shop,
28 Colquhoun St, Glasgow.

Aitken Dott & Son,
26 Castle St, Edinburgh.

Fred Aldus Ltd.,
37 Lever St, Manchester.

Alexander of Newington,
58 South Clerk St,
Edinburgh.

The Arts Centre,
71 Causeway St, Paisley.

The Arts Centre,
583 Fishponds Rd,
Fishponds, Bristol.

Art Repro,
8 De-la-Beche St, Swansea.

The Art Shop,
40 Castle St, Guildford.

The Art Shop,
54 Castle St, Trowbridge.

The Art Shop,
Great Coleman St, Ipswich.

Binney & Smith,
Ampthill Rd, Bedford.

The Blue Gallery,
16 Joy St, Barnstaple.

H. Blyth & Co.,
53 Back George St, Manchester.

Brentwood Arts,
106 London Rd, Stockton Heath,
Warrington.

Briggs Art & Book Shop,
15 Crouch St, Colchester.

The Chantry Studios,
Pauls Row, High Wycombe.

L. Cornelissen & Son,
22 Great Queen St,
Covent Garden,
London WC2B 5BH.

Cowling & Wilcox,
26 Broadwick St, London W1.

Dahle (UK) Ltd.,
37 Camford Way, Luton,
Beds LU3 3AN.

Daler Board Co. Ltd.,
Wareham, Dorset.

J. Davey & Sons Ltd.,
70 Bridge St, Manchester.

The Dollar Gallery,
22 West Burnside, Glasgow.

J. B. Duckett & Co. Ltd.,
74 Bradfield Rd, Sheffield.

The East Anglian Art Shop and Haste Gallery,
3 Great Coleman St,
Ipswich.

Falcon Art Supplies Ltd.,
26 George St, Prestwich.

Ivor Fields,
21 Stert St, Abingdon.

W. Frank Gadsby Ltd.,
9 Bradford St, Walsall.

Greyfriars Art Shop,
1 Greyfriars Place,
Edinburgh.

Gordons Gallery,
152 Victoria Rd,
Scarborough.

Handyman,
43 Tamworth St, Lichfield.

E. Hopper & Co. Ltd.,
48 Market Place, Malton,
Yorks.

Langford & Hill,
10 Warwick St, London W1.

Liverpool Fine Arts,
85a Bold St, Liverpool.

Llanelli Art Centre,
31 Market St, Llanelli.

Mair & Son,
46 The Strand, Exmouth.

John Mathieson & Co.,
48 Frederick St, Edinburgh.

A. Perkin & Son,
2a Bletchington Rd, Hove.

Reeves & Sons Ltd.,
Lincoln Rd, Enfield, Middx.

Reeves Art Materials,
178 Kensington High St,
London W8.

C. Roberson & Co. Ltd.,
71 Parkway, London NW1.

George Rowney & Co. Ltd.,
P.O. Box 10, Bracknell, Berks.

George Rowney & Co. Ltd.,
121 Percy St, London W1.

Studio 10,
10 Edleston Rd, Crewe.

Torbay Art and Craft Centre,
109 Union St, Torquay.

Trinity Galleries,
Trinity St, Colchester.

Winsor & Newton,
PO Box 91, Wealdstone,
Harrow, Middx HA3 5QN.

AUSTRALIA

Marcus Art (Australia) Pty Ltd.,
218 Hoddle Street,
Abbotsford, Victoria 3067.

J & R Walker (Bemboka),
Bemboka Paper Mill,
Bemboka, NSW.

INDEX